'This is a highly insightful book that scrutinise between gender and sport by exploring historical temic barriers for trans and gender diverse peopl lens, it amplifies the voices of a marginalised cor inclusive sporting environments. A compelling read for scholars and advocates alike, igniting conversations on equity in sports'.

– **Dr Beth Jones (she/her),** *Senior Lecturer in Psychology at Nottingham Trent University*

'An empowering read that thoughtfully and helpfully foregrounds the lived experiences of trans and nonbinary people. Through a trans feminist lens, this book offers practical insights and progressive strategies for enhancing inclusion, making it a valuable resource for sports studies scholars and those working in sport. A must-read for anyone passionate about creating a more equitable and affirming sporting community'.

– **Dr Sheree Bekker,** *Senior Lecturer at University of Bath*

'Abby Barras presents a caring and patient view on the position of trans people in sport and physical activity. The experiences and voices of trans people are centred in this book while examining how sport has reached this point – offering a compassionate perspective on an aspect of inclusion that has divided people in sporting worlds. Like Abby, I encourage readers to take their time and use the perspectives of the people who offer insight into their lives here, in order to search for unity not division'.

– **Dr Joanne Hill,** *Senior Lecturer in Physical Education and Sport Sociology at University of Bedfordshire*

'This is an important and brilliant book. With care and integrity, Barras cuts through the noisy misinformation about trans inclusion in sport – using facts, social and historical context, and the lived experiences of trans people. This book deserves to be read by everyone who cares about social justice. 'Unfortunately, some feminists are leading the charge for trans exclusion. Barras' trans feminist account will be a touchstone for those of us who know instinctively that banning trans women from sport is not a feminist thing to do, but who feel silenced by all the misinformation. A must-read'.

– **Professor Alison Phipps,** *author of* Me, Not You: The Trouble with Mainstream Feminism. *University of Newcastle*

'This book makes a valuable contribution to our understanding of gender diverse people in sport. This fascinating research overcomes divisions by connecting theory and practice. It moves freely between disciplines and centralises the lived experiences of gender diverse people to explore barriers and improve inclusion. By taking risks and engaging with the community, the book increases the visibility of marginalised people through their powerful stories. These authentic accounts are missing from the literature and deserve their place in current and future gender eligibility consultation'.

– **Dr Seema Patel,** *Associate Professor in Sports Law at Nottingham Law School, Nottingham Trent University*

TRANSGENDER AND NON-BINARY PEOPLE IN EVERYDAY SPORT

This formative work discusses transgender people's inclusion in everyday sport in the United Kingdom. It adopts a trans feminist approach to explore pivotal issues regarding the barriers to participation faced by transgender and non-binary people.

Offering a critical perspective on the current landscape surrounding this topic, the book draws from insightful interviews conducted by the author with 18 transgender and non-binary individuals. The author uses a critical social science approach to explore the heteropatriarchal construction of sport in the modern industrialised West, and how this has formed the backdrop to the continuing discrimination towards many athletes, not just those who are transgender. Using first-hand perspectives, it focuses on the three themes of the sporting body, sporting spaces and sporting communities. It investigates why conversations about fairness and safety regarding transgender athletes have become so polarised within the media, and the significance of taking a trans feminist approach to reducing barriers in sport. Lastly, the book's key findings initiate a dialogue on the importance of gender affirmation in sport, the value of supportive teammates/role models and how sporting spaces can be reimagined to promote greater inclusion for all.

Transgender and Non-Binary People in Everyday Sport is a crucial resource for researchers, academics and students in the field of social science, sports organisations, policymakers, third-sector organisations, activists and other related disciplines. The book will also be a compelling read for anyone with an interest in improving inclusion for transgender and non-binary people in everyday sport and wants to learn more about how trans feminism can achieve this.

Abby Barras is a critical social scientist based at the University of Brighton, UK, where she teaches in the School of Humanities and Social Science.

Gender and Sexualities in Psychology

Series Editors: Elizabeth Peel and Elizabeth Stokoe

Gender and Sexualities in Psychology is a book series showcasing scholarly work over a wide range of areas within gender and sexualities in psychology, and the intersection of gender, feminism, sexualities and LGBTIQ psychology with other areas of the discipline.

The series includes theoretically and empirically informed scholarship including critical, feminist, queer, trans, social, and progressive perspectives. Creative and innovative methodological approaches are encouraged, as are proposal which are intersectional and/or global in topic or reach. The series adopts an inclusive approach to the discipline of psychology (as well as its cross-cutting relationship to related disciplines) and a recognition of the diversity in research on genders and sexualities.

We welcome proposals for traditional and innovative formats, including research monographs, edited collections, textbooks, research methods, and crossover books that target both academics and/or practitioners. We also welcome proposals from researchers at all career stages.

Titles in the series:

Emergent Identities
New Sexualities, Genders and Relationships in a Digital Era
Rob Cover

Transgender and Non-Binary People in Everyday Sport
A Trans Feminist Approach to Improving Inclusion
Abby Barras

For further information about this series please visit: https://www.routledge.com/Gender-and-Sexualities-in-Psychology/book-series/GSP

TRANSGENDER AND NON-BINARY PEOPLE IN EVERYDAY SPORT

A Trans Feminist Approach to Improving Inclusion

Abby Barras

Routledge
Taylor & Francis Group
LONDON AND NEW YORK

Designed cover image: Verity Smith, trans man, activist and rugby player. Photographed by Luke Bartle, February 2024 (Lucas4Designs)

First published 2025
by Routledge
4 Park Square, Milton Park, Abingdon, Oxon OX14 4RN

and by Routledge
605 Third Avenue, New York, NY 10158

Routledge is an imprint of the Taylor & Francis Group, an informa business

British Library Cataloguing-in-Publication Data
A catalogue record for this book is available from the British Library

ISBN: 978-1-032-47299-7 (hbk)
ISBN: 978-1-032-46617-0 (pbk)
ISBN: 978-1-003-38548-6 (ebk)

DOI: 10.4324/9781003385486

Typeset in Times New Roman
by SPi Technologies India Pvt Ltd (Straive)

For Bronya – my dearest, kindest and wisest friend; for Claire, my guiding star; and for Harry, whose story I often think about.

All royalties for this book will be donated to Pride Sports, a UK organisation working to challenge LGBT+ phobia in sport and improve access to sport for all LGBT+ people across the world. You can find out more about their work here: www.pridesports.org.uk

CONTENTS

MEET THE PARTICIPANTS

Good manners go a long way in research (and in life generally), and so a short introduction to the people who kindly told me their stories is both polite and necessary. They rightly deserve to be at the beginning of this book. As discussed later in Chapter 3, regarding the erasure of trans people's histories in research which concerns them, some names have been anonymised, some are real and some have been chosen by the participant themselves. Aside from Judith and Harry, all participants are White British. Age is as confirmed at the time of the original interview (in 2018), and names and gender as (re)confirmed when I checked a year later. Sometimes people change their minds about using their real name, or their pronouns or gender identity, and that is absolutely fine and to be respected.

Sarah (she/her)
Sarah is a trans woman in her late 60s. She adores playing tennis and darts and enjoys the performing arts.

Judith (she/her)
Judith described herself as trans femme and is in her early 40s. Judith is a climber, both indoors and outdoors, and has travelled extensively.

Charlotte (she/her)
Charlotte is a trans woman in her early 30s who enjoys swimming.

Katy (she/her)
Katy is a trans woman in her early 30s and a footballer. She is a formidable activist.

Jenny (she/her)
Jenny is a trans woman in her early 50s. She is a keen mountain climber, cyclist and loves the outdoors and cake.

Freya (she/her)
Freya is a trans woman in her early 30s. Freya takes part in roller derby, goes to the gym and runs. Freya is a tea lover.

Persia (she/her)
Persia is a trans woman in her late 60s and enjoys swimming and yoga. She is very involved in community activism and highly knowledgeable about Eastern philosophy.

Eric (he/him)
Eric is trans masculine and non-binary. They are in their early 20s and keen on boxing and politics.

Craig (they/them)
Craig is trans masculine and non-binary and in their early 30s. They run and go to the gym and are whip smart.

Annie (she/her)
Annie used the term 'transsexual' to describe herself, with a feminine gender presentation. She is in her early 50s, participates in motor sports and is a talented artist.

Tom (they/them)
Tom is non-binary/trans-masculine and in their 20s. They play water polo, swim and enjoy football.

James (he/him)
James is trans masculine and in his late 20s. He is a fitness coach, runs and used to do yoga.

Miles (he/they)
Miles is a trans man and in his 20s. Miles is very active in lots of sport, but especially skateboarding and circus skills. Miles loves dogs.

Alice (she/her)
Alice is in her 40s and is very fit and active. She cycles and competes in triathlons.

Alix (they/them)

Alix is non-binary and trans masculine and in their 20s. Alix is a personal trainer and runner, and very involved in improving inclusion in fitness for trans people.

Harry (he/him)

Harry was a man in his early 50s who played badminton and football. Harry had been very involved in activism and anti-nuclear protests and described himself as mixed-race. This book is dedicated in part to him, though I have not used his real name to respect his original wishes to remain anonymous. Harry sadly passed away in 2022.

Jude (they/them)

Jude is non-binary and in their early 20s. They play rugby but were keen to get involved in other sports like gymnastics and roller derby.

Joe they/them

Joe is non-binary and trans masculine, and in their early 20s. They play water polo and rugby and had been involved in sport from a very young age. Joe had me in stitches for most of their interview and was the perfect ending to the data collection phase of the research.

ACKNOWLEDGEMENTS

There is a cast of thousands to thank in the writing of this book – how could there not be after a decade in the making? Firstly, thank you to the greatest loves of my lives: my partner Andy and our son, Eddie. I am so lucky to be your Mum, Eddie, and I am so proud of you. To my own incredible Mum, Caroline, who is the cat's pyjamas. Thank you to my brother William, his partner Carla and my nephew Illia: you three make such a beautiful family. To Katherine Johnson and Alison Phipps, for introducing me to gender studies and changing my life for the better; to Claire Collison, the Yoga Queen, for reminding me to always trust my gut, and to Kristin O'Donnell: we will always have DJing cats to remind us of how far we have come. To Gemma for all the art and chats, to Debbie for all the coffee and to Susannah for her humour, local knowledge and shared love of a quiet life. To my former work husband Verity Smith and colleagues at Mermaids, who taught me how to weather hostility with dignity and grace. Likewise, to my 'legal guardian angel' for their expertise: I salute you. To my former PhD supervisor and superstar Hannah Frith, now my dear friend, who is always willing to talk, walk and plot new things. To Nigel Jarvis and Rodrigo Lucena, my two other wonderful supervisors, for sticking with me until the bitter end when things were tough. Thank you to the University of Brighton and the Doctoral College for funding my original research, which became the book you now hold. To my absolutely brilliant mentor Paul Hanna for helping me to be less attention averse (still working on that!) and boosting my confidence. A gigantic thank you to Olu Jenzen, who became my confidant and colleague during a difficult time: I can't wait to work with you again! Thank you of course in buckets to my incredible editors at Routledge, Elizabeth Peel (also my fellow POWES

Paddler), Elizabeth Stokoe and Emilie Coin, whose support and reassurance has been golden. Thank you to Alison (again), Beth, Sheree, Seema and Joanne for your kind endorsements.

And of course, thank you to those in the Trans NB sport + media chat WhatsApp group I hang out in, and whom with patience and enormous humour offer me guidance and friendship beyond measure. Last, but never least, for always and forever, an ocean of gratitude to the participants who made this all happen and to the wider trans community who have welcomed me as an ally.

INTRODUCTION

On the last Friday in January 2023, whilst driving my son to a local trampoline park on a school INSET day, and listening to Women's Hour on BBC Radio 4, the presenter announced the launch of the Power List 2023: Women in Sport BBC, 2023. My mind went immediately to hoping this would be an inclusive list across all kinds of identities, such as disability and race, but as a gender studies scholar, what I was most paying attention to was, well, gender. To my delight, the presenter confirmed diversity was key, shortly followed by the revelation that Tanni Grey – Thompson would be on the judging panel. I actually laughed out loud, much to my son's confusion. 'What is it, Mum?', he said. 'Oh, just the usual', I replied.

'Just the usual' has become a catchphrase amongst those I know and work with, in the field of trans[1] rights. What I mean of course is, 'just the usual transphobia', whether it be the current UK Prime Minister Rishi Sunak or the former Home Secretary Suella Braverman making 'dangerous and othering' jokes (Duffy, 2023) about trans people, or the horrific 42-minute attack on pensioner Marie MacGowan in Dublin, at the hands of Alex Bailey, in September 2022, because he thought she was a trans woman (Milton, 2023). 'Just the usual' questioning of trans rights and discrimination, which are evidenced in the rise in hate crimes against trans people in the United Kingdom. On 6 October 2022, Ashitha Nagesh reported for the BBC:

> The number of hate crimes recorded by police in England and Wales has risen by 26% – to 155,841 in the year to March 2022, Home Office figures show. More than two-thirds – 109,843 – were racist hate crimes. But crimes against transgender people saw the biggest rise, with 4,355 reports, up 56% from the previous year. The rise in crimes against transgender people could

DOI: 10.4324/9781003385486-1

> also be because 'transgender issues have been heavily discussed on social media over the last year', it said.
>
> *(Nagesh, 2022)*

Baroness Tanni Grey-Thompson, DBE, DL, is, according to her Wikipedia[2] page, 'a Welsh life peeress, television presenter and former wheelchair racer'. She is a highly decorated Olympian, and unquestionably an incredible athlete. Baroness Grey-Thompson has sat on multiple boards including the National Disability Council and is the current Chair of the Board for Sport Wales. The list of her awards and achievements is long and impressive, and to many she is a much-admired role model. She rightly has much to be proud of.

However, Baroness Grey-Thompson is also a fierce opponent of trans women competing in sport against cisgender women (those who are not transgender), something many listeners to that radio piece may not know, nor appreciate the influence she had to potentially block trans women from the 2023 Power List (BBC, 2023). In 2019 Baroness Grey-Thompson attended a conference in London, a conference organised with the specific intention to invite people to 'hear from high-profile sportswomen and scientists about the impact of permitting male transgender athletes to compete against women in sports' (Sitwell, 2019, n.p.). The conference was organised by Woman's Place UK and Fair Play for Women. Both of these organisations were started in 2017, and both are self-funded through donations. According to their website (Woman's Place, 2024), Woman's Place UK was started 'to ensure women's voices would be heard in the consultation on proposals to change the Gender Recognition Act' and was opposed to these changes being made. These proposed changes to the UK Gender Recognition Act (UK, 2004) would allow people to be able to self-identify their gender and change their birth certificates without a medical diagnosis of gender dysphoria. The proposed changes were ruled out by parliamentary ministers in England and Wales in 2020. Fair Play for Women's campaign may very well have 'evolved into a broader women's rights campaign' (Fair Play for Women, 2024), but they remain opposed to gender self-identification for trans people in the United Kingdom and has advocated restricting access to women-only spaces on the basis of 'sex, not gender'.

According to their website (Fair Play for Women, 2024), Fair Play for Women started 'as a small, informal women's discussion group concerned about the impact of transgender policy on the participation of women and girls in sport' (Fair Play for Women, 2024). The group calls itself 'a campaigning and consultancy group which raises awareness, provides evidence and analysis, and supports policy-makers to protect the rights of women and girls in the UK'. It was at the London conference in 2019, reported by the *Morning Star* (Sitwell, 2019) and organised by Woman's Place UK and Fair Play for Women, that Dame Grey-Thompson gave 'endorsements' via video link, and, along with Olympic champion Dame Kelly Holmes,[3] 'sent their best wishes for the event'. In her speech to the conference attendees, Dame Grey-Thompson said, 'it's really important that everyone has the chance to discuss the future of female sport and it's only fair that women's voices are part of that as well. A factual and respectful discussion must be allowed' (Sitwell, 2019). Former Olympic swimmer Sharron Davies, MBE was a headline speaker at the event, and also present was Dr Emma Hilton. Both women are vocally opposed to trans women competing in sport with or against cis women. We will return to discuss the basis of their opposition later.

Another judge on the 2023 Power List panel, hockey player Sam Quek, has also spoken about her belief that trans women possess an unfair advantage over cis women. Quek was part of the squad which won Britain's first-ever hockey gold medal at the Rio Olympics in 2016 and was also a member of the England hockey team which won gold at the European Championships in 2015. Quek publicly backed Laurel Hubbard, a trans woman weightlifter representing New Zealand to compete at the Tokyo 2020 Olympics. Even so, Quek believes trans women have 'an unfair biological advantage'. In a piece she wrote for the newspaper *Irish Mirror* (Quek, 2021, n.p.), Quek said that she 'sympathises' with the New Zealander's situation, but, like Sharron Davies (Sitwell, 2019), criticised the International Olympic Committee's (IOC) handling of the issue, arguing that it was 'unfair' for trans women to compete against biological women. Quek wrote:

> I have absolutely no problem with Hubbard personally for being selected for Tokyo 2020. In fact, I sympathise with her situation ... she has every right to compete and with no other platform available to her as a transgender woman, she has abided by all of the IOC's guidelines and has been selected on that merit ... my issue is that I believe the IOC's guidelines aren't fit for purpose and as a result, I believe Hubbard is competing against biological female athletes with an unfair biological advantage – that is on the IOC.

As we will discuss later, the IOC play a big part in this discussion, and not everyone agrees with their approach to defining inclusion.

To be clear, I think the list of subsequent winners on the 2023 Power List is impressive and inspiring, and the challenges and triumphs of those on it are not to be understated. They are all worthy nominees , and diversity is reflected in the choice of winners. They are succeeding in what is still an industry set to the dial of men (English, 2017). Both Helen Hardy, the founder of Manchester Laces, an inclusive football club for women and non-binary people, and Lauren Rowles, the Paralympic rowing champion, are vocal trans allies. But not a single trans or non-binary person was on the list in any of the categories, either as an athlete, as an amplifier or as a change maker. This is despite there being suitable candidates, including Natalie Washington and Sophie Cook. Washington is the Campaign Lead for the Football vs Transphobia campaign, which is part of Football vs Homophobia, itself a volunteer-run 'international initiative that exists to challenge discrimination based on sexual orientation, gender identity and expression at all levels of football' (Football v Homophobia, 2024). Washington is an expert on the inclusion of trans people in sport and has spoken internationally to governments, intergovernmental organisations, sports bodies, grassroots organisations and the media. Sophie Cook is the first out trans woman to work in the Premier League and was recognised for her Outstanding Contribution to LGBT+ Life at the 2020 British LGBT Awards. There may not be many trans candidates for the Power List, but they do exist, and they are speaking back to what Mhairi Black, the National Party's deputy Westminster leader, called 'bad actors [who are] using the debate around trans people as a wedge issue to cause chaos' (Paterson, 2023). Nowhere is this chaos more visible than in the media coverage around the eligibility of trans people competing in sport.

I do not disagree with Dame Grey-Thompson on the need for factual and respectful discussions to happen. I also respect Sam Quek for agreeing that Laurel Hubbard's team selection was made on merit and that Hubbard had every right to participate at the Tokyo 2020 Olympics. Where I do not agree is that Hubbard had an unquestionable unfair biological advantage when she competed. I would imagine that both Dame Grey-Thompson and Quek would also agree with me that trans people's inclusion in sport has become bitterly polarised. You can be 'for' safety and fairness, or you can be 'for' trans people's inclusion, but it seems you cannot be both. Lost within this polarised culture wars are the ongoing issues facing women and girls globally in sport (and not just women, as we will read later): underrepresentation, sexualisation, the gender pay gap and fewer opportunities for career progression off the pitch when compared to ment. Writing in *The Guardian* (Mossier, 2022), Chris Mosier, an American advocate for trans rights and a competitive triathlete, said:

> But if policymakers really cared about fairness in sports, they'd examine the real issues plaguing their organisations. They'd investigate sexual misconduct and corruption allegations and the real inequities in terms of access, funding, development opportunities and media coverage. There are many ways the sports industry, and particularly women's sports, can be improved; banning transgender athletes is not one of them.

Sport has form for punching down on marginalised communities and reinforcing the gender inequality which originally kept women out in the first place. As this book will go on to argue, organised sport in the modern industrialised West is itself born out of male entitlement and two millennia of the heteropatriarchy. Never was this more visible when after Spain won the Women's World Cup in 2023, the head of the Spanish Football Federation, Luis Rubiales, grabbed the head of player Jennifer Hermoso and forcibly kissed her on the lips without consent in front of thousands of people. Rubliales was given a three-year ban for his actions, but continues to insist Hermoso is lying, claiming 'everyone has said the "attack" on him has been "unjustified"' (Daly, 2024). Women are frequently treated as inferior to men in sport, tolerated by those who control the power, and publicly objectified when that power is challenged (Jennifer et al., 2017).

Mapping the Aims of the Book

On 30 May 2023, Channel Four aired the documentary 'Gender Wars', described by investigative reporter Patrick Strudwick as a programme which 'fails both women and trans people, whilst missing the full story' (Strudwick, 2023). But what is the full story? The overall arching aim of this book is to simplify without minimising a topic which has become politically hostile and polarised. It is book with a purpose, to foreground the lived experiences of trans people in everyday sport and physical exercise, and to help make sense of how gender issues in sport can be explored from a range of perspectives. I do not want to unequivocally dismiss some of the arguments gender critical feminists present nor gloss over the thorny issue of competitive advantage. Questions about gender authenticity remain central at the time of writing this book, though, as we will explore, such definitions of authenticity will vary according to how one views gender in the first place. Rather, I believe in changing systems, not people (Frith and Capdevila, 2022), and like Finn Mackay (2021, p. 42), I also believe feminism is about 'building revolutionary change rather than forever building gated communities'.

Whilst there is a growing wealth of academic papers and books which cover elements of this topic, this is the first book to offer a valuable crossover, to help practitioners who are looking for advice and support. This book sits in a series of other books in the Gender and Sexuality in Psychology family. This is an interdisciplinary text and is not a book intended exclusively for psychologists or academics. As Gemma Witcomb and Elizabeth Peel write in their introduction to the 2022 book *Gender Diversity and Sport*, 'the boundaries of social science disciplines should be porous ones, and similar debates about inclusion and exclusion and the relationship between the marginalised and the mainstream occur in numerous disciplinary contexts' (2022, p. 3). This book provides an opportunity to both draw from and reflect upon literature which moves between sociology, social psychology, sports and leisure studies and the sociology of sport. The value of this is that it gives the reader full access to the 'big questions' this topic needs to address: for example, what rights in sport do trans people want/have, what exactly is competitive advantage, what are gender critical feminists asking for and what part can we all play in making sport more inclusive for everyone?

This means this book will also touch on some of the other elements which feed into those broader conversations about inclusion in sport, such as the law and policy formation, and the impact of these on trans people's lives. In doing so, I hope this book provides a balanced overview of the topic and connects the theoretical with the applied, providing equal appeal and usefulness for those inside the classroom and those outside of it. I want to help demystify some of these academic perspectives, which do not always translate easily into practice. Key to answering these questions (and generating more) is trans feminist theory, which helps to both foreground and illuminate the lived experiences of the 18 people who so kindly and generously shared their stories with me in 2018 as part of my doctoral research. My own feminism draws on a broad range of theoretical and political approaches (Bordo, 2004; Hill Collins, 1990; Phipps, 2014), and at its very core is built on the belief that feminism is a political movement for social justice, and assumes the rights of *all* those who identify as women, not just cis women. This means that my methodological approach is committed to a value position, that of accepting the rights of all persons who identify as women. It also makes room for critical thinking about sport and its heteropatriarchal origins, gender and the body, as well as key issues around social justice and human rights.

In this book, the term 'everyday sport' has been utilised as a catch-all term to define sport which is amateur, and not elite. It can be understood as the sport individuals engage with in their everyday lives and is often a highly patterned and structured set of activities. Craig and Beedie (2008, p.13) argued, 'sport does not exist other than through its active production and reproduction through people's everyday actions.' It might include for example, regular weekly attendance at a water polo club, or playing tennis with your friends every Saturday.

Jennifer, Manning, Keiper and Olrich (2017, p.5) offer this definition of sport. Sport must include play (voluntary, intrinsically motivated activity), be organised (governed by rules), include competition (outcome of a winner and loser), be comprised of skill (not chance), include physical skills (skilful and strategic use of one's body), have a broad following (beyond a local fad), and have achieved institutional stability where social institutions have rules which regulate it, stabilizing it as an important social practice.

By building on this definition this book also understands sport to be 'a usually competitive physical activity which, through casual or organised participation, aims to use, maintain or improve physical ability and skills while providing entertainment to participants, and in some cases, spectators' (Allender, Cowburn and Foster, 2006, p. 827).

Mapping the Structure of the Book

This book is divided into two halves. The first half sets the scene, beginning with Chapter 1, which provides an overview of the relationship between gender and sport. There is a particular focus on how the (sporting) body and identity has shaped historical concepts of masculinity and femininity. Whilst this book is concerned with trans people and their inclusion in sport, some historical background is needed if we are to better contextualise how the manufactured organisation of sport in the modern industrialised West has laid the foundation for the exclusion of certain social groups. We will use the lenses of gender, class, race, disability and sexuality to examine how the construction of sport created barriers to participation for those whose bodies were deemed to sit outside of normative representations in sport. This chapter engages with sociological and psychological ideas around identity, prejudice and discrimination, with attention paid to those scholars who advocate for more focus on the lived experiences of sporting participants.

Chapter 2's purpose is to examine the literature about trans people in sport and what might currently be known (or not known) about their participatory experiences. This includes a broad summary of the early literature concerning the hypothetical trans athlete and the part the International Olympic Committee has played – and continues to play – in this matter. Key here is a discussion about competitive advantage, fairness and safety and how the UK Equality Act (2010) has arguably been misinterpreted by those with the power to fully exclude trans women participating in sport in the United Kingdom. Chapter 3 begins with the methods used to inform this book. It pays attention to the ethical considerations of research with trans communities and will explain how this research was designed as trans feminist and strives to maintain those principles throughout. It considers the relevant literature and frameworks necessary to better understand the importance of lived experience when writing about trans communities, including (trans) feminist approaches to gender and inequality in sport. It will also discuss the importance of reflexivity and researcher positionality.

The second half of this book looks towards the stories gathered from participants. It starts with Chapter 4 and the people who informed this research, and the variety of ways their bodies shaped their own experience of – and relation to – participation in sport. We consider the (sporting) body and embodiment, and how important it is in the context of taking part in sport and physical exercise. We will be thinking about hegemonic masculinity and gender normativity, and what passing means. Chapter 5 covers the relevance of sporting spaces and the ways in which participants navigated these. These include both private spaces, such as changing rooms, and those more public spaces where physical activity takes place, such as the swimming pool or the gym. Chapter 6 not only introduces the topic of sporting communities, understood here as teammates, family, friends and allies, but also includes those organisations responsible for defining the rules of inclusion for trans people. We conclude with Chapter 7, where we will summarise and suggest strategies for the advocacy and advancement of trans people in everyday sport and physical exercise and ideas for future research, as well as acknowledge any limitations.

At the end of Chapters 1 through 6 are discussion questions. These can be utilised in the classroom, between work colleagues, or simply as an exercise in self-reflection. I have included these because, again, I believe in changing systems not people. After a decade of studying, thinking and writing about this topic, as well as working alongside colleagues, many of whom are both trans and/or non-binary and sporting professionals, I think that without some collective action, change will never happen.

As such, I do not have all the answers to what often feels like difficult and complex questions. The current climate towards trans people generally remains hostile; it frequently feels overwhelming, whatever your opinion about trans people in sport. I suggest working through your own thoughts, with supportive friends and colleagues; it might be painful, and it will not always be comfortable, but I believe simply that sport is a human right, and I will strive in this book to explain why achieving this matters. You might not agree with me, but modelling the advice of Victor Madrigal-Borloz – UN Independent Expert on protection against violence and discrimination based on sexual orientation and gender identity – is a good place to start. In his report after visiting the United Kingdom in May 2023, Madrigal-Borloz suggested we must 'Keep calm. Examine the evidence, Respect diversity' (Madrigal-Borloz, 2023, p. 18.94). This is sound advice.

Notes

1 This book uses the abbreviated term 'trans' to include all individuals whose gender identity sits under the transgender and non-binary umbrella. The author acknowledges that this shorthand is not a catch-all for all gender-diverse identities and is mindful to take great care where language is concerned in order not to oversimplify, flatten or promote incomplete terms. In addition, terms were used interchangeably by participants. For example, some people may identify as both transgender and non-binary, whilst recognising that non-binary is an identity in its own right. Most importantly, all gender is self-defined.

2 See https://en.wikipedia.org/wiki/Tanni_Grey-Thompson (accessed 9 August 2023).

3 Dame Kelly Holmes has since 'admitted she was previously "ignorant" about trans athletes in competitive sports' (Norris, 2023).

References

Allender, S., Cowburn, G., & Foster, C. (2006). Understanding participation in sport and physical activity among children and adults: A review of qualitative studies. *Health Education Research*, *21*(6), 826–835. https://doi.org/10.1093/her/cyl063

Craig, P., & Beedie, P. A. (2008). *Sport sociology*. Exeter: Learning Matters.

[Fair Play for Women]. (2024). https://fairplayforwomen.com

[Football v Homophobia]. (2024). https://www.footballvhomophobia.com

[UK Equality Act]. (2010). https://www.legislation.gov.uk/ukpga/2010/15/contents

[UK Gender Recognition Act]. (2004). https://www.legislation.gov.uk/ukpga/2004/7/contents

[Woman's Place UK]. (2024). www.womansplaceuk.org

BBC. (2023). *Radio 4 Woman's Hour Power List Revealed*. BBC. https://www.bbc.co.uk/programmes/articles/3qC2czM9jxfQWlb8r5g1y5h/womans-hour-power-list-2023-the-list-revealed

Bordo, S. (2004). *Unbearable weight: Feminism, western culture, and the body*. USA: University of California Press. ISBN: 9780520930711

Daly, C. (2024, January 10) *Disgraced ex-Spain football president Luis Rubiales claims 'everyone who stops me tells me that it's an injustice' after he was given a three-year ban for 'Kiss-gate' scandal - as he insists Jenni Hermoso is telling 'lies' over incident*. Daily Mail. https://www.dailymail.co.uk/sport/football/article-12948513/Disgraced-ex-Spain-football-president-Luis-Rubiales-claims-stops-tells-injustice-given-three-year-ban-Kiss-gate-scandal-insists-Jenni-Hermoso-telling-lies-incident.html

Duffy, N. (2023, July 11). *Sunak and Braverman's trans jokes 'unacceptable and dangerous' says Parliament equalities chief Caroline Nokes*. i-news. https://inews.co.uk/

news/politics/rishi-sunak-suella-braverman-trans-jokes-parliament-equalities-chief-2467613

English, C. (2017). Toward sport reform: Hegemonic masculinity and reconceptualizing competition. *Journal of the Philosophy of Sport*, *44*(2), 183–198. https://doi.org/10.1080/00948705.2017.1300538

Frith, H. & Capdevila, R. (2022). *A feminist companion to research methods in psychology: Changing the system not the person*. Open University Press. ISBN: 0335250130

Hill Collins, P. (1990). *Black feminist thought: Knowledge, consciousness, and the politics of empowerment*. New York: Routledge.

Jennifer, S. E., Manning, R. D., Keiper, M. C., & Olrich, T. W. (2017). Virtual(ly) athletes: Where eSports fit within the definition of "sport". *Quest*, *69*(1), 1–18. https://doi.org/10.1080/00336297.2016.1144517

Mackay, F. (2021). *Female masculinities and the gender wars*. London: I.B Tauris

Madrigal-Borloz, V. (2023). *Country visit to the United Kingdom of Great Britain and Northern Ireland (24 April–5 May 2023)*. Available at: https://www.ohchr.org/sites/default/files/documents/issues/sexualorientation/statements/eom-statement-UK-IE-SOGI-2023-05-10.pdf

Milton, J. (2023, May 25). *Woman, 86, shoved headfirst into wheelie bin by man who thought she was trans*. Metro. https://metro.co.uk/2023/05/25/ireland-woman-robbed-and-beaten-by-man-who-thought-she-was-trans-18840850/

Mossier, C. (2022, June 29). *As elite sports think again about trans participation, our only demand is for fairness*. The Guardian. https://www.theguardian.com/commentisfree/2022/jun/29/sports-trans-participation-transgender-women-swimming

Nagesh, A. (2022, October 6). *Hate crimes recorded by police up by more than a quarter*. BBC. https://www.bbc.co.uk/news/uk-63157965

Norris, L. (2023, January 17) *Dame Kelly Holmes admits she was ignorant about trans athletes*. Metro. https://metro.co.uk/2023/01/17/dame-kelly-holmes-admits-she-was-ignorant-about-trans-athletes-18114195/

Paterson, J. (2023, August 8). *Trans people should be 'left the hell alone', says SNP's Mhairi Black*. Standard. https://www.standard.co.uk/news/politics/mhairi-black-trans-debate-gender-sex-snp-westminster-b1099393.html

Phipps, A. (2014). *The politics of the body: Gender in a neoliberal and neoconservative age*. Polity Press: UK. ISBN: 0745648886

Quek, S. (2021, July 19). *Laurel Hubbard's Olympic efforts will set precedent for the future - I hope she wins gold*. Irish Mirror https://www.irishmirror.ie/sport/other-sport/athletics/tokyo-olympics-weighlifting-laurel-hubbard-24564118

Sitwell, R. (2019, July 19). *Self ID will stop women competing on an equal playing field*. Morning Star. https://morningstaronline.co.uk/article/self-id-will-stop-women-competing-equal-playing-field

Strudwick, P. (2023, May 29). *Channel 4's Gender Wars fails both women and trans people, whilst missing the full story*. i-news. https://inews.co.uk/opinion/channel-4s-gender-wars-fails-both-women-and-trans-people-while-missing-the-real-story-371146?fbclid=IwAR2iDUa-lZ5chUa_4IvZlLoKW2ZkKYuHO2XQFlq3xkEvUNCe_EmTiqA3r_A

Witcomb, G. & Peel, E. (2022). *Gender diversity in sport*. London: Routledge.

1

THE SOCIAL CONSTRUCTION OF MODERN SPORT

Introduction

This is a book about the lived experiences of trans people in sport and the barriers to inclusion they face. In order to understand the present status quo, we first need to turn to the past, and examine how the origins of modern sport can help us to contextualise what is happening in the present. Consideration of how the organisation of sport in the modern industrialised West was manufactured is crucial for understanding how the foundations of exclusion were laid for those individuals who do not fit the idealised image of the preferred athlete. By using gender, class, race, disability and sexuality as lenses, we can understand how the social construction of sport has created barriers to participation for those whose body was deemed to sit outside of normative representations in sport. Whilst it is not possible to conduct an exhaustive summary of all the relevant research on other marginalised groups in sport, I have strived to highlight the necessity of always looking to those who advocate for a more intersectional approach when considering the lived experiences of sport participants.

Sport Is a Social Construction

In Colleen English's 2017 paper on hegemonic masculinity and reconceptualising competition in sport, she recaps on a 2013 broadcast with San Francisco radio personality Damon Bruce, in which Bruce supported Miami Dolphin football player Richie Incognito's locker room bullying of fellow player Johnathan Martin. 'Incognito's bullying was not the problem', Bruce explained, 'it was because sports have become "feminized" and "a lot of sports has lost its

DOI: 10.4324/9781003385486-2

way and part of the reason is that women have been giving the directions"' (English, 2017, p. 183). Bruce went on to say, 'sports are set to the dial of men. Doesn't mean men only. But that's the setting. And I'm not going to allow it to be changed' (English, 2017, p. 183). As English surmised, 'Bruce blames the inclusion of women and their opinions for ruining the masculine nature of sport' (2017, p. 183).

It is important to recognise that 'sport' as we understand it is a social construction. In other words, it is a cultural creation, in the same way the categories of the family, the economy, the media, politics, education, religion and gender roles are (Burr, 2015). This does not mean that sport is not real, or meaningless. Far from it, sport is a central, influencing feature and national obsession for many societies around the globe, though any definition of sport must, as Jim McKay (1992) noted, be culturally relative. But knowing both how sport has been constructed (in the modern industrialised West, at least) and why (to benefit one specific demographic) is crucial. Appreciating the historical origins of sport and the way in which it is organised helps those of us who study social inequalities to better understand why some inequalities still exist, as well as identify how past inequalities have been challenged. Giulianotti (2016, p. 96) writes:

> Modern sport has always been a crucial cultural domain for the construction and reproduction of dominant, heterosexual masculine identities. Sports institutions at elite and grassroots level still harbour formal and informal restrictions on the full participation of women and minorities.

The relationship between sport and social inequality/social identity – including religion, race, gender, age, sexuality, class and disability – has been widely researched within the sociology of sport, often aiming to identify and challenge the ways in which sport can both reduce and reinforce social inequality for marginalised groups (Cahn, 2015; Magrath, 2017; Ratna and Samie, 2018). Much of this research has provided explanations as to why modern sport became so dominated by men, often confining all other groups to subordinate roles and positions. But how do we define 'modern sport', and what is its relationship to trans people's inclusion in it? The following section presents a brief history of sport in the United Kingdom, from pre-industrial sports to contemporary considerations of identity and inclusion (Johnes, 2020, n.p.), to help answer this question.

A History of Sport

Once the preserve of unadorned empiricism, 'sport is a major cultural phenomenon, with multiple histories [but] modern sport did not spring from nowhere [and] it has no simple, timeline-able history' (Tomlinson, 2007, p. 57).

Sport, notes Alan Tomlinson, is not the same now as it was 250 years ago, and sport history today 'mobilizes complex and sophisticated social and cultural theories to derive a vast range of meanings' (Edelman and Wilson, 2020, p. 1). But writing about sport does not just mean writing about the *kind* of sport played, for instance football or tennis. It also means, as Tomlinson advises, reading closely and critically about the ways in which such writing can illuminate and understand both human experience and the place of sport in society, in particular late modern, Western industrialised societies (Guttman, 1978; Mason, 1989). Understanding the human experience in sport continues to evolve, and includes race, ethnicity, disability, gender, globalisation, spectatorship, peace-keeping, class, social control, politics, religion, social commentary, outreach diplomacy (see ping-pong diplomacy), cultural hegemony (see Flynn for Gramsci, 2021) and social capital (Bourdieu, 1977). All of these play a part in sport's contribution to what Elias Norbert and Eric Dunning (1986, p. 43) called 'a civilising process'.

Writing in 1987, sociologist and anthropologist Jean-Marie Brohm (see Bryson, 1987), offered a Marxist and radical critique of sport, when he drew parallels between sport and capitalism, believing these to be the driving forces of society. For Brohm, sport is more than the activity; it is a means of government, and the qualities which define sport – performance, competitiveness, records – are 'clearly carried over from the driving forces of capitalism: productivity, the search for profit, rivalry and competitiveness' (Brohm, 1978, p. 16). Although gender is the primary focus in this book, we need to keep in mind Brohm's critique, especially when we are examining the past to understand the present: Just why is sport so dominated by men? And what does this have to do with trans people's inclusion?

Discussions about sport's intrinsic connection to power, culture and class (Hargreaves and Anderson, 2014) and the long shadow cast by the influence of the state on sport and vice versa are relevant here. American football (the National Football League, or NFL) is a good example of this, because the NFL has a deep connection to the US Armed Forces. As Butterworth (2016, p. 141) writes, 'from flyovers to "military appreciation" events, to live feeds showing stationed personnel overseas, NFL productions are interwoven with military themes, images and values'. In 2017 (see Barrón-López and Waldron, 2015), the *Huffington Post* reported that Arizona Senators John McCain and Jeff Flake, on looking into the US Defence Department's spending of taxpayer dollars on military tributes, found that the Pentagon had paid up to $6.8 million of taxpayer money to pro sports teams for military tributes – not only to the NFL but also to the National Basketball Association (NBA), the National Hockey League (NHL) and Major League Soccer (MLS). In 2016, Darren Rovell reported for ESPN that the NFL would be returning $724,000 of 'paid patriotism' to the US government (Rovell, 2016). The power of pageantry and hegemonic masculinity are deeply ingrained in sport. But how did sport get to this point?

Leisure and Recreation, Class and Masculinity

McCrone (1991) wrote of how the second half of the nineteenth century and the complicated processes of industrialisation and urbanisation produced a revolution in leisure and recreation of which sport was the most spectacular aspect. Prior to the model of sports and team games established in England in public schools in the nineteenth century, the terms 'leisure' and 'recreation' better describe the activities people enjoyed. These were mostly localised and lawless, and included activities such as hurling and a kind of mob football (Vamplew, 2015).

Leisure and recreation were themselves already gendered and classed, and leisure especially was central to the formation of masculine identities in working-class neighbourhoods. For example, writing about working-class culture in Salford and Manchester from 1900 to 1939, Andrew Davies described how drinking, gambling and sport, three of the cornerstones of 'traditional' working-class culture, were all heavily male dominated. Men were identified by their hobbies or by the pubs where they drank as 'regulars', as well as by their occupations and political or religious allegiances (Davies, 1992). The masculine spheres of pub vaults and sport were out of bounds for women, consigned as they were to the home and associated domesticated responsibilities such as childcare. The significant development of sport in England begins essentially from 1880 to 1900 onwards, during the Victorian period. In his policy document in sport, *Raising the Game* (Department of Education, 1995, p. 2), former British Prime Minister John Major claimed:

> We invented the majority of the world's great sports, and most of those we did not invent we codified and helped to popularise throughout the world. It could be argued 19th century Britain was the cradle of a leisure revolution every bit as significant as the agricultural and industrial revolutions we launched in the century before.

What Major wrote here has become both mythologised, ballooning into the common trope that Britain's Industrial Revolution was the flashpoint for the unique creation of sport. Whilst true for some modern sports (such as football), the narrative claiming that Britain was the *exclusive* inventor of modern sports is untrue. Victorian culture, colonialism, anti-colonial resistance and the problems of postcolonial identity remain in many sports today, most notably cricket (Hussain et al., 2022). Predictably, John Major failed to acknowledge that nineteenth-century sport had its roots in the revamping of agriculture and the exploitation of colonial people and goods from empires during the Industrial Revolution. This was because:

> With the first stages if the agrarian and industrial revolutions late in the eighteenth-century, a burgeoning and expansive middle-class elite emerged. These newly wealthy men had not gained their power and status from the

> traditional sources of military service and landed wealth. Instead they sat in offices and 'made' money. Sport then became a way to demonstrate their otherwise ambiguous strength and manliness.
>
> *(Edelman and Wilson, 2020, p. 6)*

This new wealthy middle class generated new demands upon the education system, and public schools generally reserved for the aristocracy now found themselves admitting the sons of the newly wealthy. Schools began to introduce organised sport, including cricket and rugby, onto the curriculum, a hugely successful move which spread to elite British universities (Edelman and Wilson, 2020) which was inevitably exported to the colonies. Here also are the beginnings of fair play becoming a highly valued intrinsic marker of sporting integrity (Hargreaves, 2000), and sport, cricket in particular, was seen as a method to embed (British) rules of fairness and were considered to help preserve (and control) the social and moral order amongst the colonies (Hargreaves, 2000). This public school athleticism (Mangan, 2001) reinforced traditional ideals of manhood and character, differentiating participants from the masses – and from women – resulting in the creation of the amateur–professional distinction, which then dominated British and colonial sports for over a century (Mangan, 2001; McDevitt, 2004).

At this time, it was not only the middle and upper classes who were enjoying a sporting revolution. Sport was beginning to filter down to working-class children. The Factory Act (1833) - an act which imposed a duty on employers to provide half-time education for employees under 13 - laid the foundation for creating a more organised schooling system for children. By 1874, five thousand 'Board Schools' were running, and the provision of elementary schooling for both boys and girls became compulsory in 1880. Pupils also participated in physical activity, though the only exercise received by boys was 'a monotonous form of military drill, and girls got almost no exercise at all' (McCrone, 1991, p. 159).

With the new century also came a change in the belief that vigorous exercise was no longer a danger to women. Previous Victorian beliefs that women were frail and fragile faded. Due to the increasing influence and popularity of medical leaders and physical educators in Victorian Britain, physical exercise for young women and girls was promoted. A further shift in the interwar years (1918–1939) saw a gradual change in women and girls' participation in sport, with some schools beginning to offer Physical Education (PE) for girls in the curriculum, and club-based sports such as lawn tennis for those middle-class women with more available leisure time became fashionable (Osborne and Skillen, 2014; Roberts, 2004). However, the drive for encouraging exercise for women was also closely linked to the promotion of maternal health and stamina in childbirth – it was less a radical promotion for the social inclusion of women in sport, than a drive for increasing reproduction. Sport was seen as belonging to the realm of masculinity, a space which women were not permitted to enter unless under surveillance and an obligation to benefit others (Osborne and Skillen, 2014). Whilst sport and exercise were pleasurable pursuits for men, for women physical fitness came with a directive, a means to an end which centred on reproductive control and assessment.

The First World War had had a devastating impact on the male population in the United Kingdom, with around 750,000 British servicemen killed (Royde-Smith, 2023), amounting to approximately 1.9% of the pre-war population., According to Osborne and Skillen (2014), the drive by the British government to improve the nation's fitness overall was also motivated to produce the next generation of soldiers. Nonetheless, school had profound implications for social control, and in it, as in society at large, class and gender were important variables reflecting potent power relationships. Inevitably these were also reflected in sport and were a particularly useful means of reinforcing distinctions of class and social standing. The legacy of this, the privileging of men over women, of rich over poor, of empire over colony meant sport became

> A gender factory – a site where men made themselves into men and where women fought and overcame the consequences of that historically constructed 'male bastion' ... sport is, has been, and will continue to be one of the great engines of cultural creation.
>
> *(Edelman and Wilson, 2020, p. 3)*

The introduction of sport into school brought with it the notion not only of men's 'natural' superiority over women, but over racially and class-subordinated groups of other men throughout the British Empire and her colonies (Ehrenberg, 2006). In short, the intention of women's inclusion was meant in no way to imitate men or encroach on their territory, thus reinforcing the message that sport was the preserve of men (Scraton and Flintoff, 2002). Vociferous opposition in sport to certain players has not been limited to women or the lower classes, and other marginalised groups have also experienced direct and indirect discrimination and face numerous social barriers. The expansion of the British Empire during the Victorian period opens up the problematic discussion of race, and the lasting legacy of colonialism's impact on sport.

Race

The framing of the body as a site for exclusion in sport based on difference is not limited to women, nor to those individuals from lower-class backgrounds. Sport was constructed in the image not just of masculinity but of white masculinity (Carrington, 1998, 2010). The late nineteenth century's conjoined processes of 'industrial expansion, overseas imperialism, scientific racism and ideologies of manliness and vigour' (Widener, 2017, p. 461) means that, like gender and class, race and sport are also historically intertwined. The segregated lines originally intended to distance men and boys from both femininity and homosexuality (Mangan, 2001; McDevitt, 2004) were also employed to promote a difference of exclusion based on race.

According to Widener (2017), the shifting relationship between race and sport from the late nineteenth to the early twenty-first centuries divides roughly into three periods. The first, lasting up to the Second World War, is characterised principally by racial exclusion; the second (1940s–1970s) is characterised by confrontation to the period before and the third is described as the post-racial era. Whilst all of these periods offer 'a crucial terrain for understanding unfolding patterns of race relations' (Widener, 2017, p. 462), it is the sporting, racialised body which is of importance in the context of this book, and how this relates to the sporting, trans body.

For Black people, and for other people from ethnic minority backgrounds, their bodies within a sporting context have long been a focus of both objectification and abjectification (Abdel-Shehid and Kalman-Lamb, 2017). Images of Black male athleticism has historically stereotyped Black individuals as savage, aggressive and hypersexual (Ferber, 2007). In 2021 Chelsea footballer Edouard Mendy criticised media outlets for mistakenly using his image in stories about Manchester City's Benjamin Mendy, who had been charged (and later cleared) of rape. Photos of Edouard Mendy and his cousin, Real Madrid's Ferland Mendy, were used to illustrate articles about the case, rather than those of Benjamin Mendy. On his Instagram feed (BBC, 2021b, November 18), Edouard Mendy wrote:

> Sad to see that in 2021, in France as well as in England, for some, black people have neither names nor distinct faces … these 'mistakes' of photos appear anecdotal, but actually they are quite the opposite, they are highly symbolic. It's not that complicated to differentiate two faces, especially when the football jersey is of valuable help!

The symbolism to which Mendy is referring to is clear and previously written about by Stuart Hall (2006) in his work on new ethnicities, the politics of anti-racism and the post-war Black experience in Britain: all Black men look the same, and all Black men are dangerous predators.

Similarly, Black female athletes have been subjected to the damaging intersections between race and gender, and embodied as hypersexual (Ratna and Samie, 2018). In September 2018, an Australian newspaper published a cartoon of Serena Williams, the American professional tennis player and former world No. 1 in women's single tennis, which depicted Williams jumping above a broken tennis racquet next to a baby's dummy in the 2018 US Tennis Open final. Despite receiving global criticism and complaints that the caricature used racist and sexist stereotypes of African American people, with the National Association of Black Journalists in the United States denouncing it as 'repugnant on many levels' (BBC, 2019, February 25), the Australian Press Council concluded that the image did not breach media standards. This is not the first time Williams has been the subject of racist attention. During the 2002 US Open, she wore an outfit described as a body-clinging, faux leather, black cat-suit, and as Schultz (2005, p. 338) notes:

> It was not necessarily the catsuit itself that the popular media found especially controversial but rather the visibility of her physique the outfit provided. The ways in which Serena Williams, the outfit, and her body were discussed offers a particular site at which to interrogate the production of blackness in 21st-century, U.S. society.

Whilst white female athletes have themslves been subject to sexualisation and the accompanying commodification of 'sex sells', I would argue there is, as Edouard Mendy pointed out, a more symbolic denial to Black women's rights to control their own bodies. Alice Dearing made history at the 2021 Tokyo Olympics as the first-ever Black woman to represent Team GB in a swimming event at an Olympics. Derring, who co-founded the Black Swimming Association, a non-profit organisation, set up to diversify the world of aquatics through education, advocacy, support and research, has spoken of how 'decades of cultural and institutional racism has sadly seeped into the swimming community and swimming in general for quite some time' (Goodbody, 2021). Derring has spoken of having 'been a victim of some instances of racism but it hasn't stopped me from swimming'. Nonetheless, in a display of what swimming coach Tony Cronin (BBC, 2021, July 2) called 'misunderstanding and ignorance', international swimming organisation FINA initially banned athletes from wearing a specially designed for natural black hair swimming hat. FINA claimed the hat, called a Soul Cap, did not follow 'the natural form of the head'. The ban was later overturned but the message was clear; black hair is an extension of the black body (Johnson, 2016), and for those athletes whose bodies were deemed unruly and different to white bodies, exceptions would not be made.

Successful Black athletes' bodies are often viewed as potentially threatening to the notion of white male (and female) superiority, in whose imagination both Black men and women have been reduced to their physical bodies (Magrath, 2017; Walker and Melton, 2015). The hypervisibility of the Black male athlete in particular has led to the development of a Black queer theory of sport and masculinity which moves beyond the supposedly masculinist limitations of earlier observations (Abdel-Shehid and Kalman-Lamb, 2017). Although it can be argued that the success of Black male athletes might help to undermine racism and promote positive and visible representation, 'sport represents an arena where Black men have historically been allowed to succeed on the field but never to hold positions of power and control, such as coaches or owners' (Ferber, 2007, p. 20). Sport, whilst often regarded as meritocratic and equal for all, brightly illuminates contemporary racisms and their connection with gender and other oppressions (Carrington, 2010; Bryan, Pope and Rankin-Wright, 2021).

The uneven patterns of racial exclusion and discrimination which originated over a century ago remain today (Widener, 2017), and initiatives similar to tacking inequalities and discrimination in sport for women, such as *This Girl Can* (UK, 2015) and Title IX (US, 2024), have been developed, for instance, the anti-racist UK initiative *Kick it Out* (2024). However, according Bryan, Pope & Rankin-Wright (2021), because the world of sport leadership privileges white heterosexual men, women's, particularly Black women's, access to leadership roles is severely limited (see also Carter-Francique, 2018). In 2020, the murder of George Floyd was a catalyst for the five Sports Councils responsible for investing in and growing sport across the United Kingdom, to explore racial inequalities in sport and to look at how reflective their sporting system is of UK society. Their findings revealed that 'racism and racial inequalities still exist within sport in the UK and that there are longstanding issues, which have resulted in ethnically diverse communities being consistently disadvantaged' (UK Sport, 2021). Whilst there is slow change happening to address these inequalities, they will only happen effectively and permanently by centring the lived experiences of those who are disadvantaged and in particular need of urgent reform.

Disability

Disability, arguably like gender, can be viewed on a spectrum, and multiple definitions of disability posit that disability is a social construct (Craig and Beedie, 2008). Early organised sport for people with disabilities was heavily influenced by medical discourses that favoured exercise to rehabilitate the newly disabled, particularly those recovering from spinal injuries received in military conflict (Thomas and Smith, 2008). Scholars have written about how the disabled body has been subject to the medical gaze, and the disabled body in sport, much like the transgender body, has been pathologised in opposition to able-bodied ideologies (Giulianotti, 2016; Smith and Sparkes, 2019). Florian Kiuppis (2018, p. 5) writes:

> Sport is an area of life in which people with disabilities arguably have less favourable experiences than their non-disabled peers and competitors. Typical barriers for people with disabilities to participate in sport include lack of awareness on the part of people without disabilities as to how to involve them in teams adequately; lack of opportunities and programmes for training and competition; too few accessible facilities due to physical barriers; and limited information on and access to resources.

This has led to questioning some of the ways in which modern society has imposed social and moral views of the body as a project, something to be trained, disciplined, kept healthy and monitored (Craig and Beedie, 2008). Physical and attitudinal barriers demonstrate that culture's interest in the non-normative body remains in thrall to the tyranny of the normal (Richardson and Locke, 2014). At the 2021 Tokyo Games, British Paralympian Olivia Breen, who has cerebral palsy, was told by an official that her athletic briefs were too short, highlighting how gender, sport and disability intersect when the body is on display. Breen said the incident had made her 'feel really angry and it's very wrong' (BBC, 2021a). Breen (2021a) rightly pointed out that it was unlikely male athletes would be subjected to the same level of scrutiny. Whilst both she and the news coverage focused on the sexism at play, no mention was made of Breen's disability perhaps being the real reason for the discrimination she was subjected to, which was rooted in ableist anxiety. Also unmentioned was the unnecessary time and effort undertaken to challenge such double standards in what is, after all, the workplace. Similar to trans people, disabled people continue to face profound barriers to physical activity that, in turn, exacerbate health inequalities. As Smith and Sparkes note (2019, p. 24), what is needed is 'more research on physical activity that is committed to a praxis for radical change' and to identifying barriers.

Sexuality

Because sport has been defined as 'the last bastion of male domination' (Burton Nelson, 1994, p. 6), it has, according to Rachel Bullingham et al. (2014, p. 5), 'created not only a problem for effeminate and/or gay men, but also for women'. The heteropatriarchy is central to the culture of sport, and the damaging impact this continues to have on LGBTQ+ athletes has been widely discussed (Anderson, 2016; Cleland et al., 2023; Griffin, 1998; Lenskyj, 1986). Despite an increased visibility of openly gay and lesbian athletes in elite sport, homophobia is still commonplace. British Olympic champion diver Tom Daly, who came out in 2019, spoke openly about his experiences as a gay athlete in the documentary 'Illegal to Be Me', in which he talks about the homophobia he (and others) have experienced both in sport and outside of it (Nicholson, 2022). Daly was subjected to horrific homophobic abuse after he exited the Rio Olympics in 2016, from the UK-based prayer and lobby group Christian Voice.

There is a huge disparity between the number of openly gay women and openly gay men in football and soccer. According to OutSports (2023), there were at least 96 players who were out as gay or bisexual competing in the 2023 Women's World Cup. These players were across 22 teams and included Megan Rapinoe (USA) and Marta (Brazil). Yet, openly gay or bi-sexual professional footballers on the men's team remain a rarity. In 2022 Blackpool forward Jake Daniels became the first active UK male footballer to come out as gay since

1990 and was the first to do so since Justin Fashanu.[1] Jake Daniels told Sky Sports (MackInnes, 2022) how

> For a long time, I've thought I would have to hide my truth because I wanted to be, and now I am, a professional footballer. I asked myself if I should wait until I've retired to come out. No other player in the professional game here is out.

Daniel's coming out may be 'a striking landmark' (MackInnes, 2022), but Daniel is right; he is an outlier in UK football. Homophobia is especially rife in football globally, brought sharply into focus when Qatar – where homosexuality is illegal – hosted the 2023 Men's World Cup. It seems outdated Victorian moralities continue to cast a long shadow, and the heteropatriarchy is far from being dismantled in sport. To reiterate:

> Modern sport thus emerged in Europe and its colonies in the late nineteenth and twentieth centuries as a male-supremacist 'civilizing' project that represented a backlash against the increasing power of middle-and upper-class white women, designed to emphasise sex difference, to socialise men into orthodox [hegemonic] masculinity, and enforce heterosexuality.
>
> *(Anderson and Travers, 2017, p. 651)*

With few heterosexual allies and the very real loss of income and endorsement if they are openly gay, many LGBTQ+ athletes and coaches have long felt compelled to keep their sexuality private, understanding how in an overwhelmingly heteronormative world, hiding their sexual orientation is often necessary for acceptance by teammates, spectators and sponsors (Griffin and Ouellett, 2003; Kauer and Rauscher, 2019; Symons, 2011). The culture within sports still relies on stereotypes of gender and sexuality, where men are assumed to be straight and women are assumed to be lesbians.

The Sporting Body and Feminist Thinking

Participation for many marginalised groups including women and LGBTQ+ athletes in sport has constituted 'a form of corporeal transgression, in terms of putting their bodies in places where only white, male, able-bodied athletes were authorised or "normally" expected to be present' (Giulianotti 2016, p. 121). However, it is not enough to juxtapose social categories of gender, class and race and apply them to sport. They need to be woven together, beginning with the most visual element of sport, the human body, and an investigation of social meanings. Sport, after all, as Vertinsky et al. (1998) wrote, is a form of body culture.

The hidden-from-history trope is a familiar one within feminist observations on sport, whereby women's experiences have been largely ignored or marginalised (Hargreaves, 2000; Scraton and Flintoff, 2002). The fight for women to gain equality in sport at national levels and in professional leagues in terms of better visibility, pay and training remains ongoing at the time of writing. These inequalities are also reflected off the field, with fewer female than male sports commentators, pundits, coaches and managers in high-earning roles. Women continue to be treated as inferior to men, in terms of visibility, coverage and sponsorship. Whilst the 2012 London Olympics were seen as 'the women's games' (Mansfield et al., 2017), female athletes continued to face barriers and constraints to participation., This included the initial refusal to allow Saudi women to attend, opposition to women's boxing and the suggested policy requiring competing female boxers to wear skirts/skorts, rather than the type of shorts their male counterparts were allowed to wear (Mansfield et al., 2017). These aspects are focused squarely on the body, giving weight to Bourdieu's argument that the body can express much that the mind and speech could not (Bourdieu, 1977).

As Jennifer Hargreaves and Patricia Vertinsky so beautifully articulate in their book *Physical Culture, Power, and the Body* (2006), sport is not just a diverse phenomenon; it is a cluster of phenomena. Because of this, the body offers a useful way into the topic, and bodies are used to convey a host of deep-seated cultural beliefs and values (Hargreaves and Vertinksy, 2006). Edelman and Wilson use Foucault's 1977 approach to historical knowledge as an example of this, and the way in which he 'placed the human body at the centre of scholarly concerns and deployed a concept of power that was particularly helpful to understanding how relations of domination and subordination were constituted and expressed in sport' (Edelman and Wilson, 2020, p. 2).

Feminist scholars have engaged widely with discourses concerning the body and sport, most notably in terms of conceptualising and understanding gender in psychological and sociological terms, and in the politics of the body (Cooky, 2019; Cregan, 2006; Fink, 2008; Roy and Caudwell, 2014; Throsby, 2013, 2015; Toffoletti and Thorpe, 2018). This feminist work has been instrumental in bringing to the foreground the multitude of issues many female athletes have faced when engaging with sport, particularly concerning the unruly or overlooked body. Mansfield et al. (2017, p. 7) write:

> Developments such as poststructuralism and representing the 'Other' (Aitchison, 2000), resistance (Shaw, 2001), diversity (Allison, 2000), confronting whiteness (Watson and Scraton, 2001), and intersectionality (McDonald, 2009; Watson and Scraton, 2013) were placed firmly, as feminist concerns, on the leisure studies agenda. It is clear that during the last three decades feminist leisure studies have developed as a substantive and robust framework for informed critical analyses.

Utilising a feminist perspective in sport began to emerge in the early 1980s and into the 1990s, when feminist challenges to traditional sports studies examined how gender and power interrelate. These feminist perspectives included sports and oppression (Bryson, 1983), empowerment (Theberge, 1997), and then later the philosophical questioning of traditional epistemology (Coakley, 2017). This research has been crucial in providing a strong foundation for scholars to analyse in detail particular areas in sport, including the body (Bandya, Gorib and Jinxiac, 2012; Caudwell, 2003; Cregan, 2006; Throsby, 2013).

Deeper critical analysis of sport by feminists has led to the development and application of the now-familiar concepts in sport studies such as hegemonic femininity (Krane, 2001) and hegemonic masculinity (Connell and Messerschmidt, 2005). These concepts were developed to help highlight idealised gender stereotypes of both masculinity and feminity as ubiquitous within sport, and are the product of a patriarchal society which continues to value male physicality and dominance and perpetuates the subordination and exclusion of anyone viewed as 'other' (C. Phipps, 2019). Catherine Phipps (2019, p. 11) calls this

> A paternalistic gender-based classification, whereby particular characteristics – such as women being small and men being big – are ascribed to each sex (when in reality not all people of that sex share those traits), perpetuating gender stereotypes. In other words, gender binaries may reflect hegemonic ideas about men's physical superiority over women, which is usually unquestionably accepted.

These idealised gender sterotypes often manifest in sport's frequent association with the corporeal differences between men's and women's bodies: what Tagg calls the image of 'large armoured men' versus 'thin women in short skirts' (Tagg, 2018, p. 410). Yi-Hsiu and Chen-Yueh (2013) argued not only that sports tends to masculinise women, for example the ways in which powerful athletes such as Serena Williams are deemed 'too aggressive', but also how gender stereotypes influence sport participation. This is seen in the skimpier, sexualised clothing and appearance of female gymnasts versus the covered-up and hyper-muscular appearance of their male counterparts. In turn this can affect an individual's decisions about whether to participate in gender-'appropriate' or 'inappropriate' sports, which also sees sports participation as being further influenced by

> Whether the activity characteristics are considered socially acceptable for one's gender [with] women expected to display feminine behaviours while also participating in masculine activities often facing a conflicting set of roles.
>
> *(Yi-Hsiu and Chen-Yueh, 2013, p. 5)*

Emphasising gender stereotypes within sport further essentialises the outwardly physical characteristics between men and women via these corporal differences. In addition, there remains, as Vertinsky (2020, p. 446) writes, 'a belief system that negotiates the current tensions between beliefs in equal opportunity with stubbornly persistent commitments to the idea of natural difference'. Whilst we have previously examined the (historical) causes of the exclusion of certain bodies in sport, what does this mean in real terms for the gendered body? According to Giulianotti (2016), sport was also founded on the belief of sexual dimorphism and dichotomous gender differences, creating segregated competitions. To stress, within sport the body is a central focus, with gendered structures (such as separate male and female sport teams) and normative gendered ideologies (such as the socialisation of males and females into different sports) apparent, creating a highly gendered space.

Progressive policy interventions for increasing participation rates in sport for women and girls have been successful, though not without criticism (Mansfield et al., 2017). The most well-known of these policies is the US initiative, Title IX, a federal civil rights law passed as part of the Education Amendments of 1972, which bans discrimination on the basis of sex within federally funded schools, including universities. Since its inception over 45 years ago, the impact of Title IX on women's sports cannot be overstated: the numbers of girls playing high school sports has grown considerably from fewer than 300,000 in 1974 to more than 3.1 million in 2012 (US Department of Education, 2014). The UK-situated *This Girl Can* campaign, which was developed by Sport England in 2015, was established to address the issue that more men play sport than women over the life course, and women's participation is more likely to decline with age due to caregiving commitments elsewhere. The focus of this campaign is to narrow the participation gap, whilst encouraging women to seek out alternative and creative methods of exercising, and has a commitment to showcasing non-normative bodies and promoting diversity, such as wheelchair users and Muslim participants.

For this reason, the *This Girl Can* campaign (2015) was considered groundbreaking, fresh and disruptive, and it proved successful in encouraging women and young girls to become more involved in physical exercise, no matter the activity. Since its implementation, 2.9 million women aged 14–60 have been more active (e.g. tried a new type of exercise or increased the amount of time spent exercising) as a result of seeing the campaign. Visibility and representation in sport have a measurable impact. However, both these initiatives have faced criticism, because whilst they can be applauded for their attempts to improve participation rates and visibility for women and girls in sport, they are still focused on bodies not vocation, often wrapped up in the commodification of women sports, and how women look. Nike, a long-time sponsor of Title IX, has been particularly pervasive in increasing its sales by selling empowerment and health to the growing female market (Toffoletti and Thorpe, 2018). More recently, sponsorship has been extended to trans athletes, for example Chris

Mosier for Nike, boxer Patricio Manuel for Everlast and volleyball player Tiffany Abreu for Adidas, though this has been met with accusations of rainbow washing (Dass, 2023).

Paying attention to the gendered body might encourage new perspectives on the sporting perspectives of the past, and it is important to be mindful of Catriona Parrat's (1998, cited in Vertinsky, 2020, p. 451) observations of how

> While attention to theory about gender offered a powerful way of exposing and attacking oppositions in which gender relations are based, it also poses the gender of abandoning concern with the lives of 'real women'. Sporting women of colour and ethnicity, working women, lesbian women, aging women, and those with disabilities were amongst those who remained hidden from history and whose voices needed to be heard as authentic and legitimate.

Historian Joan Wallach-Scott views gender as a question, and as an invitation to think critically of the meanings of bodies, and how they are produced, deployed and recorded in history. As she notes, 'for all its corporeality the body is not an originating point nor yet a terminus; it is a result, or an effect conceived in a specific time and place' (Wallach Scott, 2008, p. 1,423).

Vertinsky (2020, p. 453) extends this invitation further, and reminds us how important it is that we 'continue to ask, in increasingly precarious times, how new forms of gender might affect the ways we live, play and think about our sporting present, as well as our past'. I both like and agree with this idea, that rather than rely on the idea of sex/gender as

> A natural, universal and stable binary, perhaps a breaking down rather than mobilizing round conventional gender categories is necessary. This would offer a paradigmatic shift in transgender politics and discussions of human rights, making space for the very complexity, mutability and fluidity of gender.
>
> *(Vertinsky, 2020, p. 453)*

This literature has paved the way in our understanding of how gender connects to issues about the body in sport, and to barriers to inclusion. In turn, these approaches have helped to open up discussions regarding inclusion in sport for trans people (Buzuvis, 2011, 2012; Caudwell, 2014, 2020; Klein et al., 2018, 2019; Love, 2017; Travers and Deri, 2011). Most significantly for this research, they have looked towards new theoretical approaches including trans feminist theory, which contributes fresh knowledge and perspectives to the 'development, diversification and rigour of feminist approaches to gendered issues, theories and concepts in sport' (Mansfield et al., 2017, p. 7).

Discussion Questions

1 Do you think sport is socially constructed, and if not, why not? If we understand that sport has been created, what is stopping it from being recreated?
2 Some historians argue that sport is a particularly useful means of reinforcing distinctions of class, social standing and race, and also of gender. Can you think of examples from your own experiences?
3 Sport, like school, is a form of social control, and the growth of modern sport took place in the context of efforts – of varying success – by church and state to control and direct leisure. How would you explain this?

Note

1 Justin Fashanu was an English footballer who sadly took his own life in 1998. The Justin Campaign, which is a campaign against homophobia in football and promotes the inclusion of openly gay players in football, was set up in his name. www.thejustincampaign.com

References

[This Girl Can]. (2015). https://www.thisgirlcan.co.uk/
[Title IX]. (2024). https://titleix.harvard.edu/what-title-ix
Abdel-Shehid, G., & Kalman-Lamb, N. (2017). Complicating gender, sport, and social inclusion: The case for intersectionality. *Social Inclusion*, *5*(2), 159–162. https://doi.org/10.17645/si.v5i2.887
Aitchison, C. (2000). Poststructural feminist theories of representing others: A response to the 'crisis' in leisure studies' discourse. *Leisure Studies*, *19*(3), 127–144.
Allison, M. T. (2000). Leisure, diversity and social justice. *Journal of Leisure Research*, *32*(1), 2–6.
Anderson, E. (2016). *Out in sport: The experiences of openly gay and lesbian athletes in competitive sport*. London: Routledge.
Anderson, E., & Travers, A. (2017). *Transgender athletes in competitive sport*. London: Routledge.
Bandya, S.J., Gorib, G., & Jinxiac, D. (2012). From women and sport to gender and sport: Transnational, transdisciplinary, and intersectional perspectives. *The International Journal of the History of Sport*, *29*(5), 667–674. https://doi.org/10.1080/09523367.2012.687142
Barrón-López, L. & Waldron, T. (2015, April 11). *Pentagon paid up to $6.8 million of taxpayer money to pro sports teams for military tributes*. Huff Post. https://www.huffingtonpost.co.uk/entry/defense-military-tributes-professional-sports_n_5639a04ce4b0411d306eda5e
BBC. (2019, February 25). *Serena Williams: Cartoon accused of racism cleared by press watchdog*. BBC. https://www.bbc.co.uk/news/world-australia-47352854
BBC. (2021, July 2). *Soul Cap: Afro swim cap Olympic rejection 'heart-breaking' for black swimmers*. BBC. https://www.bbc.co.uk/news/newsbeat-57688380
BBC. (2021a, July 20). *Olivia Breen World champion para-athlete left angry after official said her shorts were 'too revealing'*. BBC. https://www.bbc.co.uk/sport/disability-sport/57887715

BBC. (2021b, November 18). *Edouard Mendy criticises media outlets over use of his image in stories about Benjamin Mendy*. BBC. https://www.bbc.co.uk/sport/football/59329882

Bourdieu, P. (1977). *Outline of a theory of practice*. New York: Cambridge University Press.

Brohm, J.-M. (1978). *Sport, a prison of measured time*. London: Ink Links Limited.

Bryan, A., Pope, S., & Rankin-Wright, A. J. (2021). On the periphery: Examining women's exclusion from core leadership roles in the "Extremely Gendered" organization of Men's Club Football in England. *Gender & Society*, *35*(6), 940–970. https://doi.org/10.1177/08912432211046318

Bryson, L. (1983). Sport and the oppression of women. *Journal of Sociology*. https://doi.org/10.1177%2F144078338301900303

Bryson, L. (1987). Sport and the maintenance of masculine hegemony. *Women's Studies International Forum*, *10*(4), 349–360. https://doi.org/10.1016/0277-5395(87)90052-5

Bullingham, R., Magrath, R., & Anderson, E. (2014). Sport and a cultural shift away from homohysteria. In: *Handbook of sport, gender and sexuality. Routledge International Handbooks*, pp. 275–282. London: Routledge. ISBN 9781138695047

Burr, V. (2015). *Social constructionism* (3rd ed.). New York, NY; Hove, East Sussex: Routledge.

Burton Nelson, M. (1994). *The stronger women get, the more men love football*. New York: Avon Books.

Butterworth, M.L. (2016). Everybody's all-Americans: High school football and the American military. In: D.J. Leonard, K.B. George & W. Davis (Eds). *Football, culture and power*, pp. 141–155. UK: Taylor and Francis.

Buzuvis, E. (2011). Caster Semenya and the myth of a level playing field. *The Modern American*, *6*, 36–45. https://digitalcommons.wcl.american.edu/cgi/viewcontent.cgi?article=1136&context=tma

Buzuvis, E. (2012). Including transgender athletes in sex-segregated sport: Essays from activists, coaches, and scholars, 25–31. https://digitalcommons.law.wne.edu/cgi/viewcontent.cgi?article=1248&context=facschol

Cahn, S.K. (2015). *Coming on strong: Gender and sexuality in women's sport* (2nd ed.). Urbana: University of Illinois Press.

Carrington, B. (1998). Sport, masculinity, and Black cultural resistance. *Journal of Sport and Social Issues*, *22*(3), 275–298. https://doi.org/10.1177/019372398022003004

Carrington, B. (2010). *Race, sport and politics: The sporting black diaspora*. London: SAGE.

Carter-Francique, A.R. (2018). Is excellence inclusive? The benefits of fostering Black female college athlete's sense of belonging. *Journal of Higher Education Athletics & Innovation*, *1*(3), 48–73. https://doi.org/10.15763/issn.2376-5267.2018.1.3.48-73

Caudwell, J. (2003). Sporting gender: Women's footballing bodies as sites/sights for the (re) articulation of sex, gender, and desire. *Sociology of Sport Journal*, *20*(4), 371–386. https://doi.org/10.1123/ssj.20.4.371

Caudwell, J. (2014). [Transgender] young men: Gendered subjectivities and the physically active body. *Sport, Education and Society*, *19*(4), 398–414. https://doi.org/10.1080/13573322.2012.672320

Caudwell, J. (2020). Transgender and non-binary swimming in the UK: Indoor public pool spaces and un/safety. *Frontiers in Sociology*, *5*. https://doi.org/10.3389/fsoc.2020.00064

Cleland, J., Cashmore, E., Dixon, K., & MacDonald, C. (2023). Analyzing the presence of homosexually-themed language among Association Football Fans in the United Kingdom. *Communication & Sport*, *11*(3), 551–569. https://doi.org/10.1177/2167479521l005838

Coakley, J.J. (2017). *Sports in society: Issues and controversies* (International; 12th ed.). New York: McGraw-Hill Education.

Connell, R.W., & Messerschmidt, J.W. (2005). Hegemonic masculinity: Rethinking the concept. *Gender and Society*, *19*(6), 829–859. https://doi.org/10.1177/0891243205278639

Cooky, C. (2019). Feminisms. In: B. Smith & A.C. Sparkes (Eds). *Routledge handbook of qualitative research in sport and exercise*, pp. 75–87. UK: Routledge.

Craig, P., & Beedie, P.A. (2008). *Sport sociology*. Exeter: Learning Matters.

Cregan, K. (2006). *The sociology of the body: Mapping the abstraction of embodiment*. London: SAGE.

Dass, C. (2023, April 12). *Nike called out for Dylan Mulvaney ad: Why brands are failing when it comes to trans representation in campaigns*. Marketing Interactive. https://www.marketing-interactive.com/nike-called-out-for-dylan-mulvaney-ad-why-brands-are-failing-when-it-comes-to-trans-representation-in-campaigns

Davies, A. (1992). Leisure, gender and poverty: Working-class culture in Salford and Manchester, 1900–1939. In: A. Davies & S. Wilder (Eds). UK, Buckingham: Open University Press.

Department of Education. (1995). *Raising the Game*. https://publications.parliament.uk/pa/cm201314/cmselect/cmeduc/164/164vw21.htm

Edelman, R., & Wilson, W. (2020). *The Oxford handbook of sports history*. Oxford: Oxford University Press.

Ehrenberg, M. (2006). Athletic intruders: Ethnographic research on women, culture, and exercise. *Archives of Sexual Behavior*, *35*(4), 511–513. New York. https://doi.org/10.1007/s10508-006-9051-5

English, C. (2017). Toward sport reform: Hegemonic masculinity and reconceptualizing competition. *Journal of the Philosophy of Sport*, *44*(2), 183–198. https://doi.org/10.1080/00948705.2017.1300538

Ferber, A.L. (2007). The construction of Black masculinity: White supremacy now and then. *Journal of Sport and Social Issues*, *31*(1), 11–24. https://doi.org/10.1177/0193723506296829

Fink, J.S. (2008). Gender and sex diversity in sport organizations: Concluding comments. *Sex Roles*, *58*(1), 146–147. https://doi.org/10.1007/s11199-007-9364-4

Flynn, S. (2021). Revisiting hegemony: A Gramscian analysis for contemporary social work. *Irish Journal of Sociology*, *29*(1), 77–96. https://doi.org/10.1177/0791603519884201

Foucault, M. (1977). *Discipline and punish: The birth of the prison* (2nd ed.). New York: Vintage Books.

Giulianotti, R. (2016). *Sport: a critical sociology* (2nd ed.). Cambridge: Polity Press.

Goodbody, J. (2021, June 25). *Racism has held up ethnic minorities in swimming, says Alice Dearing*. The Guardian. https://www.theguardian.com/sport/2021/jun/25/racism-has-held-up-ethnic-minorities-in-swimming-says-alice-dearing

Griffin, P. (1998). *Strong women, deep closets: Lesbians and homophobia in sport*. Champaign, Ill; Leeds: Human Kinetics.

Griffin, P., & Ouellett, M. (2003). From silence to safety and beyond: Historical trends in addressing lesbian, gay, bisexual, transgender issues in K-12 Schools. *Equity and Excellence in Education*, *36*(2), 106–114. https://doi.org/10.1080/10665680303508

Guttman, A. (1978). *From ritual to record: The nature of modern sport*. New York: Columbia University Press.

Hall, S. (2006). New ethnicities. In: *Stuart Hall*, pp. 453–462. UK: Routledge.

Hargreaves, J. (2000). *Heroines of sport: The politics of difference and identity*. London; New York: Routledge.

Hargreaves, J., & Anderson, E. (2014). *Routledge handbook of sport, gender and sexuality*. Abingdon: Routledge.

Hargreaves, J., & Vertinksy, P. (2006). *Physical culture, power, and the body*. UK: Taylor and Frances.

Hussain, M., Muzaffar, F., Lone, B.A., Hamid, S., & Loan, F.A. (2022). Racism in International Cricket: A review of selected incidents from media reports. *Antrocom: Online Journal of Anthropology*, *18*(2), 639–650.

Johnes, M. (2020). *A brief history of sport in the UK*. Available from: https://martinjohnes.com/2020/04/15/a-brief-history-of-sport-in-the-uk/

Johnson, E.J. (2016). *Resistance and empowerment in black women's hair styling*. UK: Taylor and Francis.

Kauer, K.J., & Rauscher, L. (2019). Negotiating gender among LGBTIQ athletes: Sport as a space for disruption and reproduction. In: K. Krane (Ed). *Sex, gender, and sexuality in sport: Queer inquiries*, pp. 49–66. UK: Routledge.

Kick it Out. (2024). Available at: https://www.kickitout.org/

Kiuppis, F. (2018). Inclusion in sport: Disability and participation. *Sport in Society*, *21*(1), 4–21. https://doi.org/10.1080/17430437.2016.1225882

Klein, A., Krane, V., & Paule-Koba, A.L. (2018). Bodily changes and performance effects in a transitioning transgender college athlete. *Qualitative Research in Sport, Exercise and Health*, *10*(5), 555–569. https://doi.org/10.1080/2159676X.2018.1466721

Klein, A., Paule-Koba, A.L., & Krane, V. (2019). The journey of transitioning: Being a trans male athlete in college sport. *Sport Management Review*, *22*(5), 626–639. https://doi.org/10.1016/j.smr.2018.09.006

Krane, V. (2001). We can be athletic and feminine, but do we want to? Challenging hegemonic femininity in women's sport. *Quest*, *53*(1), 115–133. https://doi.org/10.1080/00336297.2001.10491733

Lenskyj, H. (1986). *Out of bounds: Women, sport and sexuality*. Toronto: Women's Press.

Love, A. (2017). The tenuous inclusion of transgender athletes in sport. In: A. Travers & E. Anderson (Eds). *Transgender athletes in competitive sport* (Chapter 7). UK: Routledge. https://doi.org/10.4324/9781315304274-17

MackInnes, P. (2022, May 16). *Jake Daniels becomes first UK male footballer to come out as gay since 1990*. The Guardian. https://www.theguardian.com/football/2022/may/16/jake-daniels-becomes-first-uk-male-footballer-to-come-out-as-gay-since-1990

Magrath, R. (2017). The intersection of race, religion and homophobia in British football. *International Review for the Sociology of Sport*, *52*(4), 411–429. https://doi.org/10.1177/1012690215597651

Mangan, J. (2001). *Athleticism in the Victorian and Edwardian public school*. UK: Taylor and Francis.

Mansfield, L., Caudwell, J., Wheaton, B., & Watson, B. (2017). *The Palgrave handbook of feminism and sport, leisure and physical education*. Basingstoke, Hampshire: Palgrave Macmillan.

Mason, T. (1989). *Sport in Britain: A social history*. New York: Cambridge University Press.
McCrone, K.E. (1991). Class, gender, and English women's sport, c. 1890–1914. *Journal of Sport History*, *18*(1), 159–182. http://www.jstor.org/stable/43636123
McDevitt, P.F. (2004). *May the best man win: Sport, masculinity, and nationalism in Great Britain and the Empire, 1880–1935*. Basingstoke: Palgrave.
McDonald, M. G. (2009). Dialogues on whiteness, leisure and (anti)racism. *Journal of Leisure Research*, *41*(1), 5–21.
McKay, J. (1992). *Sport and the social construction of gender. In: Society and gender*. London: Palgrave. https://doi.org/10.1007/978-1-349-15168-4_11
Nicholson, R. (2022, August 9). *Tom Daley: Illegal to Be Me review – a beautiful, moving protest against homophobia*. The Guardian. https://www.theguardian.com/tv-and-radio/2022/aug/09/tom-daley-to-be-me-review-a-beautiful-moving-protest-against-homophobia
Norbert, E., & Dunning, E. (1986). *The quest for excitement: Sport and leisure in the civilizing process*. Oxford, UK: JSTOR.
Osborne, C.A., & Skillen, F. (2014). Introduction. The state of play: Women in British sports history. In: *Women in sports history*, pp. 1–6. London: Routledge.
OutSports. (2023). https://www.outsports.com/2023/7/11/23787885/world-cup-women-gay-lesbian-lgbtq-usa-australia-brazil#comments
Phipps, C. (2019). Thinking beyond the binary: Barriers to trans participation in university sport. *International Review for the Sociology of Sport*. https://doi.org/10.1177/1012690219889621
Ratna, A., & Samie, S.F. (2018). *Race, gender and sport: The politics of ethnic 'other' girls and women*. London/New York: Routledge/Taylor and Francis Group.
Richardson, N., & Locke, A. (2014). *Body studies, the basics*. UK: Routledge.
Roberts, E. (2004). 'More than Mere Amusement': Working-class women's leisure in England, 1750–1914. *The English Historical Review*, *119*(483). Oxford Academic. https://doi.org/10.1093/ehr/119.483.1078
Rovell, D. (2016, May 19). *NFL returning $723K for sponsored military tributes*. ESPN. https://www.espn.com/nfl/story/_/id/15611052/nfl-returning-723000-taxpayers-paid-military-tributes
Roy, G., & Caudwell, J. (2014). Women and surfing spaces in Newquay, UK. In: J. Hargreaves & E. Anderson (Eds). *Routledge handbook of sport, gender and sexuality (Chapter 25)*. Routledge. http://www.routledge.com/books/details/9780415522533/
Royde-Smith, J.G. (2023). *How many people died during World War I?* Available at: https://www.britannica.com/event/World-War-I
Schultz, J. (2005). Reading the catsuit: Serena Williams and the production of blackness at the 2002 US Open. *Journal of Sport and Social Issues*, *29*(3), 338–357. https://doi.org/10.1177/0193723505276230
Scraton, S., & Flintoff, A. (2002). *Gender and sport: A reader*. London: Routledge.
Shaw, S. M. (2001). Conceptualizing resistance: Women's leisure as political practice. *Journal of Leisure Research*, *33*(2), 186–201.
Smith, B., & Sparkes, A.C. (2019). Disability, sport, and physical activity. In: *Routledge handbook of disability studies* (2nd ed.), pp. 391–403. London: Routledge. ISBN 9781138365308
Symons, C. (2011). *The gay games: A history*. London: Routledge.
Tagg, B. (2018). Men's netball or mixed-gender indoor netball? *Sport in Society*, *21*(9), 1400–1415. http://dx.doi.org/10.1177/1012690214524757

Theberge, N. (1997). "It's part of the game": Physicality and the production of gender in women's hockey. *Gender and Society*, *11*(1), 69–87. UK: SAGE.

Thomas, N., & Smith, A. (2008). *Disability, sport and society: An introduction*. UK: Routledge.

Throsby, K. (2013). "If I go in a cranky sea lion, I come out like a smiling dolphin": Marathon swimming and the unexpected pleasures of being a body in water. *Feminist Review*, *103*, 5–22. UK. https://doi.org/10.1057%2Ffr.2012.23

Throsby, K. (2015). "You can't be too vain to gain if you want to swim the Channel": Marathon swimming and the construction of heroic fatness. *International Review for the Sociology of Sport*, *50*(7), 769–784. UK. https://doi.org/10.1177%2F1012690213494080

Toffoletti, K., & Thorpe, H. (2018). The athletic labour of femininity: The branding and consumption of global celebrity sportswomen on Instagram. *Journal of Consumer Culture*, *18*(2), 298–316. https://doi.org/10.1177/1469540517747068

Tomlinson, A. (2007). *The sport studies reader*. London: Routledge.

Travers, A., & Deri, J. (2011). Transgender inclusion and the changing face of lesbian softball leagues. *International Review for the Sociology of Sport*, *46*(4), 488–507. https://doi.org/10.1177/1012690210384661

UK Sport. (2021, June 23). *Tackling racism and racial inequality in sport review*. https://www.uksport.gov.uk/news/2021/06/23/tackling-racism-and-racial-inequality-in-sport-review

US Department of Education. (2014). https://www2.ed.gov/about/offices/list/ocr/docs/tix_dis.html

Vamplew, Wray. (2015). Sport, industry and industrial sport in Britain before 1914: Review and revision. *Sport in Society*, *19*, 1–16. 10.1080/17430437.2015.1057942

Vertinsky, P. (2020). Gender matters in sports history. In: R. Edelman & W. Wilson (Eds). *The Oxford handbook of sports history*, pp. 446–460. Oxford: Oxford University Press.

Vertinsky, P.A., Finzsch, N., & Schirmer, D. (1998). Body matters: Race, gender, and perceptions of physical ability from Goethe to Weininger. *Semantic Scholar*. https://doi.org/10.1017/CBO9781139052672.017

Walker, N.A., & Melton, E.N. (2015). The tipping point: The intersection of race, gender, and sexual orientation in intercollegiate sports. *Journal of Sport Management*, *29*(3), 257–271. https://doi.org/10.1123/jsm.2013-0079

Wallach Scott, J. (2008). Unanswered Questions, AHR Forum. *America Historical Review*, *113*(5), 1422–1430. https://doi.org/10.1086/ahr.113.5.1422

Watson, R., & Scraton, S. (2001). Confronting whiteness? Researching the leisure lives of South Asian mothers. *Journal of Gender Studies*, *10*(3), 265–277.

Watson, R., & Scraton, S. (2013). Leisure studies and intersectionality. *Leisure Studies*, *32*(1), 35–47.

Widener, D. (2017). Race and sport. In: R. Edelman & W. Wilson (Eds). *The Oxford handbook of sports history*, pp. 461–475. Oxford: Oxford University Press.

Yi-Hsiu, L., & Chen-Yueh, C. (2013). Masculine versus feminine sports: The effects of peer attitudes and fear of negative evaluation on sports participation among Taiwanese college students. *Revue internationale de psychologie sociale*, *26*, 5–23. https://www.cairn-int.info/journal--2013-4-page-5.htm

2

TRANSGENDER AND NON-BINARY PEOPLE IN SPORT

Introduction

The purpose of this chapter is to offer a broad overview of the literature about trans people's inclusion in elite sport, and how this now impacts everyday sport. It is necessary to give some careful consideration as to how (and why) conversations about competitive advantage, fairness and safety have become so fraught, and the problematic reliance on inconclusive science as a means to shut down, rather than open up, ideas about inclusion in sport for trans people. We will discuss puberty, testosterone, the current gender critical arguments in the United Kingdom and the significance of the UK Equality Act (EA, 2004) in relation to fairness and safety. Before this, we need to consider the earlier literature about trans people competing in elite sport.

Trans Athletes Competing at Olympic Level Prior to 2004

Publicly out trans athletes have never competed in the Olympics' 125-year modern history prior to Tokyo 2020, when weightlifter Laurel Hubbard represented New Zealand on the women's team. Trans athletes certainly existed in Olympic records, for example, the East German high jumper Dora Ratjen, who competed in the 1936 Olympics (see Harper, 2023, Hu et al., 2023, for a comprehensive history). Consequently, there is limited academic literature within the field of social science which discusses what inclusion for trans athletes involves in terms of the International Olympic Committee's (IOC) regulations during this time, as no regulations existed. Previosuly, an athlete could only compete as assigned by their sex at birth and not their gender identity. This all changed with the Stockholm Consensus in 2003.

DOI: 10.4324/9781003385486-3

The Stockholm Consensus (2003)

Whilst many discussions about trans athlete's participation in elite sport begins with the IOC's 'Stockholm Consensus' (2003), the regulation change which allowed their inclusion, the IOC were not the first organisation to make a change. The first international sports organisation to actually establish this framework was the International Association of Athletics Federations (IAAF, now World Athletics) in 1990. IOC Medical Commission Chairman Arne Ljungqvist (2004) wrote of how the IAAF (2024) convened:

> An expert seminar [who] unanimously recommended that any person who has undergone sex reassignment before puberty should be accepted in sport under the assigned gender. Individuals who have undergone sex reassignment after puberty were considered to represent a more complex problem, since they have been under the influence of hormones under their former gender during their puberty. In particular, a male puberty would mean an influence of testosterone, which could, in theory, be of importance even after a reassignment to female gender. It was, therefore, recommended that any such case be evaluated on an individual basis by competent experts before a decision be taken by the relevant sports authority.
>
> *(Ljungqvist, 2004)*

These original recommendations made by the IAAF were adapted and updated by the IOC in 2003 in what became known as the Stockholm Consensus. This update was necessary, the IAAF felt, because the IAAF's existing system of applying a case-by-case basis for athletes who had undergone gender-reaffirming surgery after puberty was insufficient. On 28 October 2003, 'an ad-hoc committee convened by the IOC Medical Commission met in Stockholm to discuss and issue recommendations on the participation of individuals who have undergone sex reassignment (male to female and vice versa) in sport' (IOC, 2004). According to the IOC, the most debated aspects were the following:

> (A) For how long will the hormonal influence of the earlier puberty be of importance? (B) Will the testosterone influence on the muscular strength during male puberty ever disappear? (C) For how long should the treatment with female hormones last in order to be considered sufficient? (D) How can one make sure that the required treatment with female hormone does really take place?

The IAAF's expert panel had previously unanimously recommended in 1990 that any person who had undergone gender-affirming surgery (then called sex reassignment surgery) before puberty should be accepted in sport under their assigned gender. The IOC acknowledged that individuals who have undergone gender-affirming surgery after puberty

> were considered to represent a more complex problem, since they have been under the influence of hormones under their former gender during their puberty. In particular, a male puberty would mean an influence of testosterone, which could, in theory, be of importance even after a reassignment to female gender.
>
> *(IOC, 2004)*

On the advice from external experts, the IOC made the following four recommendations for the inclusion of trans athletes competing in the Olympic games:

1. Surgical anatomical changes have been completed, including external genitalia changes and gonadectomy.[1]
2. Legal recognition of their assigned sex has been conferred by the appropriate official authorities.
3. Hormonal therapy appropriate for the assigned sex has been administered in a verifiable manner and for a sufficient length of time to minimise gender-related advantages in sport competitions.
4. In the opinion of the group, eligibility should begin no sooner than two years after gonadectomy.

These changes came into effect for the 2004 Olympic Games in Athens and applied to both trans men and trans women, but the IOC's focus was firmly on the part (male) puberty and testosterone played when defining the requirements. Regardless, the Stockholm Consensus allowed trans athletes to compete at the Olympics provided they qualified and met these requirements.[2]

A Snapshot of the Literature after the 2003 Stockholm Consensus

The arrival of the Stockholm Consensus brought with it a wave of new literature which focused on the possibility that a trans athlete would imminently be making their debut on the Olympic stage. In fact, this did not happen until Tokyo 2020, when Laurel Hubbard became the first trans athlete to qualify for and compete in the Olympics, representing New Zealand on the woman's weightlifting team. Hubbard failed to record a successful lift in the women's +87kg weightlifting and was placed last in her group.

With this possibility came discussions of what this might mean for a trans athlete to compete against a cis athlete, and if this would change understandings of what constitutes fairness in sport. Whilst – as discussed in the previous chapter – gender-segregated sports exist only in part due to differences between male and female bodies (it is not fair for women to compete against men because they have physical advantages considered beneficial in some sports), what constitutes as 'fair' competition was reconsidered. In light of the IOC's updated recommendations and its publication of the Stockholm Consensus, the first wave of academic literature focused on the hypothetical trans athlete competing at elite level. This earlier research is largely supportive in principle of inclusion for trans people and the ways in which they foreground the variety of barriers and challenges faced by trans athletes in their pursuit of participation in sport, and also what exactly is 'fair play' in sport? This early literature is discussed broadly next.

Gooren and Bunck's 2004 paper is the first to analyse the effects of androgen deprivation in 19 trans women and of androgen administration to 17 trans men on muscle mass, haemoglobin and insulin-like growth factor-1. What the authors found was that before the administration of what they termed 'cross-sex hormones' (gender-affirming hormones), there was a considerable overlap in muscle mass between trans men and trans women. In both trans men and trans women, height was a strong predictor of muscle mass. The authors also found that androgen deprivation in trans women decreased muscle mass, increasing the overlap with untreated trans men, but mean muscle mass remained significantly higher in trans women than in trans men. Androgen administration to trans men increased muscle mass without inducing an advantage over nontreated trans women. The conclusion Gooren and Bunck arrived at was that androgen deprivation in trans women increases the overlap in muscle mass with cis women but does not reverse it, statistically. The key point, Gooren and Bunck wrote, regarding the question of whether trans women can fairly compete with cis women depends on what degree of arbitrariness one wishes to accept, because it was necessary to keep in mind, for instance:

> That similar blood testosterone levels in men have profoundly different biologic effects on muscle properties, rendering competition in sports intrinsically a matter of how nature endows individuals for this competition.
>
> *(Gooren and Bunck, 2004, p. 429)*

In other words, establishing fairness regardless of sex, gender or hormones is complex. Interpreting fairness as a level playing field was discussed by Reeser (2005)] in what can be considered the earliest review of the literature into how organised sport has attempted to safeguard the promise of fair competition via gender-segregated events. Reeser's focus was on the

> practical consequences of the policies on gender verification and the participation of transsexuals in sport that the International Olympic Committee (IOC) and selected sports governing bodies have adopted in an effort to ensure that the sporting competitions they sanction are fair and that the athletes who compete in them do so on an equal basis.
>
> *(Reeser, 2005, p. 695)*

To do this, Reeser identified relevant articles from both the peer-reviewed scientific literature and the lay press through searches of the PubMed/Medline, OVID, SPORTDiscus, CINAHL and Evidence Based Medicine Reviews databases. After examining the literature, Reeser concluded that whilst inclusion for trans athletes appears to be 'relatively uncomplicated', the actions of the IOC were bold, and there is 'inadequate physiological performance related data to allow an unambiguous position to emerge' (Reeser, 2005, p. 699). The inclusion of trans men in sport, Reeser noted, was also overlooked in the literature. Almost two decades later, we are still in the same position as Reeser, of trying to make the best decision for everyone who competes, both cis and trans women, along with trans men and, more recently, non-binary athletes.

Cavanagh and Sykes (2006) bring to the discussion their belief that whilst the IOC's 2004 policy updates may indeed be bold, but, nonetheless, they do not a guard against discrimination and harassment towards trans athletes. Rather, they argue, the policy operates to 'maintain the popular illusion that there are two, binary gender designations' (Cavanagh and Sykes, 2006, p. 77). Their paper brings to the forefront body politics and the ways in which different modes of power govern and regulate individual bodies. Body politics usually revolves around gender, disability, sexuality, race and other minority groups. For example, Collison and De Martini Ugolotti (2022) explore Syrian Muslim women's stories of resettlement in Sweden, in which the embodied experience of yoga offers an intersectional-phenomenological perspective to understand their lived experiences of forced migration. Often body politics is used to explain how societal laws and norms limit how we use our bodies and how this can be oppressive to certain minorities (Eichberg, 1997; Martin Shaw, 2019).

Cavanagh and Sykes (2006, p. 96) echo this same point when they wrote of how anxiety about gender in Olympic communities 'intersects with contemporary anxieties about immigration (illegal and otherwise) in a postcolonial context' and the policing and politicising of bodies in the name of 'equity, access and fair competition' (ibid.). After all:

> Transsexuals and intersexed athletes – the groups most often subject to discrimination and disqualification – have always confounded a static and unchanging two sex model based on biology, and so their gendered subjectivities were erased, and/or largely ignored in competitive sport prior to the 21st century.
>
> *(Cavanagh and Sykes, 2006, p. 77)*

Cavanagh and Sykes also predicted that trans women athletes would not have an advantage over what they called genetic female competitors, which, as we will discuss a little later, remains unresolved in the current literature. One key observation they make is that given some trans men take testosterone, it is curious that the Olympic community does not consider they may have an advantage over genetic men, considering the competitive advantage testosterone is still considered to infer. I am in full agreement that such an omission – still in effect today – is symptomatic of a refusal to see trans men as men and that it also provides 'an illustration of the popular compulsion to see gender as determined by nature, not culture: made men are, thus, not to be seen as legitimate competition' (Cavanagh and Sykes, 2006, p. 78).

Teetzel (2006) acknowledges that there are conceivable advantages that an elite trans athlete might possibly possess over their competitors, but 'conclusive evidence based on long-term scientific studies has either not yet been done or fails to show any unfair advantages at the elite level with statistical significance' (Teetzel, 2006, p. 229). Teetzel's concern, rightly so, is that trans athlete's participation in sport at elite level is challenged on the basis that it is the same as doping (an accusation Sharron Davies has made, as discussed a little later). There is a marked difference, Teetzel wrote, 'between using performance-enhancing drugs to increase athleticism and using the same drugs as part of a prescribed hormone therapy' (Teetzel, 2006, p. 229; see also Donnellan, 2008, on the complexities of drug-testing and intersex athletes). This is inappropriate, she argues, because athletes who dope and take banned substances are intentionally cheating, and are not playing fairly because they are both breaking and abusing the rules. Afterall, sport, argue many, is centred on fair play, either in practice or in spirit. This is not the same as trans athletes who are following the very rules provided by the IOC, as Laurel Hubbard did, and have a legitimate right to compete.

Aura (2007) offers a retrospective legal analysis of Renee Richards, who was one of the first professional athletes to identify as trans. American Richards is a former tennis player who competed on the professional circuits in the 1970s, who after transitioning fought to compete as a woman in the 1976 US Open. When the United States Tennis Association (USTA) introduced genetic screening for female players that same year,[3] Richards challenged the policy, claiming it was gender discrimination. When she was disallowed from playing in the US Open, Wimbledon and the Italian Open in 1976, she subsequently sued the USTA. The New York Supreme Court ruled in Richards's favour, agreeing the test was a violation of her rights and grossly unfair. The introduction of genetic testing for females (but not male tennis players) by the USTA was also a discriminatory manoeuvre against cis women, too, including athletes with DSD[4] or who might be intersex. Body politics are clearly present here, in the way they make visible how certain people in sport (men) are allowed to take up more space than others, indicating which bodies are valued more.

Aura (2007, p. 110) gives consideration, as Cavanagh and Sykes (2006) did (see also Buzuvis 2012; Lucas-Carr and Krane, 2011; Sullivan, 2011), that perhaps 'not only are there cracks in the concept of sex and gender as coherent categories, but, moreover, that the concepts of sex and gender are continually created, recreated, delineated, acted out, and policed through social interaction'. Elite sport continues to evoke anxieties about gender instability and the changeability of the human body. As Sullivan (2011) noted, the power to compete is not in the hands of the trans athlete at all, but in that of the sporting governing body. Thus, 'the decision over who is included and who is excluded from sex-segregated, elite sporting competitions is imbedded in the communicative structure of our society' (Sullivan, 2011, p. 442). The case of Caster Semenya (Buzuvis, 2011) underpins this.

The Case of Caster Semenya

Caster Semenya, the South African double Olympic champion and middle-distance runner, has faced questions due to her 'suspicious' masculine perceived appearance about her eligibility to compete, and whether her appearance was an indication of her levels of the hormone testosterone being unfairly high. Semenya became embroiled in a struggle with the International Association of Athletics Federations (IAAF) after winning the World Championship's 800m gold in 2009, after the IAAF revealed she had been the subject of a gender verification process that year and subsequently was declared ineligible to compete for 11 months.

A decade of rule changes by the IAAF and appeals from Semenya followed. In 2019 Semenya lost her appeal to Switzerland's Federal Supreme Court against the restriction of testosterone levels in female runners. Semenya is not allowed to compete in events between 400m and a mile without taking testosterone-reducing drugs, following a 2019 rule change by governing body World Athletics. In a statement following the ruling by the Court of Arbitration for Sport (CAS), Semenya was asked whether she would consider such a medical intervention. Semenya said:

> Hell, no … I know that the IAAF's regulations have always targeted me specifically … for a decade the IAAF has tried to slow me down, but this has actually made me stronger … no man can tell me what to do.
>
> *(Dator, 2019, n.p.)*

In those sports settings where the cultural norms of gender normativity and hegemonic masculinity continue to dominate, some participants, such as Caster Semenya, the impact of imposing a rigid binary agenda upon those who do not conform to it, is significant. As Cornelius wrote in *The Conversation* (2019, n.p.), 'my view is that some women are being singled out because they are different. If Semenya looked different, if she was a blonde bombshell or if she didn't win, we wouldn't be having this debate today'. Like many other individuals who do not conform to gender-normative expectations, Semenya was involved in a fight against 'a rigid and violent system of sexual essentialism that renders many bodies and lives incomprehensible, forcing conformity and/or expulsion of those deemed unruly' (Olufemi, 2020, p. 51). Semenya's case had repercussions for two cis women sprinters from Namibia in 2021. Both Christine Mboma and Beatrice Masilingi were banned from running in the Olympic 400-meter dash because, whilst their high testosterone levels were deemed to be 'natural', they were too high, and thus unfair on the other competitors. These examples all reflect, as Hamad wrote in 2019, 'how easy it is to undermine women, in particularly racialized women, by shifting the goalposts and requirements for entry into womanhood' (Hamad, 2019, n.p.). What we are also seeing is a drawing of 'new iterations of older, gendered as well as racialised boundaries between "biological" femaleness and "social" womanhood' (Pearce et al., 2020, p. 688). Thus, there is no consideration for any individual, cis or trans, who may fall 'somewhere in between these dichotomous categories [and who] face social repercussions and discrimination in sport' (Lucas-Carr and Krane, 2011, p. 533).

This early literature begins to open up other complex issues of what constitutes fairness in sport, for instance socio-economic and racialised privileges. Mandating particular types of (gendered) medical treatments and testing have been historically instigated to ensure a 'level playing field', but even the limited literature (post-2004) has questioned just how reliable this is. Before we move on to discuss the IOC's 2014 policy changes, it is necessary to reflect on puberty and testosterone, both of which are at the heart of the complex issue of fairness and safety.

Puberty and Testosterone

Puberty is the physiological process whereby adolescents reach sexual maturity and become capable of reproduction. According to Susman and Rogol (2004), puberty is one of the most profound biological and social transitions in the life span, and the trajectory of the hormonal and physical changes that characterise puberty are well documented in endocrinological research. One of the hallmarks of puberty is the adolescent growth spurt and changes in body composition. Whilst differences in growth and development vary (and not just between genders; see Rogol et al., 2002, for other factors), unquestionably, puberty has a significant effect on the human body. Some of these changes effect both boys and girls (the growing of underarm and pubic hair, increased body smells and emotional changes); some do not. Such examples include shoulders widening for boys and a widening of the hips for girls. Of relevance to this book are the specific changes between boys and girls which occur at puberty and which are considered to confer a physical advantage in males over females in sport. Handelsman (2017, p. 68) writes:

> This physical advantage in performance arises during early adolescence when male puberty commences after which men acquire larger muscle mass and greater strength, larger and stronger bones, higher circulating haemoglobin as well as mental and/or psychological differences. After completion of male puberty, circulating testosterone levels in men are consistently 10–15 times higher than in children or women at any age.

During puberty the influence of testosterone in boys means they have 'a significant increase in the growth of bone and muscle with a simultaneous loss of fat in the limbs, and as adults, males have 150% of the lean body mass of the average female and twice the number of muscle cells' (Rogol et al., 2002, p. 196; see also Cheek et al., 1974). The increase in skeletal size and muscle mass (generally) leads to increased strength in males (Rogol et al., 2002). This pubertal difference and its potential to create a physical advantage were flagged by both the IAAF and the IOC as something to be considered when devising the regulations on inclusion for trans women athletes. Along with the presence of testosterone, the impact of puberty on the male bodyit sits at the heart of gender critical reasoning as to why trans women should not be competing against cis women. This is because pubertal changes such as height cannot be undone. That is, men 'generally have an inherent performance advantage over women due to their average greater height and muscle mass and power, and the result of correspondingly different exposures to androgens' (Gooren and Bunck, 2004, p. 425).

Androgen is a group of hormones that primarily influences the growth and development of the male reproductive system. The most active androgen is testosterone, which is produced by the (male) testes (Alvares et al., 2022; Sudai, 2017). People assigned female at birth produce small amounts of testosterone in their ovaries but have significantly less than those assigned male at birth. Generally, women's bodies make about 1/10th to 1/20th of the amount of testosterone as men's bodies. Because of this, testosterone has been labelled a 'male' sex hormone, whilst oestrogen, which is produced in greater quantities by people assigned female at birth, is labelled as a 'female' sex hormone. Testosterone in males (or indeed anyone) induces changes in muscle mass, strength, anthropometric variables[5] and haemoglobin levels.[6] As Sullivan (2011, p. 615) noted, 'a moderate pubertal and post pubertal excess of testosterone in a young woman can give extra muscle development and other signs of hyperandrogenism, but it would be a rude error to even suggest that this would affect her female gender identity'. Nonetheless, the biological basis for sex segregation in sports is the consequence of long-term endogenous androgen exposure in men, and thus testosterone is considered to confer competitive advantage. By setting an upper limit of the acceptable amount of testosterone present in (all) women at below 10 nanomoles per litre of blood, together with undergoing gender-affirming surgery (for trans women), an attempt to level the field was made by the IOC in 2004 This changed in 2015.

The IOC's Revised Guidelines (2015)

In January 2015 the IOC issued new guidelines allowing trans athletes to compete in the Olympics and other international events without undergoing gender-affirming surgery. Under the revised 2015 guidelines, this surgery was also not required for trans men, who were eligible to take part in (cis) men's competitions without restriction. Meanwhile, trans women athletes needed to demonstrate their testosterone level was below 10 nanomoles per litre of blood for at least one year before their first competition. Additionally, the declaration of identifying as either male or female could not be changed, for sporting purposes, for a minimum of four years.

The IOC's (2015) revised policy on the regulations for trans athletes to compete in the Olympics triggered a fresh wave of public interest, particularly in the media, with an almost exclusive focus on trans women athletes. This exclusivity is, I believe, due the IOC's decision to remove gender-affirming surgery from their recommendations for eligible inclusion. What really fuelled this media interest, was the irrefutable certainty that the retention of (male) genitalia would surely confer an unfair competitive advantage. Sex verification (the humiliating inspection of a female athlete's naked body by a medical professional to confirm they were female) was still being carried out in elite sport until the 1990s. This practice of policing women's bodies was not carried out on male athletes.

Human biology is varied, and by understanding 'there is nothing 'natural' or 'stable' about human biology helps us to dismantle the idea that women's oppression is not rooted in a singular place' (Olufemi, 2020, p. 54). My position is that the concept of fairness is not the same as the concept of sameness; we are not clones, and we are equal regardless of how we identify. Bodies vary in shape and size in competition. I do not deny the changes puberty induces, but I do question the assumption that puberty undeniably guarantees a competitive advantage in trans women against cis women. As Donnelly and Kidd (2020, n.p.) write, 'while there is a significant difference between the best performances by men as a group and women as a group in the measurable sports, those averages do not mean that every male competitor enjoys such advantage'. I certainly do not believe that trans women are men.

The following year, in May 2016, the Canadian Centre for Ethics in Sports (CCES), which manages the country's antidoping program and recommends ethical standards, issued trans-related guidelines for all Canadian sports organisations. This statement says policies which regulate eligibility, like those related to hormones, should be backed by defensible science. The CCES said there is 'simply not the evidence to suggest whether, or to what degree, hormone levels consistently confer competitive advantage' (Canadian Centre for Ethics in Sports, 2016, n.p.).Yet discussions about fairness and safety persist. I will now go on to discuss how the more recent academic literature offers little more to resolve what Patel (2021) terms a 'regulatory riddle', and the influence of gender critical feminism in the current climate. We will start with what sits at the heart of the gender critical position, the twin matters of fairness of safety.

Current Research about Competitive Advantage: Defining Fairness

The myth of the level playing field and 'fairness' in sport receives much attention in the literature far beyond the inclusion of trans people (Channon, 2014).

The notion of fairness and safety is one of the most mentioned questions raised in regard to the inclusion of trans athletes in sport in research. But whose fairness and whose safety are at stake here? According to Sheridan (2003, p. 163), fair play is 'generally understood to be important in sport and in life yet it is not clear what precisely it refers to, why it is valued, what ethical principles, if any, it is grounded upon and what kinds of good it involves'. As such, the notion of 'fair play' is a fundamentally complex issue in sport (Sheridan, 2003, Simon, 2010), and there is no universally agreed-upon definition which can place all humans into the traditional binary to guarantee this interpretation of fairness. As such, the question of competitive advantage continues to be complex (Bekker et al., 2023; Hamilton et al., 2021a, 2021b; Harper et al., 2021; Hilton and Lundberg, 2020; Patel, 2021). Inclusion for trans people and others who do not meet gender-normative representations remain perpetually suspended somewhere in the middle of discussions about 'fairness' and, increasingly, 'safety'. For clarity, safety here is understood in terms of physical safety in a sport and in what might be considered a vulnerable environment (the changing room).

This book is not about endocrinology (I am not an endocrinologist) or about using science to prove (or disprove) a point about inclusion, but it does posit that biomedical studies are overvalued in sports policies in comparison to social sciences studies. Pearce et al. (2020, p. 689) write:

> The sports example illustrates how notions of science (and especially biology) are mobilised to exclude some women from the scope of 'femaleness'... by appealing to 'biology', authorities lay claim to the 'neutrality' and 'objectivity' of science – a claim that has public appeal even if it has been contested in social scientific and humanities scholarship for decades.
>
> *(e.g. Haraway, 1988; Spanier, 1995)*

Nor is this book immune to how 'the inclusion of non-conforming individuals such as intersex and transgender athletes, has triggered a global debate mostly framed around science and athletic advantage' (Patel, 2021, p. 1). The integrity of any research should reflect its willingness to engage with the broader literature, and due to the continued public interest in this topic (and this book's inevitable inability to cover everything), it is important to offer a perspective on what this literature discusses. Four key papers are discussed next.

The study by Roberts, Smalley and Ahrendt (2021) is an examination of the effect of gender-affirming hormones on athletic performance in trans women and trans men. The authors reviewed fitness test results and medical records of 29 trans men and 46 trans women who started gender-affirming hormones whilst still in the US Air Force. This was a retrospective review of medical records and fitness tests results from 222 self-identified military personnel who filed a request to begin gender transition or continue testosterone or oestrogen while serving in the US Air Force. The rationale for this research and this study group was that, whilst these individuals are not elite athletes, enlisted service members engage in regular group exercise and are expected to meet a high level of fitness for which they are regularly tested. Whilst the IOC's 2015 guidelines recommend trans women's testosterone levels must be below 10 nanomoles per litre of blood for at least one year before their first competition, Roberts et al. (2021) concluded that 'more than 12 months of testosterone suppression may be needed to ensure that transgender women do not have an unfair competitive advantage when participating in elite level athletic competition' (Roberts et al., 2021, p. 6). The significance of this study is that whilst elite trans athletes were not recruited, trans people's fitness levels were measured.

Hilton and Lundberg's 2020 paper on trans women in the female category of sport did not measure trans athlete's fitness, nor did the authors draw their findings from any direct sport-specific studies of trans athletes. Rather, they looked at examples from cis athletes (male and female) and argued that the muscle mass and strength 'conferred by male puberty and thus enjoyed by most transgender women is only minimally reduced when testosterone is suppressed as per current sporting guidelines for transgender athletes' (Hilton and Lundberg, 2020, p. 199). The authors propose that 12 months of testosterone suppression is insufficient to mitigate their concerns about safety, arguing that the inclusion of trans women in the female category of sports would compromise 'the objective of fair and safe competition' (Hilton and Lundberg, 2020, p. 199). The authors concluded that the data they have used (with cis athletes) with which to formulate their argument 'overwhelmingly confirms that testosterone driven puberty ... underpins sporting advantages that are so large no female could reasonably hope to succeed without sex segregation in most sporting competitions' (Hilton and Lundberg, 2020, p. 204).

To frame this claim as overwhelming is unrealistic. At the time of writing the scientific literature available does not categorically support this, and the data examined by Hilton and Lunberg (202) were based on cis athletes and not trans athletes. I also believe to frame any claim as 'overwhelming' is both problematic and in this instance, rooted in biological essentialism. An essentialist viewpoint is the philosophical belief that each thing has a set of characteristics (its 'essence') that defines it and which is 'fundamental to its identity and function' (Hines and Taylor, 2018, p. 20). This perspective believes that groups of people can be sorted into permanent categories because nature has assigned them unchangeable characteristics. It is a controversial concept which fails to account for individual differences, and can lead to bias, prejudice, stereotyping and racism.

A biological essentialist perspective proposes that (cis) women and men possess distinct chromosomal and hormonal variations that impact on their specific social roles (Hines and Taylor, 2018). So powerful is the essence of masculinity and femininity that it drives men and women behave differently due not to social influences, but biological ones. Biology determines behaviour, not society, and manifests as women 'naturally' exhibiting more caring and nurturing qualities (valued as inherently maternal). Men are protectors, providers and more prone to promiscuity, driven by a 'natural' drive to create multiple offspring. This conflation of biological essentialist with 'natural' (in other words, an absolute truth) 'perpetuates a concept of inevitability of different treatment, expectations and roles for men and women and naturalizes gender inequalities' (Pinho and Gaunt, 2024, p. 5). Sport maintains these differences and expectations by gender-segregated categories and its treatment of men and women differently and unequally. The gender inequalities (along with race, class, sexuality and disability), which exist not just in sport but globally within the home, in the workplace and in education, align with a biological essentialist belief. This truth is offered as simply a natural fact of life; any other way of imagining sport is unnatural, and to include trans women in sport is thus naturally unfair.

It is not the first time that biological essentialism has been employed by those in greater positions of power to oppress those with less. In her book *Black Feminist Thought* (1990), Patricia Hill-Collins wrote that in order to preserve their power, dominant groups create and maintain a popular system of 'common sense' ideas that support their view. Often these views are so persuasive that it can be difficult to argue against them, due to their 'common sense' position. For example, the deployment of 'common sense' positions has been observed in contemporary discourses surrounding motherhood, most notably with the 'breast is best' slogan and the promotion of 'natural' childbirth (which means drug-free and vaginal) as being superior to any other method of infant feeding or birthing (Phipps, 2014). It is a compelling belief system, one which is frequently held by those in the field of evolutionary psychology.

Hamilton, Lima, Barrett et al. (2021a) examined the International Federation of Sports Medicine's (FIMS) consensus on integrating women diagnosed with DSD (differences of sexual development) and trans women athletes into elite female sport 'based on identifying, selecting, and critically appraising the very limited relevant primary research' (Hamilton et al., 2021a p. 1). The authors argue that sport's governing bodies should consider reviewing rules determining the eligibility of athletes in the female category as there may be lasting advantages of previously high testosterone concentrations for trans women athletes and currently high testosterone concentrations in DSD athletes. Hamilton et al. (2021a) are not claiming an advantage due to testosterone is not a possibility. Rather, as an objective biomarker it has limitations due to the lack of sports performance data before, during or after testosterone suppression. Rather, they argue, what needs to be made available to policymakers from all relevant communities is peer-reviewed scientific evidence, the same argument made two decades ago by Gooren and Bunck (2004).

Like the studies by Hamilton et al. (2021a, 2021b), Harper et al. (2021) looked towards existing research to further examine the issue of competitive advantage. The authors reviewed the literature from 24 studies to assess how in trans women long-term testosterone-suppressing gender-affirming hormone therapy might influence lean body mass, muscular area and strength and haemoglobin (Hgb)/haematocrit (HCT). Harper et al. (2021) concluded that in trans women hormone therapy rapidly reduces Hgb to the levels seen in cis women and decreases strength...; Lean body mass and muscle area values remain above that observed in cis women, even after 36 months. Like Roberts et al. (2021), Harper et al.'s findings suggest that '[muscle] strength may be well preserved in trans women during the first 3 years of hormone therapy' (Harper et al., 2021, p. 1).

However, as with Hilton and Lundberg's (2020) and Hamilton et al.'s (2021) papers, Harper et al.'s findings do not draw on data from sports-specific studies with trans athlete participants and so do not tell the whole story of what it means to be, say, an elite trans woman athlete competing at elite level against elite cis women athletes. Harper et al.'s (2021) paper acknowledges that the performance-related differences between trans women who have received gender-affirming hormone treatment and cis women are less clear. They conclude that 'to date, there have been no prospective studies investigating the changes in athletic performance in transgender athletes after hormonal transition' (Harper et al., 2021, p. 1). In addition, 'the levels of physical activity of the trans women compared with cis women in the study were not reported' (Harper et al., 2021, p. 7).

The four papers discussed here are done so broadly as an exercise in demonstrating that the evidence on competitive advantage in trans women is as inconclusive as it was two decades ago. On two of these papers (Hamilton et al., 2021a and Harper et al., 2021), the lead author is a trans woman with a sporting history who would welcome conclusive evidence of competitive advantage being disproved. Neither of them claims this to be the case. The lead author on the Hilton and Lundberg (2020) paper attended the London conference in 2019 organised by Fair Play for Women and Woman's Place UK and claims their paper as 'overwhelmingly' confirming the existence of competitive advantage. I acknowledge my own positionality as a trans feminist as potential for bias, though, as I will go on to discuss when considering safety in sport, my belief is that the gender-critical feminist position is often misrepresented for the purposes of stirring up division and to reduce the opportunities for feminist collaboration which would benefit all women.

It is important to remember that this is a circular argument. As Hilton and Lundberg (2020, p. 211) themselves note, 'there is certainly a need for more focused research on this topic, including more comprehensive performance tests in transgender women athletes and studies on training capacity of transgender women undergoing hormone therapy'. In November 2022, the CCES published *Transgender Women Athletes and Elite Sport: A Scientific Review* (see E. Alliance, 2023). This commissioned report is an extensive review of scientific and grey literature on trans women athlete's participation in competitive sport and comprises of research articles published in the English language between 2011 and 2021 inclusive. The report is divided into two sections: one that encompasses biomedical studies and a second that encompasses sociocultural studies.

The report found:

> Biological data are severely limited, and often methodologically flawed. It also concluded that there is limited evidence regarding the impact of

> testosterone suppression (through, for example, gender-affirming hormone therapy or surgical gonad removal) on transgender women athletes' performance, and that the available evidence indicates trans women who have undergone testosterone suppression have no clear biological advantages over cis women in elite sport.
>
> *(E. Alliance, 2023, p. 4)*

This report was nonetheless refuted by a number of gender-critical supporters, including Hilton and Lundberg, authors of the 2021 paper discussed earlier, calling it 'wholly unscientific ... another attempt to replace materially based eligibility criteria in sport with 'social identity' as a passport to inclusion' (Devine et al., 2022). Opposition to trans women being included in sport is especially antagonistic from the gender critical movement, who claim the retention of testosterone-producing genitalia (even if hormones have been taken to suppress an athlete's testosterone below 10 nanomoles per litre) still confers a competitive edge over cis women athletes due to the occurrence of (male) puberty (Fair Play for Women, 2023, n.p.). Olympic swimmer Sharron Davies has compared trans women to 'doping cheats' (Ball, 2023), arguing they should not be allowed to compete until clearer regulations are in place (see also Barras, 2019; Gilligan, 2019). At the 1980 Moscow Olympic Games, Sharron Davies came second in the 400m individual medley, winning silver behind Petra Schneider. Schneider, from East Germany, later admitted her victory was drug enhanced. Davies was an incredible athlete, and this knowledge of Schneider's cheating would have been devastating for her, and she has my sympathy. Davies, who was at the event held in London (2019), organised by Fair Play for Women and Women's Place UK, said in her headline speech of what she considers to be

> The lack of fairness under current sporting rules, which permit male-born transgender competitors who have been through male puberty to go head to head with female athletes, was reminiscent of East German Olympic doping that took place in the '70s and '80s: 'Athletes would be lined up at the start of the race and they know they're not going to win.'
>
> *(Sitwell, 2019, n.p.)*

Davies also said in her speech that it was 'not PC to talk about these things', inferring that she has been in some way silenced or prevented from discussing the issue. On the contrary, Davies is frequently in the mainstream UK press, is highly active on social media and regularly appears on television and radio shows to offer her opinion. Davies is so well known for her position that she claims to be 'facing financial ruin' for her view on trans athletes (Preston-Ellis, 2022), and uses social media to express her views (see @sharrond62 on X, formerly Twitter). Former tennis player Martina Navratilova has been equally vocal on her position, going so far as to refuse to use the term ‘cisgender’, reflecting ‘a privileged desire to control and dominate the language’ (Barras, 2019, p. 7). I would argue, as Knott-Fayle, Peel and Witcomb do in their 2023 paper on (anti-) feminism and cisgendersim in sports media, that both Davies and Navratilova are themselves, as trans-exclusionary feminists, ‘controlled by non- and anti-feminist media actors who use limited visibility to justify cisgenderist arguments without taking on any responsibility for women’s rights more broadly’ (Knott-Fayle et al., 2022, p. 1,288).

Davies is right to claim doping is cheating – it is – but, as Teetzel (2006) argued, the challenges to sport that are created by trans athletes’ participation at the elite level have become confused with anti-doping issues. This stems from the perception that to be a trans woman can provide an athlete with the same type of advantage that an athlete can gain from using substances and procedures banned under the World Anti-Doping Code. Like Teetzel, I would agree that whilst there are conceivable advantages that an elite trans woman athlete might possibly possess over their competitors, ‘conclusive evidence based on long-term scientific studies has either not yet been done or fails to show any unfair advantages at the elite level with statistical significance’ (Teetzel, 2006, p. 229). To claim the scientific evidence is overwhelming is simply untrue. Nonetheless, whilst a definition of fairness is essential to sport at every level, the weaponisation of the term continues to be used to preserve sports for those already privileged to enjoy them (Donnelly and Kidd, 2020; Gleaves and Lehrbach, 2016). We now turn to the issue of safety.

Defining Safety

Safety in sport is of great importance for any athlete. But what exactly does it mean and how is it applied in the context of trans people in sport? Fundamentally, the word refers to physical safety, the safety of an athlete’s body to not be harmed exponentially during competition. That is, the idea that to pitch two bodies of opposing weight and (assumed) strength would be both unfair and unsafe. Boxing, for example, has very strict weight divisions, to ensure safety and fairness. It is not hard to understand why some contact sports (such as rugby) and non-contact sports (such as archery) might need different considerations from each other due to the interaction of the players (Hamilton et al., 2021b). This underpins the stringent need for injury prevention and the removal of reasonable risk when playing a sport.

Yet for gender-critical feminists, the physical safety of an athlete is a concern both on and off the pitch, where single-sex spaces such as changing rooms are likely. This safety applies only to that of cis women and girls. This is not exclusive to sport, and schools, hospital wards, prisons and other institutions, which may contain single-sex facilities (like toilets) or were originally intended to support and offer sanctuary to (cis) women and their children (such as women’s refuges), have found themselves having to clarify their definition of ‘sex’ and ‘gender’ with regard to who has the right to access what service or which space.

Women's safety is central to debates about transgender equality, whereby trans women are situated as 'potential rapists who want to invade "women's space"' (A. Phipps, 2021, p. 30). Not only are trans women mispresented as men, but they are imagined to be 'the very worst of men where the threat of violence against women is enacted through "gender fraud"' (Hines, 2019, p. 155).

On this note I think it is important to acknowledge that it is likely not every gender-critical feminist supports the gender essentialist position or believes that trans women should be excluded from single-sex spaces and sport. This acknowledgement is a feminist one and a proposal for an alternative perspective. Of greater concern is the lack of clarity and government guidance on the matter, the general disregard for (all) women's safety in public and private spaces and the woeful underfunding of support systems which is failing both cis and trans women. Women, myself included, are socialised from a young age to be careful and hypervigilant around men in vulnerable situations or isolated spaces. We are instructed by parents, carers, teachers and the police to protect ourselves against this whenever possible. The Reclaim the Night movement which started in Leeds in 1977 as part of the Women's Liberation Movement, is proof of this As a University student I too joined marches alongside others, demanding that women be able to move through public spaces at night took. These marches took place across England until the 1990s. Later, the organisation was revived and sponsored annual and national marches protesting against rape and violence against women. As Mackay (2021, p. 42) writes:

> There is a context to women's fears and defensiveness against people they assume to be men sharing their intimate spaces, whether these people identify as men or not. This can equal threat and the need for caution … too many men use their, on average, extra height, musculature and strength to violently control and abuse women … it is true that biology and the body are not neutral, and for women, male bodies are seen as a threat … women have good reason to believe that this threat is real … this matters.

Davina Cooper, Research Professor in Law and Political Theory at Kings College London, notes how 'the starting point and centre of gravity for gender-critical feminism is women – a class subject to male domination' (Cooper, 2020, n.p.; Cooper et al., 2022). Cooper, as this book does, acknowledges that gender critical and trans-inclusive feminism have been pitted against each other, as if they are the only two types of feminism in existence. Gender critical feminists situate their oppression as a direct result of their sex. In other words, the 'physical, economic and social consequences of being born and living with a female body are so significant that women deserve specific rights and protections in law on that basis' (see Murray, Blackburn and Mackenzie, 2020). As such, there is a high level of suspicion and hostility towards trans women's bodies. Examples of this can also be witnessed in discourses surrounding the right to trans-parent (Dietz, 2021; Riggs, 2014), or that only biological women can be mothers. This suspicion is similar to the hostility that has been aimed at women in the past (and can be found in contemporary representations of motherhood) and has been used to deny women full status in society. Stryker and Whittle (2006) call this 'informed prejudice', which sees individuals employ oppressive rhetoric against trans people without having to face their own contradictions (Stryker and Whittle, 2006). This suspicion, wrote Alison Phipps (Phipps, 2016), means cis women view trans women not as women but as men, and the very worst kind of men at that. On 9 December 2020, Professor Stephen Whittle OBE, a legal scholar and activist with the transgender activist group Press for Change (2021), gave evidence at the Women and Equalities Select Committee inquiry into the reform of the Gender Recognition Act (House of Commons, 2020). Professor Whittle said:

> We (trans people) should not be penalised for the serious crimes some violent men choose to commit … we are totally understanding as a community of the issues raised by gender critical feminists, because we are also victims.

Whilst I have much to disagree with in gender critical narratives, I do, like Finn Mackay (2021), concede that gender critical views have (like trans rights activists or 'TRA' views) been 'frequently misrepresented and simplified' (Mackay, 2021, p. 99), perhaps in part due to the socialisation of women to fear men. Nonetheless, as I will next argue, the weaponisation of the UK Equality Act (2010) by gender critical organisations including Fair Play for Women and Woman's Place UK as a legitimate reason to exclude trans women from participating in sport cannot be ignored.

The Equality Act (UK, 2010)

The Equality Act 2010 (EA) legally protects everyone in Great Britain from social and workplace discrimination in relation to nine protected characteristics, including sex, sexual orientation and gender reassignment, among other categories, such as age and disability. Under the EA, people are not allowed to discriminate, harass or victimise another person for having (or assuming to have) these protected characteristics. There is no provision or protection for non-binary people or anyone who identifies outside of binary trans, or 'does not intend to undergo the process of reassigning their sex' (White and Newbegin, 2021, p. 11). Sex and gender are both protected characteristics within the EA, which means the law that protects a trans person from being discriminated against in sport (by being excluded) is the same law which allows a cis person to challenge their inclusion on the grounds of unfair or unsafe competition.

What Does the EA Say about Trans People in Sport?

The relevant section of the EA (2010)[7] says:

> *195 Sport*
>
> *(1) A person does not contravene this Act, so far as relating to sex, only by doing anything in relation to the participation of another as a competitor in a gender-affected activity.*
>
> *(2) A person does not contravene section 29, 33, 34 or 35, so far as relating to gender reassignment, only by doing anything in relation to the participation of a transsexual person as a competitor in a gender-affected activity if it is necessary to do so to secure in relation to the activity—*
>
> (a) *fair competition, or*
> (b) *the safety of competitors.*
>
> *(3) A gender-affected activity*[8] *is a sport, game or other activity of a competitive nature in circumstances in which the physical strength, stamina or physique of average persons of one sex would put them at a disadvantage compared to average persons of the other sex as competitors in events involving the activity.*
>
> *(4) In considering whether a sport, game or other activity is gender-affected in relation to children, it is appropriate to take account of the age and stage of development of children who are likely to be competitors.*

In other words, the Equality Act provides an exception to what would otherwise be unlawful in behaviour: excluding a person based on their sex. This is because to exclude a person from participating in sport based on their gender identity is unlawful. Yet recently a number of professional sporting organisations have dramatically revised their policies on inclusion for trans women to achieve exactly this. To illustrate how they have done this, I will be using the example of the UK organisation British Rowing. Their recent major policy revision was, I will argue, unquestionably influenced by the gender critical community, whose singular intention is the removal of trans women from participating alongside (for safety), or competing against (for fairness), cis women in sport. Fair Play for Women has been particularly keen to interpret the EA 'in such a way that trans women are understood as "male", and trans men as "female", and non-binary people as implicitly delusional' (Pearce et al., 2020, p. 688). Fair Play for Women are also quick to centre themselves as the driving agents of change, when in reality their motivations are less about equality for (cis) women and more about their goal to have 'the meaning of the term "biological sex" [instead to] define women as "women who are not trans"' (Madrigal-Borloz, 2023, p. 4.22) preserved in legislation. But first we need to look at what happened in 2020, with World Rugby.

On 9 October 2020, *The Guardian* (UK) newspaper reported that the world governing body for the sport of rugby union, World Rugby, had decided to ban trans women from the elite women's game for the foreseeable future. The report was developed by a World Rugby working group 'following research into available scientific literature, which detailed an extensive consultation where the working group heard from independent experts in the field of performance, physiology, medicine, risk, law and socio-ethics' (Ingle, 2020, n.p.). This report

> [a]ims to facilitate the participation of transgender players in rugby where it is possible to do so safely and fairly. Rugby is a sport that involves frequent physical confrontation and collision and so physiological attributes such as size, strength, power and speed are important contributors to safety/welfare and performance.
>
> *(World Rugby Transgender Guide, 2020, p. 2)*

The report also included guidelines for non-binary players, whose inclusion was determined by 'whether or not they had experienced the biological effects of testosterone during puberty or adolescence' (World Rugby Transgender Guide, 2020, p. 25). Players who had experienced these effects were not permitted to play. Trans men 'may play men's rugby having provided confirmation of physical ability, and [transgender men] may not play women's rugby after the process of sex reassignment has begun, if this reassignment includes supplementation with testosterone' (World Rugby Transgender Guide, 2020, p. 5).

The World Rugby report (2020) positions trans women and some non-binary people as a threat to their teammates' safety, but it is important to note that in the United Kingdom there are 37,000 registered cis women playing rugby (figures from Rugby Football Union, 2020) and six trans women registered to play senior rugby union (BBC, 2022). Rugby is a contact sport, and, like other contact sports (for instance football, hockey or netball) it is reliant on physical strength and speed. Contact sport reinforces essentialist ideas about men's bodies being stronger/heavier and faster than women's, and, by extension, a danger should they be participating in sport together. As Mumford (2021) argues, the public rationale for excluding trans women from sport is so that cis women can be guaranteed both a safe and a fair sporting chance, itself a rationale which is 'a manifestation of patriarchal power … its power rests in the premise that women's sport is meant to be weaker than men's' (Mumford, 2021, p. 129). This is clearly a hangover from the Victorian ideals of women's frailty and fragility.

World Rugby's inclusion of the term 'safety' in their policy needs unpacking in relation to Section 195 of the EA (2010). This section, quoted in full earlier, does not offer a definition of safety. However, the accompanying explanatory note states:[9]

> This section allows separate sporting competitions to continue to be organised for men and women where physical strength, stamina or physique are major factors in determining success or failure, and in which one sex is

> generally at a disadvantage in comparison with the other. It also makes it lawful to restrict participation of transsexual people in such competitions if this is necessary to uphold fair or safe competition, but not otherwise.

If Section 195 offers neither a definition nor an example of what *is* safe in sport, then what can be assumed? In law, when there is not a definition available, what is called common-sense causation is applied (Summers, 2018). To consider safety, we are considering what it means to be safe from unreasonable injury. In other words, if we examine the case law around sport and consent, what can an individual consent to? What is reasonable by way of such consent and what are the parameters around safe/unsafe? For instance, when walking onto a rugby pitch, a player is consenting to possible injury, inevitably as part of the game. It is not unlikely for someone to be hurt. This is very different to someone consenting to taking part in, for example, a snooker match. Broadly, the way the Equality Act operates is by looking at specific terms in the context of a particular case; thus, safety will look very different when you compare different sports. The fact is, the Equality Act does not provide a singular definition of what safety means.

In November 2021, the IOC released their *Framework on Fairness, Inclusion and Non-Discrimination on the Basis of Gender Identity and Sex Variations* (IOC, 2021). The Framework aims to support International Federations (IFs) in the development of policies in relation to the participation of transathletes and/or athletes with sex variations that are sport-specific, evidence-based and rights-respecting. It is informed, as Martowicz et al. (2023, p. 26) write, 'by three values that are foundational to the Olympic Movement: fairness, inclusion and non-discrimination'. The Framework, like this book, recognises the need for separate women's and men's categories in elite sports. It also acknowledges 'the significance of fair competition opportunities for the women's category, given the historical and contemporary struggle for gender equality in sport' (Martowicz et al., 2023, p. 25). It also offers a clear and rationale approach to defining safety in sport, which I agree with:

> The Framework recognises that safety is a concern in some sports. In such cases, eligibility criteria should not rely on an athlete's gender identity or sex variations status as a proxy for injury risk. Rather, IFs should focus on actual metrics of injury risk (eg, an individual's size and power) and take into account the variation in such risk factors that is already accommodated across all eligible athletes. Where there are risks in a given sport related to physical characteristics, mitigation measures should apply equally to all athletes who potentially pose a safety risk or are at risk of injury, and not only to those who identify as trans and/or have sex variations, since this would constitute a form of discrimination.
>
> *(Martowicz et al., 2023, p. 28)*

Even so, a number of high-profile sports organisations proceeded to publish their own policies on the matter. On 20 June 2022, Fédération internationale de natation (FINA, renamed World Aquatics in 2023) which is swimming's world governing body, voted to stop trans athletes from competing in women's elite races if they have gone through any part of the process of male puberty (BBC, 2023a). In July 2022, the British Triathlon Federation confirmed that for athletes over the age of 12, competitive women's events will be reserved 'for those who are female sex at birth' (Roan, 2022). Union Cycliste Internationale (UCI) followed later that month, calling it a 'precautionary measure' (BBC, 2023b). British Cycling did the same in May 2023, claiming female races will be 'for those whose sex was assigned female at birth' (Roan, 2023). In March 2023, UK Athletics banned trans women from competing in the female category in its competitions and events in the United Kingdom (Falkingham, 2023). Two months later, in May 2023, so did World Rowing, citing the familiar phrase, 'the review was based on current scientific evidence highlighting the significant performance differences between males and females in rowing, with the core objective of guaranteeing fair competition and participation for women in sport' (World Rowing, 2023). In August 2023, British Rowing revised their policy – less than a year after publishing a previously trans- inclusive policy – to say that trans athletes who were born female and are not undergoing hormone treatment can still enter female races, and that an 'open' category will be available to trans and non-binary rowers in competition events (BBC 2023c). Arguably, trans women are not banned from rowing completely and are technically still welcome in the open category. But again, the message is clear: despite there being no legal definition of the term 'biological sex' in the law (Madrigal-Borloz, 2023), an inference to it justifies the exclusion of trans women in the female category.

The influence of the gender critical community on sporting organisations is undeniable, so familiar is the language used in these revised policies. Pearce et al. (2020, p. 689) write:

> Yet, the authority of 'science' allows 'biological truths' about sex difference to be presented as incontestable realities trumping (merely 'social') gender. The alliance between self-proclaimed feminists … and powerful sports authorities further shows how the mobilisation of 'biology' as a basis for trans (and intersex) people's exclusion currently transcends traditional political positionalities.

'Sex', the 'latest science' and 'female' are used interchangeably in these policies and as infallible terms to justify these bans and to exclude trans women. The production of evidence to justify these revisions never happens, possibly because there is no legal requirement for sporting organisations to show their workings. Organisations are quick to allude to 'the science' underpinning their decisions, yet neither British Triathlon, World Rowing, British Rowing nor UK Athletics have publicly confirmed which science they used to base their decision on. UK Athletics convened a 'Transgender Project Group' allegedly comprising volunteers with relevant legal, medical, human rights, ethics and research expertise (Crumley, 2023). Membership of this project group or the research it considered to reach its decision has never been shared. British Triathlon's policy also does not show the research it consulted, and the policy itself simply states that 'concerns regarding non-compliance with this policy can also be sent to concern@britishtriathlon.org. Breaches of this policy will be handled under the British Triathlon Disciplinary Policy'. As previously discussed, my belief is that the science currently available is either flawed or inconclusive.

In the case of British Rowing, the influence of gender critical voices on the revised policy is especially concerning. Despite claims that British Rowing's governing body changed its policy following 'extensive and ongoing research and consultation', their Board Meeting minutes tell a different story. Minutes taken on 22 March 2023 (Section 6.1: Presentation and Discussion on the Transgender Policy)[10] record that

> Cathy Devine (CD) and Jane Sullivan (JS) joined the meeting to present research and feedback on their views on Transgender, what is happening across the sport sector, their views on British Rowing's Transgender policy and the recent change of approach announced by World Rowing. CD outlined a scientific and legal argument around why transgender women should not be included in the women's category. JS highlighted several case studies that outlined why transgender women should not be included in the women's category.

Cathy Devine is, according to her website,[11] an independent researcher and consultant whose 'academic specialism is in sport policy'. Ms Devine holds a BSc in zoology/animal biology and an MSc in nutrition and has, to the best of my knowledge, no legal qualifications which would allow her to offer expert legal advice. And yet, as the British Rowing minutes state, this was her purpose at the meeting. Ms Devine is a prominent gender critical feminist whose published work argues for the exclusion of trans women in sport. This includes a rebuttal to the previously mentioned Canadian Centre for Ethics in Sport report (2022), a rebuttal she co-authored with Dr Emma Hilton and Dr Tommy Lundberg – themselves both prominent gender critical academics whose 2020 paper was republished with a comment advising readers as such. Jane Sullivan was the Head of Rowing at the Royal Grammar School Worcester from 2013 to 2020, and is also a prominent gender critical feminist, who has called for trans women to be banned from female events (Sales, 2023).

One action from the March 2023 British Rowing meeting was that 'a survey is to take place between now and the Board meeting on 22 May, to gather the views of our community on this topic'. This survey, assumingly intended for members of British Rowing only, was published both in the press and on 12 May 2023 in a thread in the *Feminism: Sex and gender discussions* section of the parenting website Mumsnet (*British Rowing poll on transgender policy closes today*), where people were encouraged to respond. As one (anonymised) Mumsnetter posted: 'I've replied several times to try and show my strength of feeling – have no idea if it will count only once or not, doesn't seem like a robust design and is certainly not transparent' (Mumsnet, 2023). It cannot be hard to imagine this survey receiving a high number of bad-faith responses from non-members of British Rowing, with the goal of skewing the results and banning trans women from competition. A second action from the March 2023 British Rowing board meeting was for 'further expert/external sources of advice to be arranged to meet the Board ahead of the May 2023 review' (British Rowing, 2023, p. 4). To date, British Rowing have not published details of these sources, or the advice which led to their revised policy in August that same year to ban trans women from competing with cis women. In addition, Fair Play for Women tweeted British Rowing's announcement in a tweet they titled 'Fair Play for Women: Achievement unlocked' (Fair Play for Women, 2023), in which they appeared to take credit for the revised British Rowing policy. This tweet received numerous replies thanking the organisation for all they do for women and for the prevalence of common sense.

This example from British Rowing is just one of many, and I have drawn on it because of the public availability of their minutes and the transparency on who they consulted. Nonetheless they are part of a growing list of sporting organisation's trans 'inclusion' policies using arbitrary bans that are not evidence based. Bekker et al. (2023, p. 179) write: In summary,

> Bans on trans women as a class, as in the case of World Rugby (2020) elite women's rugby policy, may also be considered discriminatory and unimplementable in certain national jurisdictions. So, too, does the FINA (2022) policy raise questions regarding potential rights violations given it mandates the sex testing of all women athletes—an approach not seen since compulsory sex testing was acknowledged as grossly unscientific and abandoned by the IOC in the mid-1990s.

I do not believe there is a fundamental, medical or scientific way to clearly categorise all humans into the female–male binary. My concern is the increasing number of sporting organisations doing so on what appears to be inconclusive and flawed evidence. As ever missing from these discussions are trans men.

Trans Men

Trans men taking part in sport rarely make headlines, and there are no examples of trans men competing in the modern Olympic Games. This failure to acknowledge their presence in sport renders them invisible and implies they are insignificant. Yet this lack of consideration dismisses the reality of their successes, of which there are examples, and in sports which they might be assumed to be unable to qualify against cis men.

The most well-known of these is Chris Mosier, the first trans athlete to represent the United States in international competition, placing third in his age group in sprint triathlon at the Draft Legal Triathlon World Championship Qualifier race in 2016. Mosier is an elite-level triathlete, duathlete and race walker, earning All-American honours in duathlon in 2015. In 2020, Mosier became the first openly trans male athlete to ever compete in an Olympic trial alongside cis men; however, he was unable to finish the race due to injury. He is also the first trans athlete to be sponsored by Nike. Professional boxer Patricio Manuel is the first trans male boxer in the history of the United States to have a professional fight, and in December 2018, Manuel defeated Mexican super-featherweight Hugo Aguilarand in California.

There are three trans men of note who have competed at college-level sport. In 2010 U.S. basketball playerKye Allums became the first openly trans person to compete in a National Collegiate Athletic Association Division 1 (NCAA D-1) sport when he came out as a trans man while playing basketball for the George Washington University's women's team in 2010. Schuyler Bailar, a trans man, was the first openly trans athlete to compete on a men's swimming team in the NCAA D-1. The NCAA D-1 is the highest level of intercollegiate athletics sanctioned by the NCCA in the United States, which accepts players globally. It is fiercely competitive, and a number of NCAA D-1 swimmers, including Jack Conger and Ryan Murphy, are Olympic medallists (Conger won gold at Rio de Janeiro in 2016, and Ryan Murphy is a four-time Olympic gold medallist). Former American high school wrestler Mack Beggs has faced opposition towards his competing in girls' wrestling leagues, despite th fact that Texas state athletic rules only allowed him to compete in the league for the sex he was assigned at birth. Beggs has twice won the Texas girls state championship, wins considered controversial by some because of the low doses of testosterone Beggs was said to have been taking at the beginning of his high school freshman year. Citing the possible advantages testosterone could give Beggs over his female wrestling competitors, some wrestlers and their parents protested, with some competitors even forfeiting matches. Beggs took hormone blockers to prevent any advantage that could be provided by the synthetic testosterone (Holmes, 2021), yet as Beggs himself said, 'it's a no-win situation' (Holmes, 2021, n.p.).

It could be argued that the achievements of the four athletes who were competing alongside cis men undermines essentialist assumptions that women are inherently weaker than men and that trans men cannot equal or outperform cis men in sport (Barras, 2019). This assumption is reflected in both the IOC's policies and in the media's lack of coverage on trans men. Trans women are frequently viewed as interlopers in cis women's sports and spaces, but trans men do not seem to attract the same concern, from either the gender-critical community, from cis men, or from the public more generally (Barras, 2024). Within the IOC's Stockholm Consensus (2004), the four recommendations made for the inclusion of trans athletes competing in the Olympic Games applied to both trans men and trans women. When the IOC updated this policy in 2015, the different eligibility criteria for trans men was included, stating that 'those who transition from female to male are eligible to compete in the male category without restriction' (IOC, Consensus Statement, 2015, G.1). Only a short section on hyperandrogenism in female athletes is included in this statement, with no mention of testosterone or required hormones levels for trans men. Undoubtedly this is because trans men are assumed to possess no competitive advantage in sport over cis men, meaning there are no concerns about cis men being disadvantaged. This is because trans men's bodies are assumed to be smaller and less powerful than cis men's). Nor are trans men considered to be a threat to cis women in sex segregated spaces such as changing rooms, though as some of the trans masculine participants note later in this book, this was less a matter of inclusive behaviour and more a matter of whether a person passed in that space.

The literature concerning trans men in sport is scant (see Barras, 2024). Notable contributions include Jayne Caudwell's (2014) research (Caudwell, 2014), which examined the gendered subjectivities of two young trans men and their inclusion in sport. Of interest is how the two young men deemed cis men's sporting spaces to be unsafe for them, a theme explored later in this book. Rebecca Farber's (2017) work on trans men in online fitness forums touches on a similar theme, that of 'gymtimidation' and passing. Farber's paper is based on a content analysis of a Reddit message board about transgender men's fitness and her interviews with eight transgender men. Farber observed how the participants

> Acknowledge that interacting with others is only comfortable when they are seen and treated as male. By building muscle in a traditionally male (and therefore masculine) shape, transgender men were also more likely to be read by others as male and masculine.
>
> *(Farber, 2017, p. 261)*

Muscles are often culturally coded as male and weights areas in gyms are frequently male-dominated (Barras and Frith, 2023), and, as later discussed, the trans masculine participants in this book were themselves aware of the necessity of passing to access these spaces.

Klein, Paule-Kobaa and Krane's (2019) paper presents a case study of a trans male college athlete as he transitions from the women's to the men's team, with the authors framing their study through a trans feminist lens. The authors' contribution is significant not only because the student is a trans man but also because previous studies are retrospective accounts (e.g. Hargie et al., 2015; Lucas-Carr and Krane, 2011; Semerjian and Cohen, 2006). A key finding – one which applies across all genders as we shall read later – is the part supportive teammates and staff (such as coaches) play in an individual feeling both welcome and included in their sport. This is a similar finding in a study by Catherine Phipps (2019), who explored trans inclusion in the UK university sport context, particularly the experiences of one trans man who had socially but not yet medically transitioned. Phipps found that potential harassment and 'gossip' in women's sport teams may impact trans men to remove themselves from these spaces (see also Travers and Deri, 2011). When single-sex sporting spaces are the only option available, how best to accommodate those who risk being made to feel both unwelcome and unsafe by those who feel more entitled to be there?

Afroozeh et al. (2023) draw on cultural cisgenderism to analyse the sporting experiences of 12 trans men in Iran and their experiences of women's sport environments, and the extent to which it is embedded into Iranian culture. The authors found that whilst there was evidence of (trans) identities being socially accepted, essentialist understandings of sex and gender remained prevalent in sport environments. Gender presentation was also policed by others in sport, with expectations that it should align with ascribed biological sex (see also Karkazis, 2019).

What connects all of the literature briefly presented here is the instability and complexity of hegemonic masculinity in sport, which is clearly challenged by the inclusion of these individuals, calling into question the conflation of competitive advantage with male physiology. Raewyn Connell (2005) argued that hegemonic masculinity is embodied in all men who participate in sport and physical activity, and gender identity and the characteristics of hegemonic masculinity are inextricably linked. Despite gradual gains by women in both professional and amateur sport globally, it is still largely organised both by and for men, particularly within the most popular sports, for example football, rugby, cricket and tennis, where masculinity is linked to 'socially sanctioned aggression and physical power' (Grindtstaff and West, 2011, p. 865). Channon (2014, p. 589) wrote:

> Throughout much of the sociological literature on sport, physical education, and related activities, the presence of traditional, sexist ways of doing gender have been frequently and consistently highlighted, leading some scholars to conclude that gender divisions and men's superiority are more naturalized in sport than perhaps any other institution.

Hegemonic masculinity sits at the top of other hierarchies, including complicit masculinities, subordinate masculinities and marginalised masculinities. Ravenhill and de Visser (2017) argued that those men who accept their position in relation to hegemonic masculinity, and keep to the norms of that position, will meet social expectations of manhood. Conversely, those men who seek to maintain hegemonic masculinity's standards, but find themselves unable, may feel unworthy, incomplete and inferior (Barker and Scheele, 2020). There is an opportunity, I believe, to open up the floor to wider conversations about how masculinity might be deconstructed in sport for the benefit of all athletes, cis and trans.

Summary

Robin White and Nicola Newbegin (2021, p. xviii) write in their book *A Practical Guide to Transgender Law*, 'sex/gender/man/woman [are] such simple terms, and we would all think easy to define until we are put on the spot to do so'. Yet the Equality Act is, I argue, being utilised to attempt exactly this definition outside of its parameters. To reiterate: the Equality Act must start from a position of inclusion, and it is therefore necessary for any organisation to comply with the Equality Act if they are using it as a basis for lawful discrimination. To date no sporting organisation has been challenged on their compliance with the Equality Act, nor asked to produce 'the science' they claim to have based their decision upon. Thus, these decisions remain untested in law. I have argued there is limited scientific data to uphold the belief that trans women competing in sport is unfair due to competitive advantage. An international expert on gender discrimination in sport and sports law, Seema Patel has also argued how the fallacy of generalised strength, stamina and physique 'as the basis for such exclusion within legislation has been heavily criticised' (Patel, 2021, p. 44; see also Patel, 2022). I have also shown that safety means different things in different sports and that with no clear explanation in Section 195 of the Equality Act (2010), it can only pertain to the activity of sport, and not extend to other spaces.

I appreciate – like the IOC's Framework (2021) – how challenging this topic is, but I believe that sport, fundamentally, must start from a place of inclusion for all, and not start from one of exclusion. This means calling upon those stakeholders with responsibility for considering eligibility criteria for trans athletes (and/or athletes with sex variations), to account for any possible negative consequences for affected athletes. After all, as Sheree Bekker et al. (2023, p. 179) write:

> Even if the scientific evidence was settled, the exclusion of athletes on the basis of their gender identity or sex variations status is potentially incompatible with legal and human rights frameworks at national and international levels. For example, the requirement to undergo medical surgery or hormone treatment as a condition of sports participation contravenes numerous fundamental human rights.

Returning to the historical origins of sport and its heteropatriarchal construction, we know that it did not 'miraculously appear on earth, followed by the "natural" superiority of men in these competitions' (Aurora, 2007, p. 101). The rules crafted for certain sports, which became popular through economic investments and media attention, require specific types of physiques that, on average, are tailored to the male physique. If a body is to be banned due to the fairness and safety of others (it is stronger, faster, taller and heavier), then why not ban cis women with the same physical attributes? What is rarely taken into consideration is how trans people's lived experiences of participation in sport. Instead, what is overlooked are the effects of a lifetime of hormone injections, the direct health implications of possible surgery, and other treatments and side effects of transition, none of which 'can be trivialised as being a price people would willingly pay in an attempt to gain a competitive advantage in sports' (McArdle, 2008, p. 53).

The laborious focus on (inconclusive) science also sidelines the legal and human rights aspect of this debate (Patel 2021). In the absence of evidence, the gender critical community are preferring to choose cissexism, transphobia and transmisogyny, by ignoring how policies 'that impact trans women's participation in elite sport are the continuation of a long history of exclusion of women from competitive sport – an exclusion that resulted in the introduction of a "women's" category of sport in the first place' (E-Alliance, 2023, p. 6). It is therefore crucial that policies and regulations which determine the inclusion (or exclusion) of trans athletes 'should be free of any social and/or religious prejudice, bias, or discrimination and should be based on the best available scientific evidence from the best available scientific practice and the decisions made will also require a firm political resolve' (Cooper, 2020, n.p). Returning to Davina Cooper's reflections on sex and gender and the dangers of drawing up separate territories to defend one's own version of feminism (Cooper, 2020, n.p), perhaps it is sport itself which can offer what Cooper terms 'a more generous place for thinking about and responding to the feminist politics of others'.

Discussion Questions

1 Sally Hines (2019, p. 5) wrote that 'hostility to the self-determinism of gender identity appears to strengthen as trans people gain increased citizenship rights'. Do you think this statement holds weight still?
2 Read the short position statement by Martowicz et al. (2023) on the IOC's Framework on Fairness, Inclusion and Non-discrimination on the Basis of Gender Identity and Sex Variations (2021). Discuss the IOC's '10-Principle Approach'. Can you give a real-world example of each?
3 Do you think trans men automatically gain male privilege when they pass as male? Discuss why this may not be the case.
4 How does body politics operate in places other than sport?

Notes

1 'Gonadectomy' is a generic term referring to the surgical removal of either the testes in males or the ovaries in females, which results in a loss of gonadal production of sex steroids.
2 It was mandated that trans women's testosterone levels must remain below 10 nmol/L for a year prior to competing.
3 This screening was known as the Barr Body Test, or Buccal Screen Test, and was introduced by the IOC Medical Commission as a sex determination (gender verification) test in 1968. At the 1992 Barcelona Olympics, the Barr test was replaced by the Polymerase Chain Reaction test, but this was also deemed problematic. At the 1996 IOC World Conference on Women and Health, a decision was made to discontinue their process of gender verification during the Olympic Games. Chromosome testing was last performed at the Atlanta Olympic Games in 1996.
4 Differences in sex development (DSD) is a group of rare conditions involving genes, hormones and reproductive organs, including genitals. It means a person's sex development is different to most other people's. Sometimes the term 'Disorders of Sex Development' is used, as is Variations in Sex Characteristics (VSC) or Diverse Sex Development. Some people prefer to use the term 'intersex' (see NHS, 2023). Bennecke et al. (2021) write that any terminology used must be sensitive to concerns of individuals having these conditions, and the author takes the same position.
5 Anthopometric measures are used in the paediatric population to evaluate the general health status, nutritional adequacy and the growth and developmental pattern of the child (see Casadei and Kiel, 2024).
6 Haemoglobin levels relate to red blood cells – the higher the volume, the more efficient your aerobic capacity and sporting performance. Lance Armstrong, a former professional cyclist, was stripped of his seven Tour de France wins for doping. Armstrong as banned from competitions for life after he described taking a 'cocktail', which included 'EPO, transfusions and testosterone' (Adams, 2020, n.p.).
7 https://www.legislation.gov.uk/ukpga/2010/15/section/195#:~:text=%281%29%20A%20person%20does%20not%20contravene%20this%20Act%2C,another%20as%20a%20competitor%20in%20a%20gender-affected%20activity.
8 E.G, contact sports such as rugby and boxing would be included, along with more traditionally physical sports, such as football, cricket and rowing. One would assume chess would not (see White and Newbegin, 2021, p. 237) – but on 17 August 2023, FIDE (International Chess Federation) did exactly this.
9 https://www.legislation.gov.uk/ukpga/2010/15/notes/division/3/14/5#:~:text=Section%20195%3A%20Sport%20Effect%20614.%20This%20section%20allows,at%20a%20disadvantage%20in%20comparison%20with%20the%20other.
10 British Rowing (2023, March 22). Board Meeting Minutes (22 March 2023). Available at: https://www.britishrowing.org/wp-content/uploads/2023/05/Board-Minutes-March-2023.pdf.
11 https://cathydevine.wixsite.com/researcher.

References

[E.Alliance]. (2023). *Transgender women athletes and elite sport: A scientific review.* https://cces.ca/transgender-women-athletes-and-elite-sport-scientific-review

[House of Commons]. (2020). https://committees.parliament.uk/oralevidence/1394/default/

[International Association of Athletics Federations] (IAAF). (2024). https://www.iaaf.org/home

[International Olympic Committee]. (2004). https://stillmed.olympic.org/Documents/Reports/EN/en_report_905.pdf

[International Olympic Committee]. (2015). https://stillmed.olympic.org/Documents/Commissions_PDFfiles/Medical_commission/2015-11_ioc_consensus_meeting_on_sex_reassignment_and_hyperandrogenism-en.pdf

[International Olympic Committee]. (2021, November 16). *IOC releases Framework on Fairness, Inclusion and Non-discrimination on the basis of gender identity and sex variations*. IOC. https://olympics.com/ioc/news/ioc-releases-framework-on-fairness-inclusion-and-non-discrimination-on-the-basis-of-gender-identity-and-sex-variations

[Press for Change UK]. (2021). http://www.pfc.org.uk

[UK Equality Act]. (2010). https://www.legislation.gov.uk/ukpga/2010/15/contents

Adams, J. (2020, May 24). *Lance Armstrong doping: What kind of drugs did former cyclist take?* Heavy. https://heavy.com/sports/2020/05/lance-armstrong-doping-drugs-what-kind-epo/#:~:text=After%20years%20of%20denial%2C%20former%20cyclist%20Lance%20Armstrong,a%20%E2%80%9Ccocktail%E2%80%9D%20which%20included%20%E2%80%9CEPO%2C%20transfusions%20and%20testosterone.%E2%80%9D

Afroozeh, M.S., Phipps, C., Afrouzeh, A., Mehri, A., & Alipour Asiri, Z. (2023). "The spectators ask, is it a boy or a girl? What is it?": Cultural cisgenderism and trans men's sporting experiences in Iran. *International Review for the Sociology of Sport*. https://doi.org/10.1177/10126902231162270

Alvares, L.A.M., Santos, M.R., Souza, F.R., Santos, L.M., de Mendonça, B.B., Costa, E.M.F., & Domenice, S. (2022). Cardiopulmonary capacity and muscle strength in transgender women on long-term gender-affirming hormone therapy: a cross-sectional study. *British Journal of Sports Medicine*, *56*(22), 1292–1299. https://doi.org/10.1136/bjsports-2021-105400

Aura, S. (2007). Like any other girl: Male-to-female transsexuals and professional sports. *14 Sports Law Journal*, 95. https://heinonline.org/HOL/LandingPage?handle=hein.journals/sportlj14&div=7&id=&page=

Ball, E. (2023, March 22). *Former Plymouth Olympian Sharron Davies compares trans athletes to doping cheats*. Plymouth Herald. https://www.plymouthherald.co.uk/news/plymouth-news/former-plymouth-olympian-sharron-davies-6833459

Barker, M.J., & Scheele, J. (2020). *Gender: A graphic history*. London: Icon.

Barras, A. (2019). "We just want to be listened to": Mundane Transphobia in BBC1's the trans woman athlete dispute with Martina Navratilova. *British Mensa's Androgeny*, *3*(3), 5–15. UK: British Mensa Ltd. https://www.researchgate.net/publication/336927760_FULL_ISSUE_of_JOURNAL_British_Mensa's_ANDROGYNY_-_Volume_3_-_Issue_3_-_October_2019

Barras, A. (2024). The invisibility of trans men in sport and sporting spaces. In: S. Lawrence, J. Hill, R. Mowatt (Eds.). pp. 85 - 98.*The Routledge handbook of sport, leisure and social justice*. London: Routledge.

Barras, A., & Frith, H. (2023). 'Cos not everyone wants to talk, they prefer to do, to move': circuits of trans embodied pleasure and inclusion in sport and physical exercise. *Sport, Education and Society*. https://doi.org/10.1080/13573322.2023.2266755

BBC. (2023a, June 20). *Fina bars transgender swimmers from women's elite events if they went through male puberty*. BBC. https://www.bbc.co.uk/sport/swimming/61853450

BBC. (2023b, July 15). *Transgender women barred from female events as UCI takes 'precautionary measure'*. BBC. https://www.bbc.co.uk/sport/cycling/66203709

BBC. (2023c, August 3). *British Rowing: Transgender women banned from competing in female category*. BBC. https://www.bbc.co.uk/sport/rowing/66393959

BBC. (2022, July 30). *RFL and RFU ban transgender women from competing in female-only forms of their games*. BBC. https://www.bbc.co.uk/sport/62349297#:~:text=There%20are%20currently%20six%20transgender,women%20playing%20senior%20rugby%20union

Bekker, S., Storr, R., Patel, S., & Mitra, P. (2023). Gender inclusive sport: A paradigm shift for research, policy, and practice. *International Journal of Sport Policy and Politics*, *15*(1), 177–185. https://doi.org/10.1080/19406940.2022.2161599

Bennecke, E., Köhler, B., Röhle, R., Thyen, U., Gehrmann, K., Lee, P., & Wiesemann, C. (2021). Disorders or differences of sex development? Views of affected individuals on DSD terminology. *The Journal of Sex Research*, *58*(4), 522–531. https://doi.org/10.1080/00224499.2019.1703130

British Rowing. (2023, March 22). *Board Meeting Minutes (22 March 2023)*. Available at: https://www.britishrowing.org/wp-content/uploads/2023/05/Board-Minutes-March-2023.pdf

Buzuvis, E. (2011). Caster Semenya and the myth of a level playing field. *The Modern American*, *6*, 36–45. https://digitalcommons.wcl.american.edu/cgi/viewcontent.cgi?article=1136&context=tma

Buzuvis, E. (2012). Including transgender athletes in sex-segregated sport. *Essays from Activists, Coaches, and Scholars*, 25–31. https://digitalcommons.law.wne.edu/cgi/viewcontent.cgi?article=1248&context=facschol

Canadian Centre for Ethics in Sports. (2016). Available at: https://cces.ca/news/cces-releases-guide-creating-inclusive-environments-trans-participants-canadian-sport

Casadei, K., & Kiel, J. (2024). Anthropometric Measurement. [Updated 2022 Sep 26]. In: *StatPearls* [Internet]. Treasure Island (FL): StatPearls Publishing. https://www.ncbi.nlm.nih.gov/books/NBK537315/

Caudwell, J. (2014). [Transgender] young men: Gendered subjectivities and the physically active body. *Sport, Education and Society*, *19*(4), 398–414. https://doi.org/10.1080/13573322.2012.672320

Cavanagh, S.L., & Sykes, H. (2006). Transsexual bodies at the Olympics: The International Olympic Committee's policy on transsexual athletes at the 2004 Athens Summer Games. *Body and Society*, *12*(3), 75–102. https://doi.org/10.1177/1357034X06067157

Channon, A. (2014). Towards the "undoing" of gender in mixed-sex martial arts and combat Sports. *Societies*, *4*(4), 587–605. https://doi.org/10.3390/soc4040587

Cheek, D.B., Grumbach, M.M., Grave, G.D., et al. (1974). *Control of onset of puberty*. New York: John Wiley & Sons.

Collison, C., & De Martini Ugolotti, N. (2022). Pain, faith and yoga. In: N. De Martini Uglottii & J. Caudwell (Eds.). *Leisure and forced migration: Lives lived in asylum systems*. London: Routledge. https://doi.org/10.4324/9780429341045

Connell, R. (2005). *Masculinities* (2nd ed.). Cambridge: Polity.

Cooper, D. (2020, April 30). *Responding to gender critical feminism: On gender, sex and a generous feminist politics in anxious times*. Future of Legal Gender. https://

futureoflegalgender.kcl.ac.uk/2020/04/responding-to-gender-critical-feminism-on-gender-sex-and-a-generous-feminist-politics-in-anxious-times/

Cooper, D., Emerton, R., Grabham, E., Newman, H.J.H., Peel, E., Renz, F. & Smith, J. (2022). *Abolishing legal sex status: The challenge and consequences of gender related law reform*. Future of Legal Gender Project. Final Report. King's College London, UK.

Cornelius, S. (2019). Caster Semenya: the legal and ethical issues that should concern us all. Retrieved from: https://theconversation.com/caster-semenya-the-legal-and-ethical-issues-that-should-concern-us-all-117636

Crumley, E. (2023, February 3). *Athletics seeing law changes to allow for creation of open category*. Athletics Weekly. https://athleticsweekly.com/athletics-news/uk-athletics-seeking-law-change-to-allow-for-creation-of-open-category-1039964704/

Dator, J. (2019, May 1). *Caster Semenya's case against discriminatory testosterone testing, explained*. SB Nation. https://www.sbnation.com/2019/5/1/18525247/caster-semenya-discriminatory-testosterone-testing-track-and-field

Devine, C., Hilton, E., Howe, L., Imbrisevic, M., Lundberg, T., & Pike, J. (2022). When Ideology Trumps Science: A response to the Canadian Centre for Ethics in Sport's Review on Transwomen Athletes in the Female Category. *Idrottsforum - Nordic Sports Science Forum*, *11*, 1–18.

Dietz, E. (2021). Normal parents: Trans pregnancy and the production of reproducers. *International Journal of Transgender Health*, *22*(1–2), 191–202. doi:10.1080/26895269.2020.1834483

Donnellan, L. (2008). Gender testing at the Beijing Olympics. *Sport and the Law Journal*, *1*(16), 20–28. Available from: https://www.britishsportslaw.com/wp-content/uploads/2017/10/BASL-Vol-16-Issue-1-1.pdf

Donnelly, M.K., & Kidd, B. (2020). World Rugby's ban on trans players has nothing to do with so-called 'fairness.' Retrieved from: https://theconversation.com/world-rugbys-ban-on-trans-players-has-nothing-to-do-with-so-called-fairness-150589

Eichberg, H. (1997). A revolution in body culture. In: J. Bale & C. Philo (Eds.). *Body cultures: Essays on sport, space and identity*. https://doi.org/10.4324/9780203042700

Fair Play for Women [@fairplaywomen]. (2023, August 2). *Achievement unlocked…* [Tweet]. Twitter. https://fairplayforwomen.com/testosterone-suppression-in-elite-athletes-what-do-we-know/

Falkingham, K. (2023, March 31). *UK Athletics bans transgender women from competing in female category*. BBC. https://www.bbc.co.uk/sport/athletics/65140092

Farber, R. (2017). 'Transing' fitness and remapping transgender male masculinity in online message boards. *Journal of Gender Studies*, *26*(3), 254–268. https://doi.org/10.1080/09589236.2016.1250618

Gilligan, A. (2019, February 17). *Martina Navratilova blasts 'cheating' transgender women in sport*. The Times. https://www.thetimes.co.uk/article/martina-navratilova-blasts-cheating-transgender-women-in-sport-8fmjbnh99

Gleaves, J., & Lehrbach, T. (2016). Beyond fairness: The ethics of inclusion for transgender and intersex athletes. *Journal of the Philosophy of Sport*, *43*(2), 311–326. https://doi.org/10.1080/00948705.2016.1157485

Gooren, L.J.G., & Bunck, M.C.M. (2004). Transsexuals and competitive sports. *European Journal of Endocrinology*, *151*(4), 425–429. https://doi.org/10.1530/eje.0.1510425

Grindtstaff, L., & West, E. (2011). Hegemonic masculinity on the side-lines of sport. *Sociology Compass*, *5(10)*, 859–881. https://doi.org/10.1111/j.1751-9020.2011.00409.x

Hamad, R. (2019, September 9). *Would Caster Semenya have been banned if she was white*? SBS. https://www.sbs.com.au/topics/voices/culture/article/2019/09/02/would-caster-semenya-have-been-banned-if-she-was-white

Hamilton, B.R., Guppy, F.M., Barrett, J., Seal, L., & Pitsiladis, Y. (2021b). Integrating transwomen athletes into elite competition: The case of elite archery and shooting. *European Journal of Sport Science*, 1–10. Advance online publication. https://doi.org/10.1080/17461391.2021.1938692

Hamilton, B.R., Lima, G., Barrett, J., et al. (2021a). Integrating transwomen and female athletes with differences of sex development (DSD) into elite competition: The FIMS 2021 Consensus Statement. *Sports Medicine*, *51*, 1401–1415. https://doi.org/10.1007/s40279-021-01451-8

Handelsman, D.J. (2017). Sex differences in athletic performance emerge coinciding with the onset of male puberty. *Clin Endocrinol (Oxf)*, *87*, 68–72. https://doi.org/10.1111/cen.13350

Hargie, O.D.W., Mitchell, D.H., & Somerville, I.J.A. (2015). 'People have a knack of making you feel excluded if they catch on to your difference': Transgender experiences of exclusion in sport. *International Review for the Sociology of Sport*, *52*(2), 223–239. https://doi.org/10.1177/1012690215583283

Harper, J., O'Donnell, E., Sorouri Khorashad, B., et al. (2021). How does hormone transition in transgender women change body composition, muscle strength and haemoglobin? Systematic review with a focus on the implications for sport participation. *British Journal of Sports Medicine*. Epub ahead of print. https://doi.org/10.1136/bjsports-2020-103106

Harper, J.M. (2023). IOC transgender athlete policies and history. In: A.M. West (Ed.). *The transgender athlete* (pp. 105–116). Academic Press, ISBN 9780323916196. https://doi.org/10.1016/B978-0-323-91619-6.00007-5

Hill Collins, P. (1990). *Black feminist thought: knowledge, consciousness, and the politics of empowerment*. New York: Routledge.

Hilton, E.N., & Lundberg, T.R. (2020). Transgender women in the female category of sport: Perspectives on testosterone suppression and performance advantage. *Sports Medicine*, *51*, 199–214. https://doi.org/10.1007/s40279-020-01389-3

Hines, S. (2019). The feminist frontier: On trans and feminism. *Journal of Gender Studies*, *28*(2), 145–157. https://doi.org/10.1080/09589236.2017.1411791

Hines, S., & Taylor, M. (2018). *Is gender fluid? (The Big Idea). A primer for the 21st century*. London: Thames and Hudson. ISBN: 9780500293683

Holmes, J. (2021, March 26). *Trans wrestler Mack Beggs speaks out on being forced to compete as a girl. "It's a no-win situation"*. LGBTQ Nation. https://www.lgbtqnation.com/2021/03/trans-wrestler-mack-beggs-speaks-forced-compete-girl-no-win-situation/

Hu, C.G., Rerucha, C., & Ingram, B. (2023). The history of transgender athletes in sport. In A. West (Ed.). *The transgender athlete: A guide for sports medicine providers* (pp. 89–194). Berkley: Elsevier Press. ISBN 9780323916196.

Ingle, S. (2020, October 9). *World Rugby bans trans women from elite women's game due to injury risk*. The Guardian. https://www.theguardian.com/sport/2020/oct/09/world-rugby-bans-trans-women-from-elite-womens-game-due-to-injury-risks

Karkazis, K. (2019). The misuses of biological sex. *The Lancet*. https://doi.org/101016/S0140-6736(19)32764-3

Klein, A., Paule-Koba, A.L., & Krane, V. (2019). The journey of transitioning: Being a trans male athlete in college sport. *Sport Management Review*, *22*(5), 626–639. https://doi.org/10.1016/j.smr.2018.09.006

Knott-Fayle, G., Peel, E., & Witcomb, G.L. (2022). Prejudice in "inclusive" spaces: Cisgenderist collusion in the interview context. *Feminism & Psychology*, *32*(2), 178–198. https://doi.org/10.1177/09593535211063263

Ljungqvist, A. (2004). *Explanatory note to the recommendation on sex reassignment and sports*. https://stillmed.olympics.com/media/Document%20Library/OlympicOrg/News/20040517-IOC-Approves-Consensus-With-Regard-To-Athletes-Who-Have-Changed-Sex/EN-report-904.pdf?_ga=2.169982949.499181184.1706707735-1761903442.1706707735

Lucas-Carr, C.B., & Krane, V. (2011). What is the T in LGBT? Supporting transgender athletes through sport psychology. *The Sport Psychologist*, *25*(4), 532–548. https://doi.org/10.1123/tsp.25.4.532

Mackay, F. (2021). *Female masculinities and the gender wars*. London: I.B Tauris.

Madrigal-Borloz, V. (2023). *Country visit to the United Kingdom of Great Britain and Northern Ireland (24 April–5 May 2023)*. Available at: https://www.ohchr.org/sites/default/files/documents/issues/sexualorientation/statements/eom-statement-UK-IE-SOGI-2023-05-10.pdf

Martin Shaw, C. (2019). Body politics. In: *Encyclopedia of race and racism*. Retrieved February 07, 2024 from Encyclopedia.com: https://www.encyclopedia.com/social-sciences/encyclopedias-almanacs-transcripts-and-maps/body-politics

Martowicz, M., Budgett, R., Pape, M., et al. (2023). Position statement: IOC framework on fairness, inclusion and non-discrimination on the basis of gender identity and sex variations. *British Journal of Sports Medicine*, *57*(1), 26–32. doi:10.1136/bjsports-2022-106386

McArdle, D. (2008). Swallows and amazons, or the sporting exception to the Gender Recognition Act. *Social and Legal Studies*, *17*(1), 39–57. https://doi.org/10.1177/0964663907086455

Mumford, S. (2021). *A philosopher looks at sport*. UK: Cambridge University Press.

Mumsnet Comment (2023). on *British Rowing poll on transgender policy closes today*. (poster username redacted). 12 May 2023, https://www.mumsnet.com/talk/womens_rights/4804468-british-rowing-poll-on-transgender-policy-closes-today

Murray, K., Blackburn, L.H., & Mackenzie, L. (2020). Academic Publications. https://murrayblackburnmackenzie.org/academic-publications/

NHS. (2023, March 16). https://www.nhs.uk/conditions/differences-in-sex-development/

Olufemi, L. (2020). *Feminism interrupted*. UK: Pluto Press.

Patel, S. (2021). Gaps in the protection of athlete's gender rights in sport – a regulatory riddle. *The International Sports Law Journal*, *21*(4), 257–275. doi:10.1007/s40318-021-00182-2

Patel, S. (2022). Law and regulatory barriers to increasing inclusivity for trans athletes. In: G.L. Witcomb & E. Peel (Eds.). *Gender diversity and sport: Interdisciplinary perspectives on increasing inclusivity*. London: Routledge. ISBN 9781003050568

Pearce, R., Erikainen, S., & Vincent, B. (2020). TERF wars: An introduction. *The Sociological Review (Keele)*, *68*(4), 677–698. https://doi.org/10.1177/0038026120934713

Phipps, A. (2014). *The politics of the body: Gender in a neoliberal and neoconservative age*. UK: Polity Press. ISBN: 0745648886

Phipps, A. (2016). Whose personal is more political? *Feminist Theory*, *17*(3). https://doi.org/10.1177/1464700116663831

Phipps, A. (2021). *Me, not you: The trouble with mainstream feminism*. UK: Polity Press.
Phipps, C. (2019). Thinking beyond the binary: Barriers to trans participation in university sport. *International Review for the Sociology of Sport*. https://doi.org/10.1177/1012690219889621
Pinho, M., & Gaunt, R. (2024). Biological essentialism, gender ideologies, and the division of housework and childcare. *The Journal of Social Psychology*, *164*(1), 59–75. https://doi.org/10.1080/00224545.2021.1983508
Preston-Ellis, R. (2022, July 25). *Plymouth's Sharron Davies 'facing financial ruin' due to views on transgender athletes*. Plymouth Herald. https://www.plymouthherald.co.uk/news/celebs-tv/plymouths-sharron-davies-facing-bankruptcy-7375297
Ravenhill, J.P., & de Visser, O.R. (2017). Perceptions of gay men's masculinity are associated with their sexual self-label, voice quality and physique. *Psychology & Sexuality*, *8*(3), 208–222. https://doi.org/10.1080/19419899.2017.1343746
Reeser, J.C. (2005). Gender identity and sport: Is the playing field level? *British Journal of Sports Medicine*, *39*(10), 695–699. https://doi.org/10.1136/bjsm.2005.018119
Riggs, D.W. (2014). What makes a man? Thomas Beatie, embodiment, and 'mundane transphobia'. *Feminism and Psychology*, *24*(2), 157–171. https://doi.org/10.1177/0959353514526221
Roan, D. (2022, July 6). *British Triathlon becomes first UK sport to create 'open' category for transgender athletes*. BBC. https://www.bbc.co.uk/sport/triathlon/62063359
Roan, D. (2023, May 26). *British Cycling to ban transgender women from competing in female category*. BBC. https://www.bbc.co.uk/sport/cycling/65718748
Roberts, T.A., Smalley, J., & Ahrendt, D. (2021). Effect of gender affirming hormones on athletic performance in transwomen and transmen: Implications for sporting organisations and legislators. *British Journal of Sports Medicine*, *55*, 577–583. https://doi.org/10.1136/bjsports-2020-102329
Rogol, I.D., Roemmich, J.N., & Clark, P.A. (2002). Growth at puberty. *Journal of Adolescent Health*, *31*(6), 192–200. https://doi.org/10.1016/S1054-139X(02)00485-8
Rugby Football Union. (2020). https://www.englandrugby.com/dxdam/d7/d740ed84-b0c3-4d8f-bc23-ff3aca56fb9e/Gender%20Pay%20Report%202020.pdf
Sales, D. (2023, May 12). *Now trans clash engulfs women's rowing as coach calls for the sport to follow World Athletics in banning biological males from competing in events - amid claims umpires at regattas cannot question gender of competitors*. Daily Mail. https://www.dailymail.co.uk/news/article-12076891/Now-trans-clash-engulfs-womens-rowing-coach-calls-sport-follow-World-Athletics.html
Semerjian, T.Z., & Cohen, J.H. (2006). "FTM means female to me": transgender athletes performing gender. *Women in Sport and Physical Activity Journal*, *15*(2), 28–43. https://doi.org/10.1123/wspaj.15.2.28
Sheridan, H. (2003). Conceptualizing `fair play': A review of the literature. *European Physical Education Review*, *9*(2), 163–184. https://doi.org/10.1177/1356336X03009002003
Simon, R.L. (2010). *Fair play: The ethics of sport*. USA: Westview Press.
Sitwell, R. (2019, July 19). *Self ID will stop women competing on an equal playing field*. Morning Star. https://morningstaronline.co.uk/article/self-id-will-stop-women-competing-equal-playing-field
Stryker, S., & Whittle, S. (2006). *The transgender studies reader*. London: Routledge.
Sudai, M. (2017). The testosterone rule—constructing fairness in professional sport. *Journal of Law and the Biosciences*, *4*(1), 181–193. https://doi.org/10.1093/jlb/lsx004

Sullivan, C.F. (2011). Gender verification and gender policies in elite sport: Eligibility and "fair play". *Journal of Sport and Social Issues*, *35*(4), 400–419. https://doi.org/10.1177/0193723511426293

Summers, A. (2018). Common-sense causation in the law. *Oxford Journal of Legal Studies*, *38*(4), 793–821, Winter 2018. https://doi.org/10.1093/ojls/gqy028

Susman, E.J., & Rogol, A. (2004). Puberty and psychological development. In: R.M. Lerner & L. Steinberg (Eds.). *Handbook PF adolescent psychology* (pp. 15–44). US: Wiley. https://doi.org/10.1002/9780471726746.ch2

Teetzel, S. (2006). On transgendered athletes, fairness and doping: An international challenge. *Sport in Society*, *9*(2), 227–251. https://doi.org/10.1080/17430430500491280

Travers, A., & Deri, J. (2011). Transgender inclusion and the changing face of lesbian softball leagues. *International Review for the Sociology of Sport*, *46*(4), 488–507. https://doi.org/10.1177/1012690210384661

White, R.M., & Newbegin, N. (2021). *Transgender law: A practical guide*. UK: Law Brief Publishing. ISBN: 1913715663

World Rowing. (2023, March 15). *World Rowing adopts tighter rules for transgender women athletes*. World Rowing. https://worldrowing.com/2023/03/15/world-rowing-adopts-tighter-rules-for-transgender-women-athletes/

World Rugby Transgender Policy. (2020).

3

TOWARDS A TRANS FEMINIST METHODOLOGY AND AN ETHICS OF CARE

Introduction

The rationale for this book originates from the limited amount of empirical research which directly asks trans people about their lived experiences of participating in everyday sport. Often trans people's experiences are subsumed under the LGBTQ+ umbrella and this can – and does – result in the misinterpretation of trans people's needs frequently being decentred in research which supposedly centres them (Namaste, 2001).

This chapter discusses the methods and methodology used during this qualitative, participant-informed research. Included are my reflections on access to participants, data collection and data analysis, as well as reflections on the importance of critically examining my own cisgender researcher positionality and reflexivity. It will also discuss the necessity of an ethics of care when conducting research as an outsider involved in research with what is considered (in research ethics terms) a vulnerable community. This chapter will then go on to examine the theoretical framework which this book is built upon, trans feminist theory, and its relevance to sport, the body and improving inclusion.

Striving for a Trans Feminist Research Design

This book advocates for applying a trans feminist theoretical lens to better illuminate the lived experiences of trans people in sport. This is because, as Krane (2019, p. 50) writes,

> Trans feminism leads to questioning the emphasis on anatomy as a criterion for social organisation. Rather, I recognise and appreciate the complexity of

DOI: 10.4324/9781003385486-4

sex and gender and of lived experience with sex and gender. By including a trans feminist stance, one honours sex and gender variation and privileges self-identity.

As previously discussed, the current milieu is dominated by discussions about whether trans people should be permitted to play sport against, or alongside, cis people. This means a particular approach is required when determining which methods are sensitive and respectful (Martin and Meezan, 2003; McCoyd and Shdaimah, 2007; Vincent, 2018). This is partly due to some trans communities feeling a sense of research participation fatigue, my own wish to actively demonstrate allyship, whilst still answering the research question(s).

When conducting research which examines people's lived experiences, a qualitative approach can often generate rich, thick data. There is also a long-established affinity between research in the field of social sciences, gender/queer studies and qualitative approaches (Smith and Sparkes, 2019). But for me, the rationale was not just about justifying my decision to use qualitative methods, it was because I did not want to waste anyone's time. Qualitative research is frequently based in conversation, whose purpose is to look for latent meanings and patterns (Denzin and Lincoln, 2005; Kuklick, 1980). I was keen to nourish such conversations because there were so few in which trans people featured centrally.

The influential work of Virginia Braun and Victoria Clarke argues that one of the many benefits of qualitative research is the way in which it captures 'the complexity, mess and contradiction that characterises the real world' (Braun and Clarke, 2013, p. 10). Qualitative research is a situated activity which locates the observer in the world (Bryman, 2008; Creswell and Poth 2017), and has a long-standing history of contributing to our understanding of social structures, individuals and cultures (Ritchie et al., 2014). More than this, as Mason says (2018, p. x), qualitative research requires 'the humility to recognise that we need to listen attentively, gently and on all channels, if we are to understand the rich and vibrant world of which we are part'.

Qualitative research also complements my social constructionist epistemology and interpretivist ontological position in this book. These positions are appropriate for this study as they take a critical stance towards the 'taken-for-granted ways of understanding the world, including ourselves' (Burr, 2015, p. 3), and challenges what may be accepted as 'knowledge'. My original research was conducted with an understanding of the basic principles which underpin a social constructionist position: that is, based on the assumption that social reality is not singular or objective but is rather shaped by human experiences and social contexts. Thus, the human experiences and narratives of trans people within the context of sport are always the central focus within this book.

Social constructionism has also shaped the approach of this book by working as 'a process and a product of collective meaning-making and ongoing negotiation through complex interactions among multiple social actors in a particular social setting' (Zhao, 2018, p. 98). This is because social constructionism emphasises the socially created nature of both gender and sport. One way of understanding social constructionism is as a process in which people's experience of reality are determined by the meanings they attach to that reality. Another way of seeing social constructionism is as a social product, one that is constructed as an outcome of interactions between complex and diverse forces. Through the lens of social constructionism, we can understand both sport and gender as socially constructed concepts (Burr, 2015). This allows the lived experiences of participants to be foregrounded.

The advantage of this social constructionist epistemology here is that 'many things we take for granted and believe as objective reality are actually socially constructed, and thus, can change as society changes' (Andrews, 2011, p. 1). Gender and sport can be reimagined as both transformative and transgressive. This means taking the view that social phenomena are in a constant state of flux because they are reliant on social interactions as they take place, such as between participants and those people they encounter when involved in sport (Beckman, 2014; Walliman, 2016). Gender identity is also key when taking a social constructionist position, because as Gherovici (2017, p. 98) writes

> Trans people's experiences may force us not just to re-evaluate our notions of gender, but also to reconsider how we think about other forms of difference as it unravels identity as a construction.

This book follows an interpretivist ontology and focuses primarily on recognising and narrating the meaning of human experiences and actions (Levers, 2013). It complements a social constructionist epistemology, because together with a focus on human experience and actions, interpretivist research 'is guided by the researcher's set of beliefs and feelings about the world and how it should be understood and studied' (Denzin and Lincoln, 2005, p. 22). The significance of an interpretivist ontological position here is the way in which it helps to shape those understandings which are mediated by people's own historical and cultural environments. This book is concerned with the unique and personal lived experiences of trans people's participation in sport, and holds that 'objective reality can never be captured, [we] only know it through representations' (Denzin and Lincoln, 2005, p. 5). Interpretivism shapes this book because it helps to capture diverse experiences and recognises that these reflect people's unique and individual gender and sporting biographies.

Ethical Research Design and Recruitment

It is common in research design to rush when we write our application to our university's relevant ethics committee. We are keen to start recruiting and collecting data. We too frequently overlook how recruiting from within marginalised communities might be considered an unfair request for intellectual and emotional labour (Ahmed, 2017; Crenshaw, 1991; Vincent, 2018). I strived to avoid this, and to be mindful of not making unrealistic demands of a community I did not belong to.

After receiving ethical approval in April 2018 (from the University of Brighton's Research Ethics Committee in the School of Applied Social Science), I began advertising for participants. A recruitment poster was emailed to 20 South East- and 20 North West (UK)–based LGBTQ+ and trans only sports groups and trans organisations. An advert was printed in a Brighton-based LGBTQ+ events magazine in May 2018. Participants were also recruited via the 2018 Transgender, Non-Binary and Intersex Conference (Brighton, UK), at which I voluntered. The advert was pinned to my Twitter profile, though I did not tag any groups. This was because I did not want to create an expectation that others should retweet my advert. However, snowball sampling on Twitter) proved to be the most successful recruitment method, possibly because participants were able to 'check me out' before getting in touch (Browne and Nash, 2010). My identity as a swimmer sometimes helped me to navigate common ground and shared experiences during interviews, but I believe if prominent members of the trans community did not like or trust me, I would have had trouble recruiting participants. This was confirmed later when I interviewed Miles, who said he had asked a mutual colleague about me, and if I was trans inclusive.

Between May and September 2018, I conducted 18 semi-structured interviews with adults from around the United Kingdom, including Kent, Lancashire, Devon, Wales, Sussex and London. A total of 12 telephone interviews and 6 in-person interviews took place which ranged in length from 45 minutes to 2 hours, with the average length being 1 hour. Participant ages ranged from 20 years old up to 69, with a variety of gender identities (eight trans women, four trans men, two trans masculine/non-binary people, one transsexual woman, one trans/gender-queer/non-binary person, one trans masculine/gender non-conforming person, one non-binary person). Pronouns were varied and included ten people using she/her/hers, four using he/him/his and four using they/them/their. Information about sexual identity was not collected, though was often mentioned during interviews.

All interviews were digitally audio-recorded on a recording device provided by the University of Brighton and stored in a secure location in compliance with the university's data protection policy and relevant ethics committee regulations. Each interview was then transcribed verbatim by me (Poland, 1995) into a separate Word doucment for each, and store securely on the university one drive. It was important for me to transcribe these recordings personally, because I wanted to be diligent and attentive to the recorded voices. As Berger (2015, p. 228) writes:

> Studying the unfamiliar may also be a barrier to identifying disguised and subtle expressions of themes. Each subculture develops its own language and associations. A stranger to the culture may miss clues that are clear to an 'insider'.

During the transcription process I found returning to my field notes was a good strategy for maintaining reflexivity, creating self-supervision and an audit trail of my conduct as a researcher (Botterill, 2015). This made me especially mindful of any microaggressions I may have committed (Vincent, 2018), such as any language insensitivity or talking over the participant.

Data analysis

All analysis begins with coding the data (Bryman, 2008; Flick, 2018), the process of 'identifying the data that relate to your research question' (Braun and Clarke, 2013, p. 206). Following on from Braun and Clarke (2013), I adopted one of the two main approaches in pattern-based forms of qualitative analysis: selective coding. I made the choice to use selective coding as I had a large amount of data, so this approach meant I could better manage my data in a systematic way. Selective coding is a method which involves 'developing an inclusive corpus of items of interest across the entire data set' (Braun and Clarke, 2013, p. 202). This method of coding enabled me to identify those items of interest in relation to my research questions and aims.

The first stage of coding was to carefully and closely read back over the transcripts, re-reading them multiple times (Braun and Clarke, 2006). This was a fundamental stage of the research process, in terms of my commitment not only to the research topic but also to my status as an outsider researcher, and my wish to be diligent. This meticulous familiarisation with the transcripts also allowed me to develop my analytical skills, helping me to establish a method of easy and efficient recollection. My three supervisors also read six of my transcripts in order to ensure that an additional layer of trustworthiness, integrity and validity was provided (Korstjens and Moser, 2018).

The second stage of the coding process involved identifying relevant words, phrases, sentences, sections, concepts and opinions in all 18 transcripts. This coding process was done manually, and I broadly assigned codes using different-coloured highlighters. I did this by highlighting key words in different colours, looking specifically for words which were relevant for my research questions. These words included, but were not limited to, transgender, non-binary, hormones, surgery, body, gender, sport, exercise, barriers, participation, experiences, impact, recommendations, hegemonic masculinity, gender normativity, inclusion and exclusion. In addition to highlighting words specific to the research, I also highlighted those words which were repeated in several places and which either caught my interest, seemed important to the participant, or resonated with the literature review.

The next stage, as advised by Bryman (2008), was to review the codes a second time. Revisiting my codes allowed a rechecking of the labelling I had carried out, which I had done correctly and not used different terms to describe the same instances. I did this by transferring the extracted codes and any supporting words to a spreadsheet, which was kept to hand for frequent checking. Due to the large volume of data, I needed to streamline it into a manageable document which I could more easily and frequently refer to, almost like a bird's-eye view. The spreadsheet of codes helped me to identify the relationships among the codes, decide which codes were the most important, bring several codes together and develop new codes by combining two or more codes. In this stage, data not relevant to the study were filtered and placed in a column marked miscellaneous where they could be accessed whenever needed. This step was important and took several weeks.

In addition, I carefully re-examined the literature review, to establish links or connections I had perhaps overlooked. The final stage of coding involved grouping these codes into piles, so I could begin the process of thematic analysis. I did this by printing out all the key words and cutting them out. At this stage, basic themes were identified, and I could move on to thematic analysis.

Thematic analysis

Thematic analysis works harmoniously with qualitative research and with my epistemological and ontological positioning. Thematic analysis was an advantage in this research, allowing for both flexibility and familiarity with the data during the transcription process (Braun and Clarke, 2006, 2013; King and Horrocks, 2019). Thematic analysis can also generate unanticipated and unique insights, making it useful for informing recommendations for future uses of this study, such as public policy, which was one of the aims of this research. Thematic analysis also allows for the close observation of themes around trans people's lived experiences of participation in everyday sport and physical exercise, and the broader framework of how hegemonic masculinity and gender normativity might exclude some individuals. This approach was harmonious to the research design, as a qualitative research design often requires qualitative research methods.

Data analysis is not the end point for understanding knowledge; rather, it can be seen as the starting point at which meanings can be unpicked. Using a social constructionist/interpretivist approach helps to orientate the position from which the data are analysed, allowing us to look more closely at the data, scrutinizing the words which interest or puzzle us and lead us to thinking more deeply about the participant's lived experiences (Bryman, 2008). These perspectives also help in the way the data is treated in this research, in that it gives access to the reality of the lived experiences of participants and the activities they are engaged in. These realities may be situated or located within how the phenomena of sport and gender are being constantly constructed and reconstructed via these lived experiences, but they still exist as realities for participants, observable in the data (Craig and Beedie, 2008).

Thematic analysis sits alongside other epistemological and ontological approaches, frequently aligning with them (Braun and Clarke, 2006, 2013). Thematic analysis achieves this by allowing a deeper and more sophisticated level of critical thinking, to better understand the rules which govern society or a phenomenon (such as gender), or the norms or mechanisims of an institution (such as sport). This in turn strengthens the rigour of the qualitative research design chosen here, opening up both straightforward and sophisticated discussions (Creswell and Poth, 2017; Denzin and Lincoln, 2005). For instance, a straightforward discussion aims to give voice to the participants, one which can describe and summarise what barriers may be faced to participation in sport. A sophisticated discussion aims to tell a story, locating both the data and the participants in the wider social, cultural, historical, political and ideological contexts of the research. Most importantly, using thematic analysis to develop this sophisticated approach helps to better structure an argument and interpret the latent meanings in the data, which in turn helps to answer the research question and achieve the research aims (Flick, 2018).

Whiteness and class

My sample was overwhelmingly White British (83.3%), with only two non-British participants (Chinese and White/Irish). All but one were university educated. A note on the whiteness (and education/class) of the sample is warranted here. This ethnic make-up is reflective of the picture in England (where 15 out of the 18 participants were from). Census data from the 2011 Office of National Statistics (ONS, 2011) showed that the total population of England and Wales was 56.1 million, with 48.2 million people (86.0%) from White ethnic groups, with 45.1 million of those identifying with the White British group (80.5% of the population). A specific ethnicity was not a required criterion for the recruitment or the research, and it is not enough that participants' ages reflect a diverse range of sample. My sample is not representative of the trans community; it fails to gather the lived experiences of participation in everyday sport amongst trans people from ethnic minority backgrounds who are trans and is limited in its diversity.

It is also acknowledged that this sample was well above the national average in terms of the level of education reached, with 17 out of 18 participants holding a degree from a higher education establishment. This is exceptionally high when measured against the general UK population figure of 27.2%. According to the Office of National Statistics (ONS, 2011), 27.2% of the UK population, or 12 million people in total aged 16 to 74, have an undergraduate degree, an equivalent or a postgraduate qualification. Seventeen out of 18 participants in this sample were educated to at least undergraduate level. It is difficult at the best of times to 'measure' social class, and in this sample, I did not collect measures of income or occupation, which can be used to establish class (Great British Class Survey, 2013). Whilst these are not an exact measure of social class, some inferences can be drawn from this, and it can be tentatively concluded that this sample was skewed towards more middle-class participants.

Overall, this book is lacking in diversity and can never claim to be representative of all trans people. As Lucie Fremlova writes in her book *Queer Roma* (2022) of her own participants, many of whom came from privileged backgrounds and social positions, 'this is an important limitation and an aspect of the participants' intersectional positioning within their respective societies in terms of class and social status that need to be acknowledged' (Fremlova, 2022, p. 60). I offer the same acknowledgement here and am mindful of a similar limitation.

A (Trans Feminist) Note on Anonymity and Pseudonyms

I offered participants in this study three options when they were interviewed: complete anonymity, being able to choose their own pseudonym or to use their own name.[1] The justification for this was to help reduce the erasure of trans people's presence from research and offer agency. Out of the 18 participants, 15 signed the non-anonymous consent form. In June 2019, during my secondary Annual Progression Review, a mandatory procedure which all doctoral students must complete in order to progress in their studies, the panel raised serious concerns some names would not be anonymised, believing this was a basic safety procedure in all research, and I must address this. I came back to this advice in 2020 when writing up my PhD, as I did not want to ignore the wishes of those participants who wanted to use their own names. I also recognised that, in the hostile climate at the time, participant safety was paramount. As data collection had taken place the previous year in 2019, I felt there was a chance some participants may have changed their mind about their decision, not least as media hostility surrounding trans people in sport was growing. I sought the advice of the Chair of the Research and Ethics Committee who agreed it was sensible to ask participants again, which was in line with the university's code of ethics. I duly emailed those individuals, and received several enthusiastic responses from participants, confirming not only that they still wished their own name to be used, but they felt this was essential in helping to dismantle transphobia in sport and improve inclusion for others. Three participants also wished to update their pronouns

The lesson here is that the commitment researchers have to both upholding high ethical standards and the best interests of their participants really is more than just a tick-boxing exercise (Thomson, 2015, n.p.). With regard to the question of participant anonymity, I remain adamant that my decision to respect participants' agency in using either their own or a chosen name may be one of the most trans-inclusive acts performed in this book, and one which I am proud to have taken the time to push back on.

Data collection

Because there is a lack of empirical research which asks trans people personally (and often intimately) about their lived experiences in sport, one-to-one interviews were deemed to be the most appropriate (Opdenakker, 2006). In addition to face-to-face interviews, telephone[2] and Skype interviews were also offered, to allow for a wider geographical sample (Novick, 2008). The comfort of the participants, as well as not wanting to trigger research fatigue, was paramount in this research, and one-to-one interviews allow for this in a way that a larger group or different data gathering methods might not.

Blaikie (2009, p. 15) wrote how 'to listen to people is to empower them, but if you want to go hear it, you have to go hear it, in their space, or in a safe space'. Empowering participants and facilitating agency was a key part of this research, notably as members of the trans community have spoken openly about experiencing research fatigue (Vincent, 2018). As the participants would be sharing and reflecting on personal and at times potentially difficult stories, face-to-face interviews allowed the opportunity to 'better break down power differences and empower the research participants who no longer feel like the 'other' or subject of study' (Crean, 2018, p. 10).

Participants needed to be partaking in sport currently, in the past, or wished to, whether as a youth or as an adult. They needed to be aged 18 or over, with no upper age-limit. Participants needed to self-identify as 'transgender' and/or 'non-binary' or any other term which they felt was appropriate, such as 'gender non-conforming' or 'gender queer'. This allowed for the shifting gender identification some individuals may experience at different phases of their lives and/or stages of transition (Anderson and Travers, 2017; Farber, 2017; Holm, 2015; Vincent, 2018). The discourses and terminology surrounding this subject change rapidly, reflecting 'an increasingly popular mode of self-identification and locus of popular cultural preoccupation' (Pearce et al., 2019). The ethics and politics of self-definition for trans people can be especially fraught, and thus agency within research is crucial (Burns, 2018; Davy, 2011).

The four interview questions were guided by the general themes of sport, participation and lived experience, and related directly back to the overarching research question:

- Can you tell me about your experiences of participation in sport and exercise?
- How has your gender identity impacted on your experiences, either negatively or positively?
- Have you experienced any barriers to participation?
- Do you think any changes could be made to improve inclusivity for trans people in everyday sport and physical exercise?

Researcher positionality

As this book takes a social constructionist/interpretivist approach, being attentive to my own reflexivity is fundamentally unavoidable. My own cis identity (and outsider status) meant I wanted to keep in mind the question of who speaks for whom in research (Ryan-Flood and Gill, 2010), and the ways in which trans communities have expressed concern about research fatigue (Vincent, 2018). Cressida Heyes (2003) wrote that effective alliances can be forged in feminist spaces, and as a trans-inclusive feminist, my position as a trans-ally within this book is unequivocal. As previously noted, many trans people have expressed dealing with research fatigue (Vincent, 2018), and discussions in and outside of the academy regarding trans people's inclusion in sport continue to be debated amongst the gender critical movement. A tension arises here because the role of the researcher 'must be seen as central to the research process and revealing the personal in research then becomes a part of explaining the bases for knowledge' (Henwood and Pidgeon, 1992, p. 9). Whilst I position myself as trans-inclusive and a trans-ally, I am aware of the tensions which exist in my research generally, between being a visible trans-ally, and my commitment to producing robust, reliable research. Many trans people, especially trans women, continue to experience 'sustained antagonism from sections of feminism' (Hines and Santos, 2018, p. 52), and I did not want to add to this by being ambiguous about my allyship.

These were real concerns for me as a researcher and the choices I made about my deciding which methods to use in my study. The choices scholars make in their research about their ontological and epistemological positioning, methodological perspectives and their research methods, are bound up with the 'interpersonal, political and institutional contexts in which researchers are embedded' (Mauthner and Doucet 2003, p. 421). That is, one's personal and professional roots play a key role in shaping these decisions. Berger (2015, p. 220) writes:

> Researchers need to increasingly focus on self-knowledge and sensitivity; better understand the role of the self in the creation of knowledge; carefully self-monitor the impact of their biases, beliefs, and personal experiences on their research and maintain the balance between the personal and the universal.

I remain self-conscious about my outsider status as a cis person researching trans people (Horsburgh, 2003; Pillow, 2003; Vincent, 2018). Many researchers are often drawn to researching something which directly relates to their own life experience (Berger, 2015). What drew me to this research was slightly different and originates from an academic interest sparked during my master's degree, rather than from a shared gender identity. I was concerned initially that I would not be able to fully understand the experiences of the participants because of this and that only an insider researcher could legitimately interpret the experience(s) of that community. To confirm, I am a complete outsider, occupying what is acknowledged as a privileged position: white, cis, able-bodied, university-educated and middle class (though I did grow up in a deprived area in an economically disadvantaged household and am the first in my family to go to university). I felt awkward at times wanting to ask trans people to share their very personal stories with me so I could write a doctoral thesis (and then this book). Whilst Kuklick (1980, p. 375) wrote, 'it does not necessarily follow that researchers should be prevented or excluded from attempting to understand participants' experiences, unless it could be shown that in doing, they would cause harm,' I still felt self-conscious about my outsider status, though this did give me the opportunity to examine my own positionality. In addition, my outsider status offered me the chance to 'discover tools for understanding the dynamics of researching within and across (my) own social group or culture' (Crean, 2018, p. 2). This has meant rather than feel awkward about my outsider status, I have attempted to utilise it as 'a framework for understanding the research relationship' (Botterill, 2015, p. 1), and continue to use my social capital to demonstrate allyship within and outside of academic.

Reflexivity and being an outsider researcher

Researchers are advised that interactions between us (as researchers) and the participant affect the data. Whether one is an insider or an outsider researcher, neutrality is an impossible claim to make in the research one does. As Ryan-Flood and Gill (2010, p. 2) wrote, 'the myth of the objective, neutral observer who leaves the field without influencing the data, untouched by the research process, has been soundly critiqued by feminist social scientists'. It is not unusual for a researcher to seek common ground or empathy with those they talk to. As a trans-inclusive feminist doing research with trans people, I was mindful of these warning from other feminists, and did not want to subject participants to what Ben Vincent (2018, p. 102) calls 'a troubled history of ethically and methodologically flawed research practices'. That is, I was caught between my outsider status and my wanting to be supportive of my participant's lived experiences as a trans-ally. I was also mindful of not categorising all trans people's experiences as homogenous. Yost and Smith (2014, p. 153) suggested that those who are interested in studying trans people are urged to 'avoid generalisations, and acknowledge the multiplicity of identities held by all people rather than reducing individuals to just their trans or cis status, and engage in reflexive practices throughout their work with trans people'. This is worthwhile advice.

Equally important is acknowledging my discomfort with being an outsider researcher whilst attempting to produce research which is representative of the participants, is non-exploitative and compassionate. Botterill (2015) acknowledges that by virtue of being a researcher, one is very rarely a complete insider anywhere. There is no monolithic experience of gender, or sport, or (I can promise you) motherhood. Rather, the views, ideas, experiences and needs of trans people are both different and similar to one another's, as well as to those who identify as cis. Most importantly, these differences are 'valid in their own right' (Henwood and Pidgeon, 1992, p. 8). Vincent (2018, p. 105) writes:

> While criticisms have been made of how trans lives have been mostly investigated, and correspondingly constructed, by cisgender people, this does not mean that cis researchers are not capable of excellent trans research with emancipatory potential.

I take some comfort from Vincent's words, and with the benefit of hindsight, reassure myself that in all the 18 interviews I conducted, no one questioned my credibility to carry out the research or accused me of having a dubious agenda. As a trans-inclusive feminist, I feel I must justify taking from participants some very personal and at times private information, which in turn commits me to searching for truths and an understanding of these experiences. My role as a researcher is also to make sense of the data clearly and truthfully (Creswell and Poth, 2017). The primary purpose of this book is to fill a knowledge gap and offer theoretical and empirical contributions about the lived experiences of trans people in everyday sport. This was best achieved with trans feminist theory.

Using Trans Feminist Theory

The term 'trans feminism' was coined by US activists Emi Koyama and Diana Courant around 1992 (Bettcher, 2017). Trans feminism usually denotes a third-wave feminist sensibility 'that focuses on the personal empowerment of women and girls, embraced in an expansive way that includes trans women and girls' (Bettcher, 2017, p. 11). US activist and trans feminist scholar Julia Serano (2013) described the origins of trans feminism as being closely linked with other forms of feminist sub movements, 'specifically, sex-positive feminisms, postmodern/post structural feminism, queer theory, and intersectionality' (Serano, 2013, p. 44). Serano advises against division between feminists and trans feminists, advocating instead for a coalition between feminists and trans feminists/activists which will combat both transphobia and misogyny, arguing whilst all women are different, their experiences overlap. For Serano (2013), trans feminism is undeniably feminist, in the way it 'weaves together critiques of male privilege, traditional sexism, heterosexism, monosexism, masculine-centrism, and other forms of sexism, while acknowledging the influence of racism, classism, and other forms of marginalisation' (Yost and Smith, 2014, p. 148). Martinez-San Miguel and Tobias (2016, p. 5) say trans feminism is 'trans-specific in a way that nothing else is. It expands, complicates and enriches, and is embedded in activism too'.

Trans feminism's origins are rooted in trans studies, which emerged as a specific discipline in the late 1990s, in response to critiques from both inside and outside the academy of the ways in which trans issues were both represented and subsumed within gender and LGB studies (Stryker, Currah and Moore, 2008). Trans studies shares its roots with queer theory. Stryker et al. (2008, p. 212) noted:

> If queer theory was born of the union of sexuality studies and feminism, transgender studies can be considered queer theory's evil twin: it has the same parentage but wilfully disrupts the privileged family narratives that favor sexual identity labels (like gay, lesbian, bisexual, and heterosexual) over the gender categories (like man and woman) that enable desire to take shape and find its aim.

Scholars in trans studies argue what positions it as a unique discipline, and not just an extension of queer theory, 'is the way trans bodies are centred epistemologically in the discipline' (Nagoshi and Brzuzy, 2010, p. 56). Because of this epistemological centring trans studies enriches debates with queer studies, in the way in which it has introduced new language (such as the term 'cis'), varied gender expressions and the importance of gender self-identification. These additions 'have totally revitalised the debates about the cultural, social, and political constructions of gender in past and contemporary historical debates' (Martinez-San Miguel and Tobias, 2016, p. 5). Trans feminist theorists have also highlighted the specific kinds of violence faced by trans women, including 'transmisogyny'. Coined in 2007 by Serano in her book *Whipping Girl*, this term refers to the unique intersection of transphobia and misogyny. Transmisogyny describes 'the intensification of misogyny that trans women experience because their femininity is viewed as fraudulent, inherently passive and existing solely in service of men and masculinity' (Olufemi, 2020, p. 63).

This expanded gender lexicon has enabled trans studies to develop in such a way as to bring inside the academy trans feminism, which like queer theory has roots in activism. From both trans studies and queer theory, trans feminism evolved, established as an academic area of inquiry, 'often seen as having developed from queer and postmodern theory and LGBTQ+ studies, that can be used to further interrogate the very concepts of sex, gender and identity' (Yost and Smith, 2014, p. 148).

The publication of Sandy Stone's 1991 paper 'The Empire Strikes Back' in response to Janice Raymond's (1979) anti-trans book *The Transsexual Empire* on trans women is widely acknowledged as the start of what became known as the first articulation of trans feminism. Together with Kate Bornstein's book

Gender Outlaw (1994), these two works formed the first key pieces exploring trans feminist ideas and issues. In 2001, Koyama's 'The Transfeminist Manifesto' offered further response on the feminist critique that trans women are unable to escape the male privilege they have been raised with. Gender critical) feminists have argued that trans perspectives cannot be aligned with feminist goals (Yost and Smith, 2014). In her work, Koyama argues that there is a larger context of privilege and oppression to consider, writing of how there are 'multiple types of privilege and oppression, and that all feminists must take accountability for their forms of privilege while also feeling justified in speaking from their experiences with oppression' (Koyama, 2001, p. 1). Koyama wrote:

> Trans feminism is primarily a movement by and for trans women who view their liberation to be intrinsically linked to the liberation of all women and beyond. It is also open to other queers, intersex people, trans men, non-trans women, non-trans men and others who are sympathetic toward needs of trans women and consider their alliance with trans women to be essential for their own liberation.

Koyama acknowledges the possibility that, whilst some trans women may have experienced male privilege, they face other forms of societal oppression, most notably around race and social class, though disability, sexuality and weight are also considered. For Koyama, the integral core of trans feminism is that it is based in both scholarship and activism, to better examine more closely the intersections of feminism and trans feminism (Yost and Smith, 2014). As Halberstam (2017) says, separate paths exist for many levels of the population to reach the same destination of equality, and just like cis feminists, trans feminists fight for the right to have their genders, names and pronouns treated with respect, and to be safe within spaces which can be openly hostile towards them (Heyes, 2003). In addition, trans feminists seek to enrich and deepen feminism by drawing on their own lived experiences about gender, sexuality and power (Hines, 2019).

Trans feminism and the body

Trans feminism can be seen to be working with some elements of feminist theory to further challenge assumptions about the gender binary and the body, and about what it means to be a 'man' or a 'woman'. Trans feminism fights against larger structures of power, such as health care systems, which are often accused of medically pathologizing trans people and withhold life-affirming resources from them (Holm, 2015). Returning to Krane (2019), what set trans feminism slightly apart from queer theory, is its questioning of the emphasis on anatomy as a criterion for social organisation (Krane, 2019, p.50). Enke,

2012 This is why it is the most appropriate theoretical approach in this study. Many trans feminist academics and writers have also argued how perceptions of gender are socially moulded, rather than biologically situated (Bornstein, 1994; Koyama, 2001; Pearce et al., 2019; Serano, 2013; Stone, 1992; Stryker and Whittle, 2006).

Even so, exploring the diversity of trans subjectivities and different lived experiences is not just about accommodating bodies which are situated outside of binary thinking (Hines, 2010). In addition, trans feminism looks to actively push back against 'the essentialist ideas of both academic and non-academic understandings of sex and gender' (Yost and Smith, 2014). A number of postmodern feminists, most notably those engaged in Black feminist thought (Crenshaw, 1991; Hill Collins, 1990; hooks, 1987), have argued exactly this, that second-wave feminism is essentialist in its claim that women's experiences are universal, 'highlighting the problematic universalising of social positions within relations of power and ignoring intersectionality' (Crenshaw, 1991, p. 4).

Other feminist scholars (Green, 2006; Haggerty and McGarry, 2007; Heyes, 2003) have identified the necessity of focusing on a variety of lived experiences – as trans feminism does – rather than using the monolithic category of 'women' to promote one principal claim of shared experience. This has allowed a counterhegemonic discourse to flourish, and argues for a less-repressive society, one which offers a more complete and empirically preferable account of all women's experiences and which encourages all women to come together to work for specific political goals (Hill Collins, 1990; Stryker and Whittle, 2006). For example, Koyama's trans feminist manifesto (Koyama, 2001) also argued feminists should recognise that the body-image and gender dysphoria some trans women (and men) struggle with should be considered as much a feminist issue as the unrealistic beauty standards experienced by many cis women.

Trans feminism and sport

It is important to reiterate that sporting practices are historically produced, socially constructed and culturally defined to serve the interests and needs of powerful groups of society (Bandya et al., 2012). Gender normativity and hegemonic masculinity in sport prevail, and sport remains one of the most segregated aspects of society. Those who experience gender incongruity will often face significant barriers when attempting to participate in sport and physical activity (Morris and Van Raalte, 2016). The participation rates in sport and physical exercise for trans people are cited as being lower than for cis people (Jones et al., 2017a, 2017b, 2018, Jones and Arcelus, 2017), resulting in less opportunities to enjoy the associated health and well-being benefits exercise may bring, including gender euphoria (Austin et al., 2022). The way in which trans people's bodies have become politicised within media discourses concerning their inclusion in elite level sport has filtered down to everyday sport(Barras et al., 2021). Sport carries with it what Klein, Paule-Koba and Krane (2019, p. 627) term 'the automatic assumptions surrounding sex and gender, which opens up the possibilities of additional and new ways of conceptualizing them'. When considering trans people's participation in sport, Whaley and Krane (2011, p. 204) argued there has been 'a hierarchical privileging of the positivist paradigm in sport and exercise psychology, and would benefit from other perspectives, such as trans feminism'. Farber (2017) says that trans identities remain marginalised even within more recent contributions from queer studies of sport. This is because these contributions often fail to place the voices and lived experiences of trans people centrally, nor do they capture 'the day to day reality of trans lives, nor do they make contributions that have the potential to improve trans people's lives' (Yost and Smith, 2014, p. 151). This means trans feminist theory has the potential to offer a stronger epistemological foundation on which to expand these narratives and work towards greater inclusion for trans people in everyday sport.

Whilst there are very few authors who have specifically adopted a trans feminist perspective in sport, those who have (or have alluded to it) claim it has the potential to provide a unique and original perspective and a valuable foundation when considering the socially constructed categories of the two sex system in sport (Caudwell, 2014, 2020; Enke, 2012; Klein, Paule-Koba and Krane 2019; C. Phipps, 2019; Query and Krane, 2017; Travers, 2006, 2014; Travers and Deri, 2011; Waldron, 2019). This leads me to conclude that a trans feminist perspective brings these three key contributions to sport:

1. The belief individuals should be addressed in accordance with their preferred language and/or identity;
2. Inserting the voice of the athletes themselves by looking beyond the common or popularised narratives in sport;
3. Respecting the way in which an individual may 'transgress conventional or binary boundaries of sex and/or gender in sport and face a demand to conform with a binary sex for sport competition.'

(Krane, 2019, p. 214)

These three aspects are important components of trans feminism in the way they all work together to both understand and support trans people's participation in sport. According to Enke (2012), trans feminism is grounded in a critique of binary sex and gender in which only two sexes (male and female) and two genders (masculine and feminine) are acknowledged. Enke (2012) also said, 'trans-literacy remains low' when it comes to research involving trans people, so, as such, a trans feminist perspective in this research goes some way to mitigate this. Caudwell (2020, p. 3) writes, 'for trans feminists, it is the confines and coercive nature of the sex-gender binary structure, especially in physical activity and sport, which is problematic and in need of change'. In short, employing a trans feminist perspective allows researchers to place their primary focus on the importance of the lived experiences of those who do not fit within the sex and gender binaries, whilst recognising the complexity of sex and gender in sporting contexts (Lucas-Carr and Krane, 2011; Nagoshi and Brzuzy, 2010; Query and Krane, 2017).

As such, Klein, Paule-Koba and Krane's paper aims to fill this gap. They write (2019, p. 628):

> A trans feminist perspective privileges self-determined sex and gender, and recognizes social constraints sometimes limiting trans self-expression. Accordingly, we resist language and approaches that medically pathologize trans bodies or that lead to surveillance of trans bodies often subsumed within policies guiding sport participation for transgender athletes. Through the lens of transfeminism, we question the conventional or binary boundaries of sex and/or gender that impact participation in sport.

By documenting the transition of a trans athlete using a trans feminist lens, Klein, Paule-Koba and Krane (2019) invite us to question more deeply the frequent assumptions made about trans people's inclusion in sport. Some of these assumptions include the reliance on regulations which focus on how to fit trans athletes into binary sport categories, the immutable physiology which confers an assumed competitive advantage, and the act of transition and its impact on the sporting body. Trans feminism welcomes a more sensitive understanding of the challenges these barriers present to some trans athletes, by placing trans people's voices at the centre of any research.

Summary: from an ethics of care to compassionate inclusion

Krane et al. (2015), when broadly discussing gender nonconformity, sex variation and sport, apply what they term 'a critical trans feminist perspective to explore the interplay among sex, gender, and fair play, as well as present a critical approach to inclusion in sport' (Krane et al., 2015, p. 49). Through examining policies which claim to be inclusive of gender nonconforming and sex variant athletes, the authors highlight how 'these policies reproduce common stereotypes and misconceptions surrounding sex, gender, athletic bodies, and sport' (Krane et al., 2015, p. 49). Krane et al., (2015) draw heavily on Scott-Dixon (2009) and Enke (2012), whose 'conceptualizations of trans feminism are a multidisciplinary blend of feminism and transgender studies' (Krane et al., 2015, p. 50). Krane et al., (2015) concludes that what is needed when considering participation for trans athletes is both an ethics of inclusion *and* compassionate inclusion. Trans athletes have to meet a rigid criteria for inclusion with little understanding for what this means for an individual's self-defined gender identity. Adopting an ethics of inclusion, or 'compassionate inclusion' (Krane, 2019, pp. 58), prioritises lived experience over binary assumptions and gender normativity, assumptions which can have damaging outcomes.

A trans feminist perspective can advance our understanding of trans people who push conventional boundaries of sex and gender categorisations in sport, and who often face sex and gender policing due to sport adhering to binary sex categorisation of participants, recognising only that there is boys'/men's sport, and girls'/women's sport (Lucas-Carr and Krane, 2011). Krane (2019) says a trans feminist approach has an emphasis on respect, dignity and inclusion, welcoming all athletes across the spectrum of diversity, reframing discussions about advantage and fairness to those who celebrate compassion and prioritise experience. Krane (2019, p. 60) writes:

> What a trans feminist perspective teaches us is the need to consider the broad social and cultural issues surrounding policy and decisions regarding inclusion and exclusion…at the centre of this debate should be the well-being of all athletes … it can also lead us towards privileging inclusion without imposing narrow Western, heteronormative expectations on elite athletes.

To conclude, a trans feminist perspective encourages looking beyond the common or popularised sporting narratives, privileging the voices of the athletes themselves. Ahmed (2017) sees trans feminism – as Caudwell (2020, p. 4) does – 'as theory, politics and activism … trans feminism has potential for trans allies to contest the normative sex-gender system and concomitant transphobia'. Trans feminism asks more questions about the organisation of sport and the gender-segregated categories of men and women. Through this method of organisation, the full range of human reality is

> Framed within the limits of heteronormativity, establishing two distinct, complementary and hierarchical models of intelligible gender: man/masculine/heterosexual and woman/female/heterosexual. Beyond the margins of this hegemony we find the unintelligible realities, which include intersex (which exceed the sexual binary) and trans, which threaten the coherence between the corporeal body and experienced gender.
>
> *(Carrera-Fernández and DePalma, 2020, p. 747)*

The next chapter explores the sporting body through the lived experiences of the participants.

Discussion Question

According to Krane (2019), trans feminism contributes three things to sport. Make a list of the ways in which these three things can be applied in your own sport, classroom or organisation.

Notes

1 This was approved by the University of Brighton's Research Ethics Committee.
2 I wrote about my experience of conducting telephone interviews here: Barras, A. (2019). The Embodied Researcher & the Disembodied Participant: Navigating Telephone Interviews with Trans &/or Non-Binary People. https://medium.com/the-politics-of-representation/the-embodied-researcher-and-the-disembodied-participant-navigating-telephone-interviews-with-77909362956f

References

[Great British Class Survey]. (2013). https://blog.ukdataservice.ac.uk/the-great-british-class-survey-now-available-from-the-uk-data-service/

[Office for National Statistics]. (2011). https://www.ons.gov.uk/

Ahmed. S. (2017). *Living a feminist life*. USA: Duke University Press.

Anderson, E., & Travers, A. (2017). *Transgender athletes in competitive sport*. London: Routledge.

Andrews, T. (2011). What is social constructionism? *Grounded Theory Review*, *1*(11). http://groundedtheoryreview.com/2012/06/01/what-is-social-constructionism/

Austin, A., Papciak, R., & Lovins, L. (2022). Gender euphoria: A grounded theory exploration of experiencing gender affirmation. *Psychology & Sexuality*, 13. https://doi.org/10.1080/19419899.2022.2049632

Bandya, S.J., Gorib, G., & Jinxiac, D. (2012). From women and sport to gender and sport: Transnational, transdisciplinary, and intersectional perspectives. *The International Journal of the History of Sport*, *29*(5), 667–674. https://doi.org/10.1080/09523367.2012.687142

Barras, A., Frith, H., Jarvis, N., & Lucena, R. (2021). Timelines and transitions: Understanding transgender and non-binary people's participation in everyday sport and physical exercise through a temporal lens. In: S. Bekker, I. Costas Batlle, B.C. Clift, J. Gore, S. Gustafsson & J. Hatchard (Eds.). *Temporality in qualitative inquiry: Theories, methods and practices* (pp. 57–71). London: Routledge.

Beckman, L.J. (2014). Training in feminist research methodology: Doing research on the margins. *Women and Therapy*, *37*(1–2), 164–177. https://doi.org/10.1080/02703149.2014.850347

Berger, R. (2015). Now I see it, now I don't: Researcher's position and reflexivity in qualitative research. *Qualitative Research*, *15*(2), 219–234. https://doi.org/10.1177/1468794112468475

Bettcher, T.M. (2017). Trans feminism: Recent philosophical developments. *Philosophy Compass*, *12* (11). https://doi.org/10.1111/phc3.12438

Blaikie, N.W.H. (2009). *Designing social research: The logic of anticipation* (2nd ed.). Cambridge: Polity.

Bornstein, K. (1994). *Gender outlaw: On men, women, and the rest of us*. London; New York: Routledge.
Botterill, K. (2015). "We don't see things as they are, we see things as we are": Questioning the "outsider" in Polish migration research. *Forum: Qualitative Social Research*, *16*(2). https://doi.org/10.17169/fqs-16.2.2331
Braun, V., & Clarke, V. (2006). Using thematic analysis in psychology. *Qualitative Research in Psychology*, *3*(2), 77–101. UK: SAGE. https://doi.org/10.1191/1478088706qp063oa
Braun, V., & Clarke, V. (2013). *Successful qualitative research: A practical guide for beginners*. London: SAGE.
Browne, K., & Nash, C. (2010). *Queer methods and methodologies: Intersecting queer theories and social science research*. Farnham: Ashgate.
Bryman, A. (2008). *Social research methods* (3rd ed.). Oxford: Oxford University Press.
Burns, C. (2018). *Trans Britain: Our journey from the shadows*. London: Unbound.
Burr, V. (2015). *Social constructionism* (3rd ed.). New York, N.Y; Hove, East Sussex: Routledge.
Carrera-Fernández, M.V., & DePalma, R. (2020). Feminism will be trans-inclusive or it will not be: Why do two cis-hetero woman educators support transfeminism? *The Sociological Review*, *68*(4). UK: SAGE. https://doi.org/10.1177/0038026120934686
Caudwell, J. (2014). [Transgender] young men: Gendered subjectivities and the physically active body. *Sport, Education and Society*, *19*(4), 398–414. https://doi.org/10.1080/13573322.2012.672320
Caudwell, J. (2020). Transgender and non-binary swimming in the UK: Indoor public pool spaces and un/safety. *Frontiers in Sociology*, *5*. https://doi.org/10.3389/fsoc.2020.00064
Craig, P., & Beedie, P.A. (2008). *Sport sociology*. Exeter: Learning Matters.
Crean, M. (2018). Minority scholars and insider-outsider researcher status: Challenges along a personal, professional and political continuum. *Forum: Qualitative Social Research*, *19*(1). http://dx.doi.org/10.17169/fqs-19.1.2874
Crenshaw, K. (1991). Mapping the margins: Intersectionality, identity politics, and violence against women of color. *Stanford Law Review*, *43*(6), 1241–1299. https://doi.org/10.2307/1229039
Creswell, J.W., & Poth, C.N. (2017). *Qualitative inquiry and research design: Choosing among five approaches* (International Student; 4th ed.). Los Angeles: SAGE.
Davy, Z. (2011). *Recognizing transsexuals: Personal, political and medicolegal embodiment*. Farnham: Ashgate.
Denzin, N.K., & Lincoln, Y.S. (2005). *Strategies of qualitative inquiry* (2nd ed.). Thousand Oaks, CA; London: SAGE.
Enke, A. (2012). *Transfeminist perspectives in and beyond transgender and gender studies*. Philadelphia: Temple University Press.
Farber, R. (2017). 'Transing' fitness and remapping transgender male masculinity in online message boards. *Journal of Gender Studies*, *26*(3), 254–268. https://doi.org/10.1080/09589236.2016.1250618
Flick, U. (2018). *An introduction to qualitative research* (6th ed.). London: SAGE.
Fremlova, L. (2022). *Queer Roma*. UK: Routledge.
Gherovici, P. (2017). *Transgender psychoanalysis: A Lacanian perspective on sexual difference*. UK: Taylor & Francis.

Green, E.R. (2006). Debating trans inclusion in the feminist movement: A trans-positive analysis. *Journal of Lesbian Studies*, *10*(1–2), 231–248. https://doi.org/10.1300/J155v10n01_12

Haggerty, G.E., & McGarry, M. (2007). *A companion to lesbian, gay, bisexual, transgender, and queer studies*. Oxford: Blackwell.

Halberstam, J. (2017). *Trans: A quick and quirky account of gender variability*. USA: University of California Press.

Henwood, K.L., & Pidgeon, N.F. (1992). Qualitative research and psychological theorizing: (Pt 1). *British Journal of Psychology*, *83*(1), 97–111. https://doi.org/10.1111/j.2044-8295.1992.tb02426.x

Heyes, C.J. (2003). Feminist solidarity after queer theory: The case of transgender. *Signs*, *28*(4), 1093–1120. https://doi.org/10.1086/343132

Hill Collins, P. (1990). *Black feminist thought: Knowledge, consciousness, and the politics of empowerment*. New York: Routledge.

Hines, S. (2010). Queerly situated? Exploring negotiations of trans queer subjectivities at work and within community spaces in the UK. *Gender, Place and Culture*, *17*(5), 597–613. https://doi.org/10.1080/0966369X.2010.503116

Hines, S. (2019). The feminist frontier: On trans and feminism. *Journal of Gender Studies*, *28*(2), 145–157. https://doi.org/10.1080/09589236.2017.1411791

Hines, S., & Santos, A.C. (2018). Trans policy, politics and research: The UK and Portugal. *Critical Social Policy*, *38*(1), 35–56. https://doi.org/10.1177/0261018317732880

Holm, M.-L. (2015). *Transgender experience: Place, ethnicity, and visibility*, Vol. 110, p. e15–e16. London: SAGE.

Hooks, B. (1987). *Ain't I a woman: Black women and feminism* (2nd ed.). New York: Routledge.

Horsburgh, D. (2003). Evaluation of qualitative research. *Journal of Clinical Nursing*, *12*(2), 307–312. https://doi.org/10.1046/j.1365-2702.2003.00683.x

Jones, B.A., & Arcelus, J. (2017). Physical activity and sport engagement in the transgender population. In: W.P. Bouman & J. Arcelus (Eds.). *The transgender handbook – A guide for transgender people, their families and professionals* (pp. 373–395). New York: Nova Publishers.

Jones, B.A., Arcelus, J., Bouman, W.P., & Haycraft, E. (2017a). Sport and transgender people: A systematic review of the literature relating to sport participation and competitive sport policies. *Sports Medicine*, *47*(4), 701–716. https://doi.org/10.1007/s40279-016-0621-y

Jones, B.A., Arcelus, J., Bouman, W.P., & Haycraft, E. (2017b). Barriers and facilitators of physical activity and sport participation among young transgender adults who are medically transitioning. *International Journal of Transgenderism*, *18*(2), 227–238. https://doi.org/10.1080/15532739.2017.1293581

Jones, B.A., Haycraft, E., Bouman, W.P. & Arcelus, J. (2018). The levels and predictors of physical activity engagement within the transgender population: A matched control study. *Journal of Physical Activity and Health*, *15*(2), 99–107. https://doi.org/10.1123/jpah.2017-0298

King, N., & Horrocks, C. (2019). *Interviews in qualitative research* (2nd ed.). London: SAGE.

Klein, A., Paule-Koba, A.L., & Krane, V. (2019). The journey of transitioning: Being a trans male athlete in college sport. *Sport Management Review*, *22*(5), 626–639. https://doi.org/10.1016/j.smr.2018.09.006

Korstjens, I., & Moser, K. (2018). Series: Practical guidance to qualitative research. Part 4: Trustworthiness and publishing. *European Journal of General Practice*, *24*(1), 120–124. https://doi.org/10.1080/13814788.2017.1375092

Koyama, E. (2001). The transfeminist manifesto. https://transreads.org/wp-content/uploads/2019/03/2019-03-16_5c8d1897c5d96_15tfmanifesto.pdf

Krane, V. (2019). *Sex, gender, and sexuality in sport: Queer inquiries*. Abingdon: Routledge.

Krane, V., Schinke, R.J., & McGannon, K.R. (Eds.). (2015). *The psychology of sub-culture in sport and physical activity: Critical perspectives*. Hove: Routledge.

Kuklick, H. (1980). On becoming a social scientist. *The Annals of the American Academy of Political and Social Science*, *448*(1). USA: Jossey-Bass. doi:10.1177/000271628044800155

Levers, M.J.D. (2013). Philosophical paradigms, grounded theory, and perspectives on emergence. *SAGE Open*, 1–6. https://doi.org/10.1177/2158244013517243

Lucas-Carr, C.B., & Krane, V. (2011). What is the T in LGBT? Supporting transgender athletes through sport psychology. *The Sport Psychologist*, *25*(4), 532–548. https://doi.org/10.1123/tsp.25.4.532

Martin, J.I., & Meezan, W. (2003). Applying ethical standards to research and evaluations involving lesbian, gay, bisexual, and transgender populations. *Journal of Gay and Lesbian Social Services*, *15*(1–2), 181–201. https://doi.org/10.1300/J041v15n01_12

Martinez-San Miguel, Y., & Tobias, S. (2016). *Trans studies: The challenge to hetero/homo normativities*. US: Rutgers.

Mason, J. (2018). *Qualitative researching* (3rd ed.). Los Angeles: SAGE.

Mauthner, N.S., & Doucet, A. (2003). Reflexive accounts and accounts of reflexivity in qualitative data analysis. *Sociology*, *37*(3), 413–431. https://doi.org/10.1177/00380385030373002

McCoyd, J.L.M., & Shdaimah, C.S. (2007). Revisiting the benefits debate: Does qualitative social work research produce salubrious effects? *Social Work*, *52*(4), 340–349. https://doi.org/10.1093/sw/52.4.340

Morris, J.F., & Van Raalte, J.L. (2016). Transgender and gender non-conforming athletes: Creating safe spaces for all. *Journal of Sport Psychology in Action*, *7*(2), 121–132. https://doi.org/10.1080/21520704.2016.1184732

Nagoshi, J.L., & Brzuzy, S. (2010). Transgender theory: Embodying research and practice. *Affilia*, *25*(4), 431–443. https://doi.org/10.1177/0886109910384068

Namaste, V. (2001). Invisible lives: The erasure of transsexual and transgendered people. USA: University of Chicago Press.

Novick, G. (2008). Is there a bias against telephone interviews in qualitative research? *Research in Nursing and Health*, *31*(4), 391–398. https://doi.org/10.1002/nur.20259

Olufemi, L. (2020). *Feminism interrupted*. UK: Pluto Press.

Opdenakker, R. (2006). Advantages and disadvantages of four interview techniques in qualitative research. *Forum for Qualitative Research*, *7*(4).

Pearce, R., Steinberg, D.L., & Moon, I. (2019). Introduction: The emergence of 'trans'. *Sexualities*, *22*(1–2), 3–12. https://doi.org/10.1177/1363460717740261

Phipps, C. (2019). Thinking beyond the binary: Barriers to trans participation in university sport. *International Review for the Sociology of Sport*. https://doi.org/10.1177/1012690219889621

Pillow, W. (2003). Confession, catharsis, or cure? Rethinking the uses of reflexivity as methodological power in qualitative research. *International Journal of Qualitative Studies in Education*, *16*(2), 175–196. https://doi.org/10.1080/0951839032000060635

Poland, B.D. (1995). Transcription quality as an aspect of rigor in qualitative research. *Qualitative Inquiry*, *1*(3). UK: SAGE. https://doi.org/10.1177/107780049500100302

Query, C.C., & Krane, V. (2017). 'Well everyone has something': A case study of a collegiate athlete with congenital adrenal hyperplasia. *Qualitative Research in Sport, Exercise and Health*, *9*(1), 87–98. https://doi.org/10.1080/2159676X.2016.1210206

Raymond, J. (1979). *The transsexual empire*. USA: Beacon Press. https://read.dukeupress.edu/camera-obscura/article-abstract/10/2(29)/150/31158/The-Empire-Strikes-Back-A-Posttranssexual?redirectedFrom=fulltext

Ritchie, J., Lewis, J., McNaughton Nicholls, C., Ormston, R., & National Centre for Social, R. (2014). *Qualitative research practice: A guide for social science students and researchers* (2nd ed.). London: SAGE.

Ryan-Flood, R., & Gill, R. (2010). *Secrecy and silence in the research process: Feminist reflections*. London: Routledge.

Scott-Dixon, K. (2009), Public health, private parts: A feminist public-health approach to trans issues. *Hypatia*, *24*, 33–55. https://doi.org/10.1111/j.1527-2001.2009.01044.x

Serano, J. (2007). *Whipping girl: A transsexual woman on sexism and the scapegoating of femininity*. USA: Seal.

Serano, J. (2013). *Excluded*. USA: Seal.

Smith, B., & Sparkes, A.C. (2019). *Routledge handbook of qualitative research in sport and exercise*. UK: Routledge.

Stone, S. (1992). The 'Empire' strikes back: A posttranssexual manifesto. *Camera Obscura*, *10*(2(29)), 150–176. USA: Duke University Press. https://doi.org/10.1215/02705346-10-2_29-150

Stryker, S., Currah, P., & Moore, L.J. (2008). Introduction: Trans-, trans, or transgender? *Women's Studies Quarterly*, *36*(3/4), 11–22. https://doi.org/10.1353/wsq.0.0112

Stryker, S., & Whittle, S. (2006). *The transgender studies reader*. London: Routledge.

Thomson, P. (2015, February 23). *Thesis know how: reporting on ethics*. Available from: https://patthomson.net/2015/02/23/thesis-know-how-reporting-on-ethics/

Travers, A. (2006). Queering sport: Lesbian softball leagues and the transgender challenge. *International Review for the Sociology of Sport*, *41*(3–4), 431–446. https://doi.org/10.1177/1012690207078070

Travers, A. (2014). Sports. *Transgender Studies Quarterly*, *1*(1–2), 194–196. https://doi.org/10.1215/23289252-2400001

Travers, A., & Deri, J. (2011). Transgender inclusion and the changing face of lesbian softball leagues. *International Review for the Sociology of Sport*, *46*(4), 488–507. https://doi.org/10.1177/1012690210384661

Vincent, B.W. (2018). Studying trans: Recommendations for ethical recruitment and collaboration with transgender participants in academic research. *Psychology and Sexuality*, *9*(2), 102–116. https://doi.org/10.1080/19419899.2018.1434558

Waldron, J. (2019). Four perspectives for understanding LGBTIQ people in sport. In: V. Krane (Ed.). *Sex, gender, and sexuality in sport: Queer inquiries* (pp. 15–32). Abingdon: Routledge.

Walliman, N. (2016). *Social research methods: The essentials* (2nd ed.). Los Angeles: SAGE.

Whaley, D.E., & Krane, V. (2011). Now that we all agree, let's talk epistemology: A commentary on the invited articles. *Qualitative Research in Sport, Exercise and Health*, *3*(3), 394–403. https://doi.org/10.1080/2159676X.2011.607186

Yost, M.R., & Smith, T.E. (2014). Transfeminist psychology. *Feminism and Psychology*, *24*(2), 145–156. https://doi.org/10.1177/0959353514529392

Zhao, H. (2018). Explicating the social constructionist perspective on crisis communication and crisis management research: A review of communication and business journals. *Journal of Public Relations Journal*, *32*(3–4), 98–119. UK: Taylor and Francis. https://doi.org/10.1080/1062726X.2020.1802732

4

SPORTING BODIES

Introduction

We are now in the second half of the book, where we hear about the lived experiences of the participants and the stories they shared. They are introduced using their first name (see page x-xii for a reminder of who they are). This chapter is about the body, and the part it plays in the context of participation in sport and physical exercise. Earlier in this book we reviewed some of the key literature around 'the body' in sport, paying particular attention to non-normative bodies, including considerations about race, disability, sexuality, class and gender. Here gender is key, because sport is most frequently organised by gender, that is, men compete against (or with) other men, and women compete against (or with) other women. There are exceptions, for example, with mixed teams such as tennis and badminton, and the 2020 Tokyo Olympics welcomed mixed-gender events in athletics, swimming, table tennis and triathlon for the first time to positive reviews from the athletes who competed (Belam, 2021; Leithäuser and Beneke, 2022).

Crucially, this chapter is about the people who informed this research, and the variety of ways their bodies shaped their own experience of – and relation to – participation in sport. Sport is an embodied experience; our body moves when it exercises. It might sweat, ache, stretch, make us feel good, tired or powerful. It might also do the opposite. Often, the type of exercise we do, the clothes we wear, where we do it and who we do it with can affect our experience. Such factors determine how we feel about our body in a multitude of ways. After all, 'along with sex and dance, sport is the most corporeal of human activities' (Edelman and Wilson, 2020, p. 2).

Much has been written about the body in sport and the ways in which the inclusion of those bodies which sit outside of normative depictions is not

DOI: 10.4324/9781003385486-5

limited to trans athletes. Emphasising gender stereotypes within sport further essentialises the outwardly physical characteristics between men and women via physical differences, often resulting in inequality for those athletes who do not conform to the heterosexual matrix (Butler, 2004). Because gender-normative bodies are privileged in sport, those bodies positioned as 'other' in sport frequently receive less visibility, reinforcing barriers which reduce inclusion (Tagg, 2012). The following section explores how discussions about the body and the ways in which people's explicit lived experiences about their body were connected to their participation in sport. It concludes with a trans feminist analysis of the data, reflections on the key themes and some questions to help provoke your own thinking about your own body and its interaction in sport.

The Complexities of Transition, Bodily Changes and Participation in Sport

When talking about their lived experiences of participating in sport, the most frequently mentioned topic for participants was their body, and how their gender identity was read by others in sporting spaces. That is, what it meant to be a trans person in a sporting environment, and how their gender identity mattered to them, to others in sporting spaces and amongst their sporting community. Heather Sykes (2006, p. 22) wrote:

> Identity is 'fluid', it is not 'fixed'. Also, that identity is 'partial', 'incomplete' and 'fragmented' ... these descriptions may not seem real, it may not be what we 'really feel.' Yet again such notions of the self can provide rich insights into the tensions and contractions of a vast range of sports experiences.

Feelings of gender dysphoria were experienced by over half of the participants, and they described how their engagement in sport heightened these feelings about their own body. Gender identity can be linked to gender presentation for some people (Fisher and Fisher, 2018), that is, identifying as a woman means looking like and consequently being read as a woman. Judith said that when she socialises, she tries to make sure she is 'wearing feminine earrings and have make up on, rather than the nude look where you look like you don't have make up on'. Judith explained this was because 'so people don't get confused whether it's a he or she when they see me?' Fourteen participants spoke of how transitioning, either socially, surgically or medically, alleviated feelings of gender dysphoria and helped with feeling more comfortable about themselves and their body. Eric explained how they were 'just waiting for surgery, basically, I'm waiting for top surgery for my life to begin'.

For some participants, this gender dysphoria is resolved through gender transition. Transition might include a range of bodily interventions, including social and legal transition, taking hormones or gender-affirming surgery.

The act of transitioning in any of these ways signifies a change in a person's body; for example, they may have surgery to remove breasts, or change their name to one which is culturally understood as being either a female or a male name, rather than a gender-neutral one. Changing pronouns is also tied to the body in the way it signals a complete shift in the language used by an individual to refer to themselves, and how they are addressed by other people. Freya said:

> I like being 'she' because I'm not non-binary, sometimes as a trans woman I can feel when someone is using 'they' are kind of hedging their bets...and I would like actually them to pin their beliefs or view of me to the mast and use 'she' and 'her.'

Talking about their body in relation to transitioning was frequently a starting point in the conversation, whereby an individual would both reflect on and expand on their experiences of participating in sport. Participants expressed different transition journeys to one another, where transition caused a temporary disruption to participation, and a return to sport later on. Charlotte, who swims, 'didn't really do a lot of sport between school and transition', due to feeling what she termed 'uncomfortable with my body'.

For Charlotte, transition changed how she felt about going swimming; she no longer felt 'uncomfortable with my body', now she felt 'confident'. These changes to Charlotte's body helped her to re-engage in swimming once her transition had reached the stage where she felt 'confident' about her body. Katy spoke of her decision to transition in similar terms to Charlotte, whose own participation in sport was also temporarily disrupted due to her feelings of discomfort about her body and starting the transition process. Katy said:

> I stopped playing men's football when I knew I was going to transition. I stopped playing men's football at the end of one season, and then I didn't start playing women's football for another couple of seasons, because I wasn't sure if I would be welcome, I wasn't sure if I was allowed, or I could get involved with it.

Here, Katy describes transition as a distinct event that happens over a finite period of time (in this case, measured in terms of the length of a couple of football seasons), during which she shifts from being recognised as male to being recognised as female. Her sporting identity – as a footballer – is similarly depicted in terms of a brief interruption with an apparently seamless shift from playing on the men's teams to playing on the women's (Barras et al., 2021). This sounds like a straightforward, linear, progression from past to present, male to female, male footballer to female footballer. As Katy puts it, 'football wise I play competitively, and I have always played competitively, I played pre-transition, I played post-transition'. Although Katy was still unsure about being 'welcome' (on the women's team), transitioning meant that she was able to consider rejoining football because her sporting body and her gender identity now aligned with the other players. Similar to Semerjian and Cohen (2006), who conducted semi-structured interviews with four trans athletes, here sport can be seen as a site where sport is both a site for transformation of the self and is itself a socially transformative act.

For Jenny, completing her transition was incredibly important on many levels and enabled her to re-engage with cycling on her own terms, terms which she felt were 'based on my own merits' and which was a 'normal performance'. Jenny needed to be sure her hormone levels reflected what she already knew, that she could 'do it [compete] in a way that, not only that other people said it was fair, but that I felt I was being fair as well'. Jenny's self-surveillance in relation to her participation in sport is based on her own measurements of eligibility, because she needed 'to have certain things in place for me, it wasn't just about being out and jumping through a hoop, I needed to know in myself I could go back into this thing I enjoy doing'.

No one on her team had questioned Jenny or asked her to do this; rather, it was her decision to approach her re-entry back into sport in a way which made sense to her, based on her own experience as a cyclist. This was a similar decision made by Eric who wondered which boxing class to attend once he started taking testosterone. When I asked Eric the question, 'is there an element that people feel that you are cheating?' he replied, 'the only reason I haven't felt that is because I have removed myself from some spaces where that might be levelled at me'.

Gender identity is frequently linked to the body (Anderson and Travers, 2017), and much has been written about the importance of gender identity and trans authenticity in trans feminist theoretical literature (de Vries, 2015; Saeidzadeh, 2020). Trans bodies remain subject to 'a politics of authenticity … and the continued influence of a medical model of 'transgender' [demands] congruity between gendered bodies and gendered identities' (Hines, 2007, p. 607). Being able to show one's true social identity is intrinsic to an individual's emotional health and well-being, and for Katy and Charlotte, transition and then playing sport as trans women provided this. This chimes with the way Lawler (2008, p. 104) describes identity as being 'part of a social and collective endeavour, not an individual odyssey'.

For Joe, transitioning was also a specific goal they wanted to work towards. Joe formerly played water polo on the women's team and was desperate to return to the sport they loved, even though they knew it would not be on the same team. Rather, they would have to join the men's team. Joe's experience of their body in relation to sport changed for them when 'trans feelings appeared' at university. They said of how they had been 'captain of one of the teams at uni, it was all good. I did four years at uni, the first two years playing water polo…er, then trans feelings appeared, and everything went tits up!'

Until that point, Joe had felt happy playing water polo on the women's team, because they presented as female and could fit in. Once Joe's 'trans feelings' appeared, they became hyper-aware of their gendered body. Joe felt that participating in sport became 'difficult' because they became 'very, very aware of my own body when I was playing, and that wasn't a thing before'. Although at the time they still physically presented as female, Joe was socially identifying as male, and consequently felt their physical body did not match their gender identity, prompting their decision to surgically transition.

Joe's experience reflects how it was sometimes difficult during a transition period, to hold onto a coherent sense of self, due to the way 'identities and identifications are the effect of socially produced embodied narratives which misrecognise, hierarchically organise and individuate bodies' (Capuzza and Spencer, 2015, p. 41). Society and sport in the West have been established on a process of assignment and categorisation along gendered binary lines in order to (arguably) make it intelligible to people. If there are only two categories,

> It is easier for us to organise the world and attach feelings, emotions and ways of being to each one. Those feelings, emotions and ways of being are commonly referred to as 'gender'.
>
> *(Olufemi, 2020, p. 51)*

Like Charlotte, Joe described feeling 'uncomfortable' and did not feel they would be able to 'fit in' until their gender presentation matched the other players. The act of transitioning is not one dimensional for people and does not immediately resolve a person's discomfort or confidence about their body. Starting transition, at least the early stages of transition and taking hormones, meant Joe anticipated a barrier being created, because water polo teams are gender segregated, and deciding which team to play on during transition was difficult for Joe.

This experience was shared by Eric, who had started his transition and was taking testosterone and presenting as masculine. Eric also wore a binder during exercise to flatten his chest and to give the illusion of a more masculine silhouette. He said:

> It's not my identity that's stopping me from participating in sports, it's my physicality. Because my identity hasn't changed since I started transition, I still feel like a non-binary, masculine centred sort of man, and when I feel like that, I have a problem participating in women's and non-binary inclusive sport, but my physicality has changed and that causes me an issue.

For Eric, transition was necessary for him to alleviate his gender dysphoria, but it also resulted in the formation of a new barrier in sport, the renegotiating of which space to access whilst he transitioned because his body was changing. Katy shared similar concerns of what the outcome of transition would be for her in sport. She was worried and 'wasn't sure if I would be allowed' to join the women's football team until she had completed her transition and was presenting as female. For Katy, transition was necessary, as it would allow her to play on the women's team, because she was visibly female. Consequently, she dropped out of football (but still went running) until her transition was finished and she was able to rejoin football, now playing on the women's team. Miles had been worried that starting transition meant giving up his sporting friendships. This was because transition would result in his body changing in ways that were noticeably different, signalling that he would not be able to play, or 'hang out with' the girls he skateboarded with. He said:

> I think a part of me not wanting to [transition] … not just because I was scared and didn't know who to turn to, I was worried I wouldn't be able to hang out with other girls. Um, in sports and outside of sports.

Miles's concerns about how transition would change his body, which could in turn lead to his being excluded from playing sport with his (female) friends, draws our attention back to understanding the ways in which dominant societal beliefs about bodies and the ways in which they are portrayed impact on an individual's lived experience. Transition for Miles might lead to a disconnection for him to sport. But for Persia it was completing her transition which helped her to reconnect to swimming after a long absence, which subsequently contributed to her loving her body. Persia reflected on how she 'did some solid good exercise, walking and stuff, but nothing really until I transitioned, then I started swimming…I even see it as now I can love my body'.

This forms what Fiani and Han (2019, p. 188) call 'a foundation of resilience' upon which Persia is able to validate her gender identity when she goes swimming. Similarly, completing the transition for Jenny wimproved her mental and psychological well-being, and allowed her to reconnect with sport. Jenny, who participates in a wide range of outdoor activities such as climbing and cycling, is similar to both Persia and Katy in that her participation in sport was put on hold whilst she went through her transition, and she only took part in activities she could do alone. Like Katy, Jenny did not return to cycling on the women's team, until she had transitioned. Once she did return, she found her transition, like Persia, had enhanced her enjoyment of and participation in sport. She explained:

> So, there's been absolutely no, no hint of impact, um, on climbing etcetera as a result of my transition, or the transition process, and in fact I'd go so

> far to say that all activities have been a life saver when I was growing up with shame, dysphoria, and things like that … when you climb you can't focus on anything else. It's a great distraction activity.

For Freya, the decision to transition triggered an engagement with a new sport, roller derby. Freya said participating in roller derby, her favourite sport, was her 'reward to myself' for starting to socially transition and openly identify as female. Persia also found she had a deeper connection to sport after she had transitioned. Once Freya had come into what she called 'a comfortable space with being trans', she began swimming, helping her to get healthier and taking up yoga. 'These two things,' Freya said, 'really happened in a big way after I'd come through the transition period.'

A person's transition is a very individual process and does not happen at the flick of a switch (Humphrey, 2020, n.p.), and 'the decision of which sex characteristics count (and which do not) is very much a social matter' (Serano, 2013, p. 9). The ways in which some participants located their changing gender identity within a continuous set of decisions helped facilitate their participation. Sometimes this happened instantly, and they would radically alter their gender presentation to align with their gender identity, for example Joe, who cut their hair very short. Others took their time and were reluctant to start the process of changing how they looked in case it meant they had to stop playing sport with their friends. Five participants said how the mid-stage part of transition could be particularly hard to navigate in relationship to passing. As Eric said, 'the middle period of transitioning is really hard, unless you look normative'. Judith, for instance, adapted her gender identity and gender presentation depending on if she was climbing or if she was socialising.

Transition could be an important factor in reducing gender dysphoria. Even so, transition did not necessarily guarantee passing in a sporting space, and participants often had to negotiate their inclusion in sport in relation to how other people responded to them. Transition was not always an option for every participant, and for the trans men especially, changing the appearance of their body to faciliate participation in sport was more complex than the experiences of the trans women.

The lived experiences of participants, and their own gender identities, may share similarities in how they navigated sport and sports settings, but their stories were all individual and personal. Sometimes 'gender and sex can move across a continuum and are not static, with identities being negotiated' (C. Phipps, 2019, p. 5). Other times, for instance after transition, some participants happily accepted a binary model of gender both in sport and in their day-to-day life. As Farber (2017, p. 257) explains, 'transition is not a linear process to reach a certain endpoint but can instead move (citing Horack, 2014,

p. 580) forward, backward, sideways, tangential'. Participants' identities were complex and not homogeneous.

Passing and the body in sport

These narratives about transition connect to how trans bodies are perceived in sport and what barriers people faced to inclusion (Jones et al., 2017, 2018). In this way, the data presented thus fits with my social constructionist epistemological position and maintains that people mostly perform in ways expected of them by their particular culture, with traditional performances of gender (and sexuality) usually privileged over non-normative ones. This was observed in participants' lived experiences of passing and passing privilege. Butler (1990, 2004) has argued that gender is not as simple as masculinity and femininity; like sexuality, it cannot be polarised in this way (see also Cohn and Zeichner, 2006). Gender is not necessarily fixed, and can be fluid, covering a whole spectrum of gender identities (Lester, 2017; Roche, 2020). However, some participants whose transition followed a 'classic trans narrative' (Barras et al. 2021) felt their gender identity to be fixed once they had transitioned. Some participants had shifting embodied gender identities, which consequently 'affects identity development and stimulates concealment strategies, such as passing' (Elling-Machartzki, 2017, p. 257).

'Passing' is the commonly used term for when a trans person is correctly gendered by strangers. Goffman (1963, p. 73) described passing 'as a practice by which a social identity that is deemed socially abnormal is nicely invisible and known only to the person who possesses it'. Nicolazzo (2016) argues that passing occurs within various communities and includes racial passing, disability passing and gender-based passing. Bernstein Sycamore (2006) offers a critical analysis of what passing means across a variety of identities, including race and disability, not only trans. Bernstein Sycamore (2006) explores and critiques passing through 'the various systems of power seen (or not seen) in the act of passing' (2006, p. 1), concluding that 'in a pass/fail situation, standards may vary, but somebody always gets trampled' (2006, p. 1).

Being read, or 'passing' as one's gender, can bring with it what is referred to in the trans community as 'passing privilege'. Passing is linked to a person's body in a very specific and intimate way; a body which passes (by cis normative standards) is succeeding at being read as the gender its owner feels aligned with. Failing to pass could in some situations trigger hostile confrontation from strangers in a space or situation, as well as trigger gender dysphoria. Passing in sport could facilitate safety and prevent misgendering.

Persia spoke of how her being able to pass and be read as female offered her 'hassle free' access to the swimming pool. She said:

> I go to the pool. And I don't go to trans swimming [classes which are for trans people only]. I don't need to. I'm fine. I mean, I've got small hips and a wider top, like swimmers, women swimmers are like that ... I just go the pool and swim, nobody notices.

For Persia, there is her passing both as a woman when she goes swimming and as a female swimmer. As Persia said, she has 'small hips and a wider top', all physical attributes which are commonly associated with a swimmer's physique. There is a meaningful intersection at play in Persia's reflection here, which further highlights the connection between a person's physical body, their gender identity *and* their sporting identity. Persia's body passes, giving her freedom to move freely in the space, with no fear of confrontation or misgendering: it is 'hassle free'. This is especially relevant in sport and sporting spaces, for instance the swimming pool, where intense social interactions between people often take place, becoming sites of meaning for individuals to perform and confirm their gender (Barras, 2022).

Alix preferred being read as trans (as opposed to being read as cis), saying:

> Whenever I meet somebody new, they just assume I'm a cisgender person, either because of the way that I look or the way that I sound. And I'm very keen for that not to the case, 'cos I don't think cis men are a particularly nice group of people, and I don't like being grouped with that group of people?

Alix's experience shows how complex and embedded in social norms the intersections of gender identity, cis normativity, sport and passing privilege are. Whilst passing gives Alix a certain amount of privilege and they can move in sports settings unchallenged, they preferred not to be associated with the majority of cis men who occupy such settings. Although Alix reflected on the problematic aspects of passing, they also acknowledged its necessity in facilitating access to the gym. Nonetheless, the 'gender performativity of transgender people is often aimed at 'passing' within a hegemonic binary sex/gender system' (Elling-Machartzki, 2017, p. 258).

Clothing

Whilst it was Joe's trans identity – their 'trans feelings'– which was the reason for them wanting to transition, the gender-segregated structure of sport triggered their gender dysphoria, due to the clothing swimmers wear. Because the women's water polo team wore swimming costumes, and the men's team wore swimming trunks, Joe became more self-conscious of their own gendered body and the visible divisions between the teams. They said:

> It was a woman's team; it as all very, very gendered. We'd train with the men sometimes, but mostly they were bigger and stronger and better than us, it

> was really divided, we were in swimming costumes and they were in trunks, so it was an obvious physical divide.

This 'obvious physical divide' manifested once Joe began questioning their own gender identity. Whilst deciding to transition allowed most participants to begin feeling better about themselves generally, it could sometimes trigger issues not previously considered within the context of sport, such as with Joe's gender dysphoria being triggered by the gendered swimming attire. The gender divide between swimmers is marked by obvious clothing options, swimming costumes versus trunks, and that men generally swim bare-chested and women do not highlights a visible difference. Gendered swimming attire brings an awareness to Joe's body during sport which was not there before.

Clothing is a distinguishable marker of gender, much like a beard or breasts (Frith and Gleeson, 2004), and what a person wears when they play sport can make a big difference to managing their gender identity, preventing others from misgendering them. This can be especially important for those people who transgress the gender binary (Doan, 2011, 2015). Many sports facilities, especially swimming pools, consist of large open spaces where bodies are more exposed, often due to less clothing being worn, or because it is form-fitting. It is not unusual for some gyms and swimming pools to have clothes restrictions such as banning the wearing of t-shirts and other loose clothing in the water for safety reasons. Significant numbers of people are uncomfortable with exposing their bodies in public places, including those who may need to cover their bodies for cultural or religious reasons (Spandler et al., 2020). It is easy to feel self-conscious.

This was reflected in a comment Joe makes about their body not fitting in physically when wanting to play water polo until they had transitioned. They said:

> I know that I probably didn't fit in with the women's team because they would see me as a male, 'cos that was how I was presenting … I want to get back into water polo [once] I had top surgery…even if I was on a rubbish team, I would still fit in … I couldn't without top surgery … I'd be too uncomfortable in a swimming costume, and other people would think it was weird! So, it would be a problem. And I'd be uncomfortable.

For Miles, passing was an important factor for him in feeling confident enough to participate in sport, and packing[1] his harness and swimming trunks helped him to achieve this. As a circus performer prior to coming out as trans, Miles had to deal with high levels of gender dysphoria due to the gendered clothing performers were required to wear. He said:

> At university my dysphoria was very high, because … if you are a female bodied person, you have to wear more girly outfits to get more work. So, at

corporate events, sparkly tights, leotard. I don't know if it was because my dysphoria was so bad when I was there [at circus class] 'cos, I had to wear tight leggings. Cisgender male aerialists tend to get away with wearing joggers ... a female body person, you'd be told off right away for having joggers on ... you'd be told to take them off or go and get some shorter, tighter shorts.

Once Miles was able to perform in 'baggier clothes', he felt much more comfortable, even before coming out to his friends as trans, which made a profound difference to his experience when participating, because he felt more physically comfortable. The way some sports clothing is designed, for example swimming costumes and tight-fitting clothing such as leotards, accentuate the body and allow freedom of movement in certain sports. However, there is no reason why other clothing could not be worn, which both allows the activity to be done and the participant to feel comfortable and relaxed. For example, Jude wondered why gymnastics outfits could not just be more neutral, 'like, you could wear a gymnastics leotard with tights or with loose shorts if you wanted ... adapting that would be so easy'.

Passing can bring with it what is referred to in the trans community as 'passing privilege'. The participants in this book talked about whether or not they could 'pass' or be 'read' correctly by strangers and how this affected their engagement in physical activity. Within the trans community, 'passing' is sometimes a contested term because it implies there is something shameful in 'looking trans'. Thus, passing is not always a desirable or wanted practice, and a trans person who passes as cisgender may feel a loss due to not being seen by others as their authentic trans self (Nicolazzo, 2016). Butler's (1990) work on gender performativity draws parallels between how the impossible sociocultural standards by which individuals are expected to pass can bring with it negative effects on a person's life and livelihood. As this chapter goes on to discuss, this has material impact on some of the participants, who talked about their experiences of participating in sport.

Bernstein Sycamore's (2006) perspectives on passing mirror trans author and activist Julia Serrano's, whose own theories on gender interpretations posit that the necessity to change one's appearance to conform to a (Western) gender-normative representation is perpetuated by the cisgender population and their 'incessant need to gender every person they see as either female or male' (Serano, 2007, p. 177). As Butler (1990) argued, sex, gender and sexuality are performative acts which individuals constantly display through their clothing choices, mannerisms and behaviours. Although individuals can choose how they want to dress, act, behave and identify through their performative acts, they may 'feel compelled to repeat performances of the heterosexual matrix of woman-feminine-heterosexual or man-masculine-heterosexual' (Butler, 1990, p. 312). This in turn embeds a pressure to pass in relation to hegemonic discourses of masculinity and femininity embedded in sport (McBride, 2021; McBride and Neary, 2021).

These performances were reflected in the lived experiences of the participants, where passing in sporting spaces was a laborious necessity, requiring the constant repetition of gendered behaviours considered normative by others, which 'support gender inequality through mechanisms of exclusion and violence toward those who transgress these norms' (Carrera-Fernández and DePalma, 2020, p. 748). Passing becomes a tool for perpetuating cisgender privilege, and whilst it might not be a desired goal for some participants, it was often unavoidable in the context of sport and the body. Considering how exposed bodies can be in sport, it is easy to understand how the passing privilege Persia describes when she goes swimming makes day to day life easier. When Persia's experience of swimming is contrasted to Freya's experience, the importance of being able to pass as female intersects with being able to access a specific sporting space: the swimming pool.

Freya was mid-transition, unlike Persia, who had, in her words, 'gone through' her transition many years ago. Being at this mid-transition stage for Freya meant she experienced a barrier to her participation in swimming, because she was not always read as female. She said:

> I like swimming, but there is a barrier there...I would have to develop body confidence. There are a few places in Manchester which do trans swimming sessions ... because personally I would feel uncomfortable going to a mainstream swimming pool as a trans person. I might still feel uncomfortable going to a trans swimming session as a trans person, but at least I'd be more inclined to go to that.

The term 'uncomfortable' is used here again, this time by Freya, her experience of passing having a direct impact her body confidence and whether she felt comfortable enough to go swimming. James talked about how before he was read and subsequently passed as male, participation in sport was difficult for him. James spoke of how, after having top-surgery, his passing privilege meant he was now read as male when he goes to the gym. This was not the case previously. He spoke of feeling 'very self-conscious ... it was quite early on in my transition, and I was identifying as trans...and identifying as male but wasn't being read as such'. Once James had recovered from top surgery, he felt more comfortable in sport, after which, 'it got easier, just because, you know, I pass'.

The different ways in which participants navigated their gender identity in relation to sport and sporting spaces supports Butler's belief that 'gender is kind of imitation for which there is no original' (Butler, 1990, p. 99). Passing privilege was often experienced at different stages of transition, such as pre- or post-surgery, and was more of a challenge for the trans masculine participants than the trans women in the research. Transitioning is a deeply personal and intimate process, yet still requires a degree of public unveiling. In her paper which discussed trans young men's social, physical and embodied experiences of sport, Caudwell (2014, p. 402) found that, for her participants, 'gender has involved, and continues to involve on-going processes of negotiation'.

Passing is not then limited only to trans women, and discrimination and abuse towards trans men and non-binary people was also experienced. Returning to the act of binding, a number of trans masculine and non-binary participants talked about doing this. Wearing a binder can provide a degree of safety for people, not just in sport but in other places (such as toilets), as it facilitates passing by flattening the chest. Alix said a way to reduce barriers for those wanting to wear a binder during sport is for a person to feel comfortable enough to tell their teammates or instructor they are wearing one. That way allowances could be made for exercising safely. Alix said:

> It's being aware of it, making sure you're working out alone so that person doesn't have to wear that binder, or be less intense, so they don't have to work so hard, or wear a looser binder, and finding ways to make them feel comfortable and safe.

Binders were not the only item utilised to help reduce gender dysphoria and facilitate participation in sport. Wearing a packer or particular item of clothing also helped some participants to change their silhouette. This was because the highly gendered and form-fitting clothing required to participate in their sport increased their gender dysphoria. Judith and Miles, who both go indoor climbing, reflected upon the harness they had to wear for safety. Judith said:

> It can be a bit tricky … because in climbing you wear a harness. When you're male to female trans you tend to have to tape up your bits, and the bits might get squashed in the harness (*laughs*).

Miles said, 'before top surgery I didn't swim. I specifically kept away from swimming pools or swimming in public'. Like Freya, Miles did not have enough body confidence to participate in swimming prior to surgery, a sporting activity which involves the body being on public display. Judith remarked, 'not many people go to the climbing centre or gym with lots of makeup', and so she 'climbs as a guy'. Judith's gender presentation is hyper-feminine, and she uses 'feminine' clothes and make-up to ensure she is read as female, things she does not use when she is climbing. Judith said she needs to feel she 'looks like a girl to climb as a girl … I'm trying not to have people be confused when they look at me, if that makes sense?'

One interpretation of Judith's experience is that because she climbs 'as a guy', she avoids 'confusing' people and thus avoids the stress of worrying about passing. Because Judith's gender presentation is hyper-feminine, she enjoyed using clothes and make-up to pass, but did not want to attract attention whilst she was climbing. It is worth remembering that passing is very often connected to avoiding the possibility of experiencing abuse and violence, and this may subconsciously be part of Judith's decision to 'climb as a guy'. This was an experience also shared by Miles. Miles talked about how his gender identity was read by others, and the consequenes when this was done correctly, but in the wrong place. For example, Miles's decision to use the female changing rooms before he had top surgery at his gym resulted in him being challenged by other users of this space, resulting in him having to disrupt his own passing privilege. Miles explained that the middle stage of transition was 'awful' because, if he was confronted in a women's changing room, he would have to say, 'I'm not a boy and then I'd feel really awful. I felt like I had to pretend to be female to use it because I knew that, if I used the men's, I'd probably be in a worse situation'. As Miles's transition progressed and he grew a beard, he was able to feel more comfortable in the men's changing room, but he never felt quite safe there either.

On one occasion Miles was even confronted by some teenage girls, resulting in him having to 'flatten' his jumper so his breasts were noticeable. Miles said:

> Even before coming out as trans, I was still using female spaces … even though I looked [he means he passed as male]. Women would ask me, and usually it would be mothers or older women. It doesn't tend to be younger people unless they're like with a group … and the leader of the group will be like, excuse me, this is the women's changing rooms? I never liked saying well I am, 'cos I never felt that way, it made me feel weird saying that I was a woman. They wouldn't believe me … so I'd have to flatten my jumper back to show them I had a chest.

For Miles, having a body which others found hard to read made him feel both scared generally and worried about being excluded from a sport. In contrast, to Miles, Tom (who is trans masculine/gender queer and played on a male water polo team) said:

> Felt completely included and involved … I think people see me differently in the pool … part of that is to do with my body and, um, there is definitely some hesitation around, um, people with breasts or people, erm … who maybe have had some surgery. Because there's a big reluctance to touch people with breasts and I know that makes those people feel less included and involved when they are playing … because they are not playing it on quite the same level as everyone else.

The body in sport, as these experiences show, is highly visible, either through the clothing some sport requires (such as swimwear) or through its interaction with others. Such visibility opens up the possibility of scrutiny, interpretation and at times comments from others. Passing and passing privilege and the ways in which sport is segregated by gender intensifies this. For Craig, even though 'I'm beginning to pass as male, but I really identify as non-binary', passing does not necessarily make participation in sport easier, because, as Craig said, 'sports are so kind of segregated'. As Craig remarked, 'I think there's a weird correlation between being physically visible and your trans heritage being physically visible'.

This visibility, and the way in which passing allows one to be visible (by which Craig means passing safely), whilst also not attracting attention, was mentioned by Harry. Once, when he was getting changed after football training, Harry was asked about his top surgery scars by a colleague. Harry said:

> I pass very easily … I don't think people would know unless I told them. Oh! Somebody at work, he saw me take my top off, and he said, this is at one of the clubs after work, and he said, oh have you had heart surgery?

In that moment, Harry said, 'I just made the decision there and then to tell him…and he, he, he was ok about it'. Harry was secure enough with his passing privilege (and perhaps also on his established place on the football team and at work), to tell his colleague the true reason for his scars, and not be concerned about their reaction. This sudden and uninvited request for a personal biographical disclosure was also experienced by Alix. Whilst on a training course to become a personal trainer, Alix participated in a group exercise which involved the men removing their shirts to practise using callipers on one another. Alix also removed their shirt, 'because why shouldn't I?', at which point another member of the group pointed out their top surgery scars and commented on them. Alix described what happened:

> Alix: And she was like, I didn't know that you'd had THAT done, and the guy who I was also working with was oblivious like, what, what, what are those scars from … I think she told him that I'd had a boob job or something (laughs), like, oh my god.
>
> Abby: Completely without your permission?
>
> Alix: Just talking about me … then for the rest of the course … she'd be like, you're so brave … I can't believe you did that, I can't believe you took your shirt off … I'm so proud of you, like, could you just stop? That whole, you're so brave thing…please stop.

As Craig observed earlier in relation to 'the weird correlation between being physically visible and yours trans heritage being physically visible', on the one hand Alix benefitted from passing privilege, but only until their scars were revealed, at which point they had to share (like Harry) their trans identity. For Alix, although they pass as male, passing was not something they desired; rather, they would prefer to simply 'look trans'.

Returning to the connection of identity to gender presentation and its importance to participants, whether this was aligned through transition and/or passing (or not), identity's precise definition 'proves slippery' (Lawler, 2008, p. 1). Part of this slipperiness resides in the way identity hinges on 'the apparently paradoxical combination of sameness and difference' (Lawler, 2008, p. 2), a description which is especially relevant in relation to this research and the lived experiences of participants. This is because for all the participants, their sporting and/or gender identity was both the same and different to other users within sports settings. Tom, for example, played on a cis team, presented as the gender they were assigned at birth but described their gender identity as trans/gender queer.

It might be assumed that all sporting bodies are the same, and there is a 'taken-for-granted assumption that a coherent LGBT collective exists, and that transgender is a fixed, definable and agreed-upon category' (Caudwell, 2014, p. 398). Reflecting upon how some people's gender identities and pronouns shifted and developed over time (or even instantly, like Joe described) offers an important insight, showing how in reality gender is not fixed at one point in one place, for all time or for all people. Rather, gender is a social construct; it is fluid and on a spectrum. Even those participants whose gender identity followed a classic binary trans narrative (Barras et al., 2021) still had to engage with this construction and settle on a binary gender presentation in sport. Gender identity and presentation are both broad churches and, as in the lived experiences of the participants, can be defined in whatever terms a person chooses at any time. However, because gender segregation in sport exists, the ability to pass in sports settings often facilitated inclusion. This book is in many ways drawing on Butler's writings on gender performativity (1990, 2004): the ways in which we interpret (male and female) sex are determined more by our cultural concepts of gender than by actual biological reality. This presents an opportunity for change and development for trans people's participation in sport, a way to celebrate these differences, rather than be defined and constrained by them.

Competitive Advantage, Lived Experience and the Body

This book concerns itself with the lived experiences of trans people in everyday sport, and as such, is written from a social science perspective and not an endocrinological one. This is because there is a lack of empirical research which asks trans people directly about their experiences and what barriers they may face to inclusion. Historically, much of the literature about trans people's inclusion in sport has focused on the hypothetical elite athlete and questions about competitive advantage. This literature has in the main concluded that no physiological competitive advantage exists for trans women athletes, and that, in relation to what constitutes an advantage in sport, biology and the physical body are only one aspect of this.

However, over the course of conducting the original research and writing this book, public interest in this topic has grown considerably. There continues to be intense focus from the media about the inclusion of trans women competing in all levels of sport. Trans men are visibly absent from discussions, though as previously noted, elite trans men athletes Chris Mosier and Patricio Manuel are outperforming their cis teammates. Whilst this book focuses on everyday sport, it is not immune to the discussions happening in the media. This is due to the question of competitive advantage being highly charged, and, as Hamilton, Lima, and Barrett et al. (2021. p. 1401) note, 'integrating athletes who previously experienced male puberty into elite female sport is far from straight forward and remains highly contentious'.

Many of these discussions in the media have been directed by gender critical feminists, whose position frequently advocates for the exclusion of trans women from sport due to questions about fairness, safety and the erasure of women and girls in sport. This erasure is focused on places being 'taken' by trans women athletes. It is a thorny one to navigate, and this book acknowledges that it has become increasingly difficult to separate legitimate, evidence-based discussions about what competitive advantage actually is from those who advocate for banning trans women from all sport, not just at elite level. This discussion saw a spike in interest after Laurel Hubbard, who is a trans woman and a weightlifter, qualified to compete in the 2021 Tokyo Olympics.

One of the arguments for the exclusion of trans women from elite female sport is that individuals assigned male at birth benefit from the androgenising effects of male puberty (Hilton and Lundberg, 2020). Chapter 2 has discussed this and acknowledges research is complex and inconclusive. Indeed, these arguments, write Erikainen, Vincent and Hopkins (2020, p. 6),

> Are not only foregrounded by enduring conceptualizations of (implicitly White) women as the 'weaker sex,' but they are also, of course, not categorically true: Some women are bigger, stronger, faster, and perform better in sport than some men, and women competing at top levels of sports perform better than most men.

I think it is possible to be both receptive to and critical of the literature which argues for further evidence to justify banning trans women from competing alongside and against cis women. I also believe it is possible to do so whilst occupying a trans-feminist and trans-inclusive position, which advocates for the inclusion of trans athletes at all levels of sport. This means listening to what the gender critical feminist position is, followed by the lived experiences of the participants.

Gender critical feminism

Olufemi (2020, p. 51) writes how 'feminists have been rightly concerned with the process of sex assignment: they recognise that, throughout history, to be "female" has often meant death, mutilation and oppression. Sex categorisation has been the starting point for well-known feminist theories'. Sport is a hot button topic, and tensions between gender critical feminists and trans inclusive feminists are well known in the public sphere. But where does this tension originate, and how might it be mitigated?

The term 'gender critical feminist' is a fairly recent upcycle of the term trans-exclusionary radical feminist (TERF). Many gender critical feminists claim the term 'TERF' is a slur, despite it being a largely accurate description of their beliefs, preferring the term 'gender critical feminist' instead. 'TERF' originated in the late 2000s, growing from the feminist circles of the 1970s as a way to distinguish radical feminists who support trans people from those who do not (Carrera-Fernández et al., 2018; Hines, 2019). TERF was commonly used both inside and outside of academia, though is on the decline (Pearce et al., 2020).

Gender critical feminists oppose the key demands of trans women, including sharing women's spaces and a refusal to believe a person's sex can be changed. Gender critical beliefs are protected under the 2010 UK Equality Act (2010) (see Brione, 2022). Gender critical feminists locate the source of women's oppression as their biology, an oppression they feel trans women have no experience of, and thus no claim to. Gender critical feminists see trans 'ideology' as a threat to feminist advancement and gloss over intersectional approaches so fundamental in feminism, such as Black feminism and class (Cooper, 2020). Put simply, gender critical feminists view trans women's rights as a threat to cis women's rights and the movement is populated with a number of high-profile supporters, including J.K. Rowling, Professor Kathleen Stock, Julie Bindel and Germaine Greer. During an interview with the BBC in 2014, author Greer said, 'many cisgender women think trans women do not look, sound, or act like women' (BBC, 2014).

Gender critical feminism originates from Janice Raymond's book *The Transsexual Empire* (1979), in which Raymond claimed gender is an expression of biological sex, impossible to change and something which is fixed at birth. Chromosomal sex, argued Raymond, in addition to being both fixed and impossible to change, is strengthened by women's life experiences, including being socialised as female and by experiencing gender discrimination. For Raymond, trans women can never be 'real' women because they cannot ever know what it means to be oppressed as a woman. The experiences of trans men are largely of overlooked by gender critical feminists, though Bev Jackson, co-founder of LGB Alliance,[2] has said she believes young gay people are being encouraged to 'trans away the gay' rather than identify as gay (Care, 2024). In other words, lesbians are choosing to be trans men, rather than gay women, in the belief this confers them greater privilege.

Participant's views on competitive advantage

The lived experiences of five of the trans women in this study offer a remarkably different perspective to those of many gender critical feminists on the question of competitive advantage. For three trans women participants, no competitive advantage materialised. Rather, there was a realisation for these participants that they had internalised the essentialist view that all men are naturally better at sport than all women, based only on being assigned male at birth. Freya, Jenny and Charlotte found, to their surprise, the innate physiological advantage all trans women are assumed to have simply did not exist for them. They each discovered any advantage they possessed was acquired through practice and other skills not associated with innate physiology. In fact, all three felt the debilitating nature of taking hormones and medically transitioning instead put them at a disadvantage, due to their reduced muscle mass and larger frames, meaning they had to work harder, and took longer to recover than their cis teammates.

When I asked Charlotte how she felt about discussions around competitive advantage and if they impacted on her participation, she said how there is 'just this assumption that you must have such an unfair advantage, that you're a danger on the pitch, which is nonsense … so unless you really, really want to play that sport, you end up just giving up'. Jenny agreed:

> This assumption that any trans woman is wanting to compete as a woman … for some sort of competitive advantage, and 99 times out of 100 … she just wants to compete, or enter a sport for herself, because she's doing something she loves, because she's meeting friends, because it's a structured way of taking some exercise, or a way of benchmarking her performance … no one would go through this process just for some perceived competitive advantage.

When I asked Sarah if she had ever faced questions about competitive advantage at her tennis club, she said, 'no one's questioned it, and um, it's very strange because I thought, physically, um, they might see me as having an advantage, you know, being trans and you can't really change certain bits about your physique (*gestures to shoulders*)'. Gender critical feminists often believe being socialised as male confers the advantage of male privilege. On the existence of male privilege, gender critical feminists are not wrong, and this is well-supported in feminist literature and activism. However, what it means to 'be socialised' varies hugely, and expectations of masculinity and maleness can also be sources of stigma and vulnerability for those individuals assigned male at birth who 'fail' at being gender normative (Carrera-Fernández and DePalma, 2020; Schilt, 2010). It is also important to remember that 'Western conceptions of gender are not and never have been, universal. Gender has no single story' (Olufemi, 2020, p. 54).

A key concern for five trans women was the worry that they may possess an unfair competitive advantage in sport by being assigned male at birth. This concern was still present even after they had transitioned, even if they had not possessed this before. This concern often manifested itself as a worry they may be excluded from sport for being trans and this assumed competitive advantage. This was the case for Freya, who said that because of her 'physiologically male body' she had worried about joining her local roller derby team. She said:

> I struggled with that at the beginning, I didn't want to be too good, in case people would think I was only good because I'm trans. There have been some barriers where if I try too hard, I'm going to be stronger than them or I'm going to have an unfair advantage. And I think that was a bit of a barrier for me to overcome when I kind of realised I wasn't the strongest, I wasn't the fittest because of that. I had to train hard to be good enough to join the team.

Roller derby is a notoriously fast and physical sport and requires a high level of fitness. Freya was concerned that having been assigned male at birth, her body would be 'naturally' stronger than the cis women players on the team and she would be better at roller derby. Instead, she was surprised she had to 'train hard to be good enough'. This was the same experience as Jenny, who said of her return to cycling on a women's team. She said:

> It was problematic for me. I thought having gone through a male puberty and being exposed to all that testosterone, it almost felt like being a massive drugs cheat. But I'm not very good! There are a lot of people who are much faster than me. Any advantage I get is solely down to my own ability and skill rather than any sort of gender affected advantage of having been exposed to testosterone when I was younger.

Freya reflected upon her lack of sporting ability as a child and said she was 'never very good at sports' and would 'do events against boys, but I regularly finished last'. Even though she herself did not have the experience of being good at sports as a child, Freya had still internalised the essentialist assumption that all men are better than all women at sport, irrespective of anything else, a view commonly held by many gender critical feminists. Katy also talked at great length about how her own internalised fear about retaining a competitive advantage in sport (Katy plays on a woman's football team) had originated when she was younger. She talked about her experiences of growing up, and of how she 'would have internalised that whole 'men are better than women' thing, and I have to get over myself ... I was worried I've got this unfair advantage which I don't believe I have. I guess people's perceptions are so strong'.

Gender critical feminists believe trans women's inherent (male) biology and socialisation constitute deliberate cheating. Such cheating, they claim, as former Olympic swimmer Sharron Davies does, is unforgivable because it overshadows the strides women and girls have made in sport. Trans women are painted as being inadequate male athletes, who have found a loophole to exploit and are 'entitled cheats' (Hutchinson, 2023). Sport, gender critical feminists claim, is being appropriated by trans women, trying to seize any opportunity to excel in sport by identifying as female (Barras, 2019a, 2019b). To defend such power grabs, notes Alison Phipps (2020), makes you no better than a handmaiden of the patriarchy. No matter that gender critical feminists are themselves keen to 'couch their opposition to trans equality in the language of women's rights' (A. Phipps, 2020, p. 138). Concerns of female erasure are central to gender-critical arguments, and by claiming to be marginalised and pushed out of sport, gender-critical feminists are able to reframe themselves as the real victims in this discussion, 'the recipients of a kind of onslaught from a group of people who make up less than 1% of the population' (Olufemi, 2020, p. 60).

Trans men and testosterone

The presence of testosterone in the human bofy is not an automatic guarantee of better athletic performance, yet it is consistently framed as such. For three trans masculine participants, there was the surprise that taking the hormone testosterone did not automatically provide improved performance and a newfound competitive advantage. Rather, it was their presenting (and passing) as male which conferred this advantage on them over their female presenting teammates. In other words, because they passed as men, opposing teammates treated them as men, and even in one case congratulated them on it. Here, Joe talks about playing on a women's rugby team whilst openly taking testosterone. They said:

> I know that I was only like marginally bigger than I was before I started [taking testosterone], my voice was deeper and I looked more masculine, but I felt that people had established I was the strong one and would think twice about tackling me and that gave me an advantage.

Starting the process of taking testosterone sometimes opened up new worries and concerns about barriers to inclusion. For example, Joe said that staring testosterone was a worry because it might dimish how much they enjoyed playing water polo. 'It was a contradiction for me', they said, 'so I was like, if I enjoy this, why do I need to change it?'

For the three individuals who talked about taking testosterone, they were certainly worried that the possible changes to their body, such as increased muscle mass, would instantly produce an unfair physical advantage over their cis teammates. Eric talked about his experience of taking testosterone and feeling unable to remain in the women's boxing class when they presented as more masculine – no matter if his strength remained unchanged. Eric said it was because 'there's the whole issue of assumed strength, or average strength based on gender'. Joe was similarly worried about being 'a masculine threat to our team or the other team … in terms of my strength and my size. I didn't want to be that annoying guy that was there and shouldn't be'. Yet, neither Eric nor Joe's testosterone-fuelled, unfair advantage ever manifested. Rather, Joe said the male advantage was 'all in my head', and they had 'internalised, like, that thing of being taught that men in sport, it's a men's game', and their ability to 'pass easily' was what gave them an advantage in rugby.

This perception of being a threat due to looking masculine is similar to Eric's feelings about remaining on the women's boxing team after also starting testosterone. He said:

> Now I'm on testosterone for a year I don't feel comfortable going to this class and people immediately say, oh are you saying you are stronger than the women? And I'm not saying that. BUT [author's emphasis] I want to avoid that kind of feeling basically … I felt so strongly that people would say that, that I pre-emptively removed myself from those spaces.

People navigate and negotiate their inclusion in sport in many different ways, and this was no different for many people in this book, too. Katy, for example, had to wait almost two years from starting transitioning to joining the women's football team, to be sure her hormone levels complied with the Football Association's policy on inclusion for trans players. This is despite the fact her own football team had not requested the need for such a compliance. This resulted in her testosterone levels being much lower even than those of cis women players, because she did not want any questions about her perceived of competitive advantage. Katy said:

> But if my testosterone level is so low, it impacts on my energy levels, and that can be a bit of a day-to-day problem … I'm reticent to … look into testosterone supplementation because, for me as a trans woman playing women's football, to be on any testosterone supplementation is quite Daily Mail worthy! I don't really want to be dealing with that…

The detrimental impact of transition (whether surgically or hormonally) upon a person's body, and the subsequent changes it can make to an individual's sporting ability and energy levels as mentioned here by Katy, were also mentioned by other participants. Judith, who was still undecided about whether she would take hormones, felt it could mean 'medically, life would be a bit shit'. Eric said how he had 'run up against a lot of physical and mental issues' once he started transitioning. It was clear the effects of a lifetime of hormone injections, the direct health implications of possible surgery, other treatments and potential side effects are rarely given enough consideration in discussions about how hard qualifying (and continuing) in sport is for trans people. Katy said her testosterone levels (for playing football) are still 'well below that, so, to be honest, if they [the doctor] said to me … if I was cis, they would probably be putting me onto testosterone supplements'.

These participants have shown how the embedded societal and internalised assumptions that all masculine (looking) bodies are stronger than all feminine (looking) ones are a lived reality. In Joe's experience, their body was only 'marginally bigger' than before starting testosterone. For Joe, it was the perception of them being stronger that conferred an advantage for them, which in men's sports would not be subject to the same level of scrutiny as it has been in women's sports. Joe said they knew 'there would come a point where I would be stronger than a lot of the other women players, and that would not be fair'. As Katy said, people's perceptions 'are so strong' about trans people in sport, the question of competitive advantage is now being discussed at recreational level.

The majority of participants found a way to mitigate their own internalised feelings about what competitive advantage felt like, by seeking out their own way of testing fairness. Jenny described her return to competitive cycling once she had transitioned:

> I could have turned up and just competed and not said anything, but I didn't want to do that … I wanted to be able to take part as I always have done … I've done well based on my merits, not because I've got some biological advantage … this year I've started competing again in mountain bike orienteering and I came first in the first event by virtue of the fact I was the only woman in it (*both laugh*).

Half of the participants mentioned how they monitored their sporting performance to ascertain if they were able to migrate from their previous team to a new team. This was most often the case when they were part of single-sex team, such as in Katy's case. Katy talked about moving from the men's football team to the women's, after transitioning, and the conversation she had with friends about it. She said:

> Even when I have conversations with friends I've known for some time…it's not them having a go at me, but I do often get questions … do you feel you've got an advantage,… is it 100% fair and most of it is framed as well at

> your level it's fine 'cos it's low level, but in elite sport I'm not sure whether it could be fair.

Katy has hinted at a common misconception here, that trans people are often treated as a homogenous group of people, where the experiences of one individual are identical to the whole community. Rather, like all individuals, experiences of gender identity are diverse and rich. There is no such thing as a level playing field in sport, and many athletes bring their own advantages which are unrelated to gender to the starting line. I am supportive of further research in the name of widening the discussion and adding new knowledge, but trans athletes should not be excluded from sport without exception until a definitive outcome is reached. Nor should, studies focus only on trans women (Caudwell, 2020). Gender critical feminists have created a manufactured moral panic between themselves and trans women, and do not seek solutions to address the gender discrimination women and girls face in sport as discussed previously. Whilst gender critical feminists fail to acknowledge the oppressions and concerns facing trans men in sporting spaces, I offer my own limitations in book which does not consider more carefully the intersections of race and other communities. As Caudwell (2020, p. 20) says:

> We cannot ignore that the existing lens is mostly on cultures pertaining to the west and global north. As such, it is easy to conclude that white transgender experiences currently dominate our knowledge; it is essential that we recognize this and make subsequent efforts to change the bias.

It is clear that the ongoing debate about competitive advantage inevitably entered some participant's thoughts, feelings and experiences of taking part in sport as a trans person. The discussions about competitive advantage, fairness and safety are important in this book, but it cannot (and does not seek to) answer the question of whether trans people do or do not possess a competitive advantage over cis people, let alone how this advantage is measured. Rather, what the book can offer is reflection on the ways in which beliefs about gender, and about men having a competitive advantage over women by virtue of biology and/or male puberty/socialisation, shape the ways in which some participants made sense of themselves as people who engage in sport. Saini (2021, n.p.) notes that because science is so frequently called upon in discussions about what constitutes as biologically male or female in these discussions 'perhaps [this] betrays how uncertain the boundaries of gender truly are'. Returning to a trans feminist position in this book, one which tries to interrogate the complexity of competitive advantage in sport, unless a trans epistemological perspective is taken, then cisgender privilege and transphobia will remain in these discussions. As Ahmed (2016, p. 22) writes, 'such transphobia works as a rebuttal system, one that, demands trans people provide evidence of their existence'.

Non-Binary Experiences

Because a person's gender identity is intrinsic to their own personal sense of self (Anderson and Travers, 2017; Lawler, 2008), every participant had a different experience of what gender identity meant to them. For some, their gender identity was placed firmly at one end of the gender binary. This meant they wished to both identify and present as the gender they were not assigned at birth, and would usually adopt the relevant pronouns, though not always. For example, eight participants who were assigned male at birth, now identified as female and wished to be read as such and use feminine pronouns. Others felt themselves to be masculine presenting, but did not identify as trans male, but as non-binary.

For those who identified as non-binary, their gender identity became something which sometimes needed additional consideration when they participated in sport. This was because whilst a person may present as masculine or feminine, this was not necessarily how they identified. Although non-binary identities have become more visible in recent years in popular culture and the media (Cosgrove, 2021; Twist et al., 2020), non-binary people in sport are less visible. Sport is a very gendered activity, where male and female categories are heavily regulated and enforced, and for non-binary people this can cause a barrier to participation (Spandler et al., 2020). Within sport there are often hierarchies, values, expectations and practices which are specifically gendered, and which need to be attended to if a person wishes to participate, mostly by adopting gender-accordant behaviour. These include the clothing that is worn in sport, the choice of changing room and the team played on (Whitehouse, 2022).

As several participants had expressed feeling worried about being confronted about their gender identity in sporting spaces, being able to access a space without concern was an important consideration. As Catherine Phipps writes (2019, p. 3), 'the binary structures of sport can create accessibility issues for everyone, but particularly for those who are trans'. The places where sport and physical activity take place most frequently only accommodate or are designed for those people who conform to the gender binary, and not every individual fits neatly into a category. For some non-binary participants, this meant they were involved in

> The continual effort to convince others (as well as to oneself) that one is a 'real' man or woman, relative to cultural stereotypes of what such a 'real' man or woman should be like.
>
> *(Channon, 2014, p. 588)*

Non-binary participants, regardless of how they identified, found themselves having to conform in sporting settings to what binary gender-normative representations of male and female bodies most often look and act like (Carrera-Fernández and DePalma, 2020; Wellard, 2006, 2016). Often a non-binary participant was subject to similar regulations as those participants whose gender identity and presentation was firmly situated on the gender binary, even though they felt uncomfortable doing this. The habitual use of binary gendered language or clothing in sporting settings (or, for example, in the absence of gender-neutral changing rooms) stressed how their gender identity was compromised, resulting in them having to either correct being mis-gendered or temporarily align with a gender to facilitate their participation in sport. Jude questioned the gendered clothing in sport and wanted to wear what felt comfortable when they were involved in gymnastics, saying, 'I don't see why there has to be a men's and women's outfit or a uniform'. Teammates using gender-neutral pronouns for everyone allowed non-binary participants to feel more included, whilst, for others, being addressed as 'she' or 'he' in sport helped affirm a binary trans identity and added to their sense of belonging (Caudwell, 2014, 2020; C. Phipps, 2019; C. Phipps and Blackall, 2021; Spandler et al., 2020; Whitehouse et al., 2022). Jude suggested if everyone 'got out of the habit of using gendered pronouns, it's just better for everyone'. Jude's own experiences when playing rugby were that 'everyone is so surprisingly good with pronouns'. Jude's experience offers a practical solution in which inclusion for non-binary people can be facilitated, just by tailoring language.

Not using gender-neutral language in sports settings is one way in which gendered social practices are reinforced daily (Doan, 2011). This was often experienced as a microaggression particularly for those non-binary participants, who felt binary gendered pronouns did not match their own gender identity. However, it is important to note that for the 12 participants whose gender identity was situated on the binary, and identified as trans men or trans women, they found being gendered this way self-affirming. In this way, gender binaries in sports settings were comforting for some participants, but uncomfortable for others, depending on how they presented and their own sense of gender identity.

Levels of participation in sport amongst trans people are generally low, with people often dropping out of sport during school and finding it difficult to return to it (Jones et al., 2017, 2018; Lawler, 2008; Perez-Samaniego et al., 2016). There is a growing body of literature which explores improving inclusion for non-binary people's sporting experiences and non-binary youth in school-based sports and Physical Education which warrants attention (see Barras and Frith, 2023, for a broad summary of this literature). One way to achieve greater inclusion for non-binary athletes would be to approach sport by 'starting from the presumption of non-binary inclusion instead of gender binarization, can facilitate inclusion not just for non-binary people but diverse subjects with different kinds of bodies and needs' (Erikainen et al., 2020, p. 23).

This book is testament to the fact that not all trans people shy away from sport. Instead, some either remained involved in sport during transition or returned to it despite at times finding it hard to do so. All the participants during the course of their interviews reflected upon how their gender identity often impacted on their participation in sport, sometimes due to a complex mix of past and present experiences, and their relationship to being able to 'pass'. As the next two chapters discuss, these experiences often intersected with the ways in which sporting spaces and communities are gendered, yet most participants had successfully renegotiated their current involvement in everyday sport. In this way for many individuals, their gender identity and their sporting body really mattered when it came to their participation in sport.

Summary

Trans feminism has helped with achieving the fundamental aim of the book – the placing of trans people's voices centrally in research which they have contributed to and which concerns them. In addition, as Krane (2019, p. 60) writes:

> What a trans feminist perspective teaches us is the need to consider the broad social and cultural issues surrounding policy and decisions regarding inclusion and exclusion … at the centre of this debate should be the well-being of all athletes … it can also lead us towards privileging inclusion without imposing narrow, Western, heteronormative expectations on elite athletes.

This chapter has argued participating in sport enables an individual to develop a certain identity which can become symbolic of personal growth or self-actualisation, meaning participants' individual gender identities are much more complex if they are constantly being remade in the context of sport. For trans people, who may have formed one type of sporting identity in their youth, negotiating a new one can be complex, fraught with uncertainty but still empowering. Being a trans person in sport could also be pleasurable, enjoyable and gender affirming. These lived experiences have been instrumental in recognising that 'being trans' does not simply mean moving from one gender binary to the other. Rather, the deeply personal relationship between gender identity and gender presentation for some participants is much more complex (Beischel et al., 2022; Olufemi, 2020).

Whilst trans feminist theory, like the data itself, is grounded in lived experience, it is not without the occasional tension. In keeping with the aims and the integrity of the book, it offers a strong foundation for interpreting the latent meanings behind the data presented in this chapter. The foregrounding of lived experiences enables a deeper understanding of why barriers to participation in everyday sport for trans and non-binary people can be both understood and challenged. Adopting a trans feminist theoretical approach then is more than a theoretical decision. It is also both a political position and a personal choice, enabling new ways to identify the socially constructed concepts of gender normativity in sport, as experienced by the participants.

In September 2020, Judith Butler wrote in *The New Statesman* (Ferber, 2020, n.p.), of how 'we have to renew the feminist commitment to gender equality and gender freedom in order to affirm the complexity of gendered lives as they are currently being lived'. As this chapter has shown, trans people's sporting bodies, their gender identity, gender presentation and pronouns all matter. These are broad churches, ever-changing for some, fixed for others, but always open to individual interpretation. Engaging with trans feminist theory, as this book does, means there is a necessity to constantly revisit 'the ways in which the medical determination of sex functions in relation to the lived and historical reality of gender' (Ferber, 2020, n.p.). After all, the lived experiences of participants in relation to sport have illuminated some key insights around bodies and the discursive assumptions made about them by others based on gender presentation.

A trans feminist perspective can advance our understanding of the needs of trans people who push conventional boundaries of sex and gender categorisations in sport. As Krane (2019) notes, a trans feminist approach has an emphasis on respect, dignity and inclusion, welcoming all athletes across the spectrum of diversity, reframing discussions about advantage and fairness, celebrating compassion and prioritising lived experience. However, this respect and dignity has to be extended to all individuals in sport, if barriers are to be reduced and alliances formed.

Discussion Questions

1. How would you describe 'passing privilege' when talking about gender? How might it intersect with other identities who have experienced passing?
2. Jude questioned the gendered clothing in sport and wanted to wear what felt comfortable when they were involved in gymnastics, saying, 'I don't see why there has to be a men's and women's outfit or a uniform'. Thinking about gendered sports clothing – what sports could accommodate a change of outfit, and what might this look like?
3. What can trans feminist theory teach us about other institutions which are historically androcentric, like medicine or education?

Notes

1 See Glossary for a definition of this term.
2 LGB Alliance is a charity founded in 2019. According to their website, they exist to provide support, advice, information and community to men and women who are same-sex-attracted. See www.lgballiance.org.uk.

References

Ahmed, S. (2016). An affinity of hammers. *TSQ*, *3*(1–2), 22–34. https://doi.org/10.1215/23289252-3334151

Anderson, E., & Travers, A. (2017). *Transgender athletes in competitive sport*. London: Routledge.

Barras, A. (2019a). *Hostility to elite trans athletes is having a negative impact on participation in everyday sport*. Retrieved from: https://theconversation.com/hostility-to-elite-trans-athletes-is-having-a-negative-impact-on-participation-in-everyday-sport-113296

Barras, A. (2019b). "We just want to be listened to": Mundane Transphobia in BBC1's the trans woman athlete dispute with Martina Navratilova. *British Mensa's Androgeny*, *3*(3), 5–15. UK: British Mensa Ltd. https://www.researchgate.net/publication/336927760_FULL_ISSUE_of_JOURNAL_British_Mensa's_ANDROGYNY_-_Volume_3_-_Issue_3_-_October_2019

Barras, A. (2022). "Yeah, Congratulations! You Look like a Cis Person, Well Done!" The politics of passing for trans and non-binary people in physical activity in the UK. In: G. Molnár & R. Bullingham (Eds.). *The Routledge handbook of gender politics in sport and physical activity* (pp. 234–245). London: Routledge.

Barras, A., & Frith, H. (2023). 'Cos not everyone wants to talk, they prefer to do, to move': Circuits of trans embodied pleasure and inclusion in sport and physical exercise. *Sport, Education and Society*. https://doi.org/10.1080/13573322.2023.2266755

Barras, A., Frith, H., Jarvis, N., & Lucena, R. (2021). Timelines and transitions: Understanding transgender and non-binary people's participation in everyday sport and physical exercise through a temporal lens. In: S. Bekker, I. Costas Batlle, B.C. Clift, J. Gore, S. Gustafsson & J. Hatchard (Eds.). *Temporality in qualitative inquiry: Theories, methods and practices* (pp. 57–71). London: Routledge.

BBC. (2014, October 14). *Germaine Greer: Transgender women are not women*. BBC. https://www.bbc.co.uk/news/av/uk-34625512

Beischel, W.J., Gauvin, S.E., & van Anders, S.M. (2022). "A little shiny gender breakthrough": Community understandings of gender euphoria. *International Journal of Transgender Health*, *23*(3), 274–294. https://doi.org/10.1080/26895269.2021.1915223

Belam, M. (2021, August 1). *Olympic mixed team events bring the fun – and the golds – back to Britain*. The Guardian. Available at: https://www.theguardian.com/sport/2021/aug/01/olympic-mixed-team-events-britain-triathlon-swimming-ioc-gender-tokyo

Bernstein Sycamore, M. (2006). *NOBODY PASSES: Rejecting the rules of gender and conformity*. New York: Seal Press.

Brione, P. (2022, December 7). *House of Commons Library*. https://commonslibrary.parliament.uk/employment-tribunal-rulings-on-gender-critical-beliefs-in-the-workplace/

Butler, J. (1990). *Gender trouble*. UK: Routledge.

Butler, J. (2004). *Undoing gender*. UK: Routledge.

Capuzza, J.C., & Spencer, L.G. (2015). *Transgender communication studies: Histories, trends, and trajectories*. Lanham: Lexington Books.

Care for What you Believe. (2024). *Gay young people being told they are transgender, says Kemi Badenoch*. https://care.org.uk/news/2024/02/gay-young-people-are-being-told-they-are-transgender-says-kemi-badenoch

Carrera-Fernández, M.V., & DePalma, R. (2020). Feminism will be trans-inclusive or it will not be: Why do two cis-hetero woman educators support transfeminism? *The Sociological Review*, *68*(4). UK: SAGE. https://doi.org/10.1177/0038026120934686

Carrera-Fernández, M.V., Lameiras-Fernández, M., & Rodríguez-Castro, Y. (2018). Performing intelligible genders through violence: Bullying as gender practice and heteronormative control. *Gender and Education*, *30*(3), 341–359. https://doi.org/10.1080/09540253.2016.1203884

Caudwell, J. (2014). [Transgender] young men: Gendered subjectivities and the physically active body. *Sport, Education and Society*, *19*(4), 398–414. https://doi.org/10.1080/13573322.2012.672320

Caudwell, J. (2020). Transgender and non-binary swimming in the UK: Indoor public pool spaces and un/safety. *Frontiers in Sociology*, *5*. https://doi.org/10.3389/fsoc.2020.00064

Channon, A. (2014). Towards the "undoing" of gender in mixed-sex martial arts and combat Sports. *Societies*, *4*(4), 587–605. https://doi.org/10.3390/soc4040587

Cohn, A., & Zeichner, A. (2006). Effects of masculine identity and gender role stress on aggression in men. *Psychology of Men & Masculinity*, *7*(4), 179–190. https://doi.org/10.1037/1524-9220.7.4.179

Cooper, D. (2020, April 30). *Responding to gender critical feminism: On gender, sex and a generous feminist politics in anxious times*. Future of Legal Gender. https://futureoflegalgender.kcl.ac.uk/2020/04/responding-to-gender-critical-feminism-on-gender-sex-and-a-generous-feminist-politics-in-anxious-times/

Cosgrove, D. (2021). "I am allowed to be myself": A photovoice exploration of non-binary identity development and meaning-making. *Journal of Gay & Lesbian Social Services*, *33*(1), 78–102. https://doi.org/10.1080/10538720.2020.1850385

de Vries, Kylan Mattias (2015). Transgender people of color at the center: Conceptualizing a new intersectional model. *Ethnicities*, *15*(1), 3–27. https://doi.org/10.1177/1468796814547058

Doan, P.L. (Ed.). (2011). *Queerying planning: Challenging heteronormative assumptions and reframing planning practice*. Farnham: Ashgate.

Doan, P.L. (Ed.) (2015). *Planning and LGBTQ communities: The need for inclusive queer space*. London: Routledge.

Edelman, R., & Wilson, W. (2020). *The Oxford handbook of sports history*. Oxford: Oxford University Press.

Elling-Machartzki, A. (2017). Extraordinary body-self narratives: Sport and physical activity in the lives of transgender people. *Leisure Studies*, *36*(2), 256–268. https://doi.org/10.1080/02614367.2015.1128474

Erikainen, S., Vincent, B., & Hopkins, A. (2020). Specific detriment: Barriers and opportunities for non-binary inclusive sports in Scotland. *Journal of Sport and Social Issues*. https://doi.org/10.1177/0193723520962937

Farber, R. (2017). 'Transing' fitness and remapping transgender male masculinity in online message boards. *Journal of Gender Studies*, *26*(3), 254–268. https://doi.org/10.1080/09589236.2016.1250618

Ferber, A. (2020, September 22). *Judith Butler on the culture wars, J K Rowling and living in "anti-intellectual times."* New Statesman. https://www.google.com/search?client=firefox-b-dandq=the+new+stsatesman+butler

Fiani, C.N., & Han, H.J. (2019). Navigating identity: Experiences of binary and non-binary transgender and gender non-conforming (TGNC) adults. *International Journal of Transgenderism*, *20*(2–3), 181–194. https://doi.org/10.1080/15532739.2018.1426074

Fisher, F., & Fisher, O. (2018). *Trans teen survival guide*. London: Jessica Kingsley Publishers.

Frith, H., & Gleeson, K. (2004). Clothing and embodiment: Men managing body image and appearance. *Psychology of Men & Masculinity*, *5*(1), 40–48. https://doi.org/10.1037/1524-9220.5.1.40

Goffman, E. (1963). *The presentation of self in everyday life*. London: Penguin.

Hamilton, B.R., Lima, G., Barrett, J., et al. (2021). Integrating transwomen and female athletes with differences of sex development (DSD) into elite competition: The FIMS 2021 Consensus Statement. *Sports Medicine*, *51*, 1401–1415. https://doi.org/10.1007/s40279-021-01451-8

Hilton, E.N., & Lundberg, T.R. (2020). Transgender women in the female category of sport: Perspectives on testosterone suppression and performance advantage. *Sports Medicine*, *51*, 199–214. https://doi.org/10.1007/s40279-020-01389-3

Hines, S. (2007). *TransForming gender: Transgender practices of identity, intimacy and care*. Bristol: Policy.

Hines, S. (2019). The feminist frontier: On trans and feminism. *Journal of Gender Studies*, *28*(2), 145–157. https://doi.org/10.1080/09589236.2017.1411791

Horack, L. (2014). Trans on YouTube. Intimacy, visibility, temporality. *TSQ 1*(4), 572–585. https://doi.org/10.1215/23289252-2815255

Humphrey, K. (2020, July 7). *Trans rights have been pitted against feminism but we're not enemies*. The Guardian. https://www.theguardian.com/commentisfree/2020/jul/07/trans-rights-have-been-pitted-against-feminism-but-were-not-enemies

Hutchinson, J. (2023, October 17). *Riley Gaines labels trans fencer Liz Kocab 'entitled cheat' for winning her EIGHTH world championship*. Daily Mail. https://www.msn.com/en-us/sports/more-sports/riley-gaines-labels-trans-fencer-liz-kocab-entitled-cheat-for-winning-her-eighth-world-championship/ar-AA1imGRc

Jones, B.A., Arcelus, J., Bouman, W.P., & Haycraft, E. (2017). Sport and transgender people: A systematic review of the literature relating to sport participation and competitive sport policies. *Sports Medicine*, *47(*4), 701–716. https://doi.org/10.1007/s40279-016-0621-y

Krane, V. (2019). *Sex, gender, and sexuality in sport: Queer inquiries*. Abingdon: Routledge.

Lawler, S. (2008). *Identity: Sociological perspectives*. UK: Polity Press.

Leithäuser, R.M., & Beneke, R. (2022). Is it time for a new category in competitive sports? *International Journal of Sports Physiology and Performance*, *17*, 1157–1158.

Lester, C.N. (2017). *Trans like me: A journey for all of us*. London: Virago.

McBride, R.S. (2021). A literature review of the secondary school experiences of trans youth. *Journal of LGBT Youth*, *18*(2), 103–134. https://doi.org/10.1080/19361653.2020.1727815

McBride, R.-S., & Neary, A. (2021). Trans and gender diverse youth resisting cisnormativity in school. *Gender and Education*, *33*(8), 1090–1107. https://doi.org/10.1080/09540253.2021.1884201

Nicolazzo, Z. (2016). Trans* in college: Transgender students' strategies for navigating campus life and the institutional politics of inclusion. *Journal of College Student Retention: Research, Theory & Practice*, *20*(3), 406–412. https://doi.org/10.1177/1521025117720391

Olufemi, L. (2020). *Feminism interrupted.* UK: Pluto Press.

Pearce, R., Erikainen, S., & Vincent, B. (2020). TERF wars: An introduction. *The Sociological Review (Keele)*, *68*(4), 677–698. https://doi.org/10.1177/0038026120934713

Pérez-Samaniego, V., Fuentes-Miguel, J., Pereira-García, S., & Devís-Devís, J. (2016). Abjection and alterity in the imagining of transgender in physical education and sport: A pedagogical approach in higher education. *Sport, Education and Society*, *21*(7), 985–1002. https://doi.org/10.1080/13573322.2014.981253

Phipps, A. (2020). *Me, not you: The trouble with mainstream feminism.* UK: Polity Press.

Phipps, C. (2019). Thinking beyond the binary: Barriers to trans participation in university sport. *International Review for the Sociology of Sport.* https://doi.org/10.1177/1012690219889621

Phipps, C., & Blackall, C.J. (2021). 'I wasn't allowed to join the boys': The ideology of cultural cisgenderism in a UK school. *Pedagogy, Culture & Society.* https://doi.org/10.1080/14681366.2021.2000012

Raymond, J. (1979). *The transsexual empire.* USA: Beacon Press.

Roche, J. (2020). *Trans power: Own your gender.* London: Jessica Kingsley Publishers.

Saeidzadeh, Z. (2020). "Are trans men the manliest of men?" Gender practices, trans masculinity and mardānegī in contemporary Iran. *Journal of Gender Studies*, *29*(3), 295–309. https://doi.org/10.1080/09589236.2019.1635439

Saini, A. (2021, July 10) *What is a woman?* Prospect Magazine. https://www.prospectmagazine.co.uk/magazine/what-is-a-woman

Schilt, K. (2010). *Just one of the guys?* USA: University of Chicago Press.

Semerjian, T.Z., & Cohen, J.H. (2006). "FTM means female to me": Transgender athletes performing gender. *Women in Sport and Physical Activity Journal*, *15*(2), 28–43. https://doi.org/10.1123/wspaj.15.2.28

Serano, J. (2007). *Whipping girl: A transsexual woman on sexism and the scapegoating of femininity.* USA: Seal.

Serano, J. (2013). *Excluded.* USA: Seal.

Spandler, H., Erikainen, S., Hopkins, A., Caudwell, J., Newman, H., & Whitehouse, L. (2020). *Non-binary inclusion in sport.* Leap Sports. https://leapsports.org/files/4225-Non-Binary%20Inclusion%20in%20sport%20Booklet.pdf

Sykes, H. (2006). Transsexual and transgender policies in sport. *Women in Sport and Physical Activity Journal*, *15*(1), 3–13. https://doi.org/10.1123/wspaj.15.1.3

Tagg, B. (2012). Transgender netballers: ethical issues and lived realities. *Sociology of Sport Journal*, *29*(2), 151–167. https://doi.org/10.1123/ssj.29.2.151

Twist, J., Vincent, B., Barker, M.-J., & Gupta, K. (2020). *Non-binary lives: An anthology of intersecting identities.* London: Jessica Kingsley Publishers.

[UK Equality Act]. (2010). https://www.legislation.gov.uk/ukpga/2010/15/contents

Wellard, I. (2006). Able bodies and sport participation: Social constructions of physical ability for gendered and sexually identified bodies. *Sport, Education and Society*, *11*(2), 105–119. https://doi.org/10.1080/13573320600640645

Wellard, I. (2016). Gendered performances in sport: An embodied approach. *Palgrave Communications*, *2*, 16003. https://doi.org/10.1057/palcomms.2016.3

Whitehouse, L. (2022). Genderqueer in the sporting sphere: An oral history project of non-binary sporting lives. Loughborough University. Thesis. https://doi.org/10.26174/thesis.lboro.20486136.v1

Whitehouse, L., Armstrong, C., & Cooke, J. (2022). The navigation of non-binary expression through sports kit. In: G. Witcomb & E. Peel (Eds.). *Gender diversity in sport* (pp. 77–96). London: Routledge.

5

SPORTING SPACES

Introduction

The highly gendered organisation of sport continues to create barriers to participation for trans people. This is partly because participating in physical activity can be regarded as particularly challenging (Elling-Machartzki, 2017) with a lack of safe and comfortable spaces and changing rooms, with transphobia and bullying cited as key issues for lower inclusion rates (Caudwell, 2020; Hargie, Mitchell and Somerville, 2015; Morris and Van Raalte, 2016; Pérez-Samaniego et al., 2016; Phipps, 2019). Changing rooms can form social barriers, creating 'a situation of self-evaluation and the evaluation by others, regulated and influenced by emotional and cognitive factors' (Hook, Valentiner and Connelly, 2013, p. 203).

Trans people often need to manage and perform their own gender identity in sport differently to cis people. Sometimes this is about helping to govern their own comfort in relation to their gender identity, for example through transition or wearing a binder to alleviate their gender dysphoria. Other times it is to avoid potential confrontation, due to the way 'public space is imbued with power relations which operate to enable dominance, control and regulation' (Caudwell, 2020, p. 6).

In this chapter, we will be considering the theme of sporting spaces and the ways in which participants navigated them. These include both private spaces, such as changing rooms, and those more public spaces where physical activity takes place, such as the swimming pool and the gym. The sporting spaces people exercised in and occupied had a big impact on their participatory experiences due to them being shared by other users.

DOI: 10.4324/9781003385486-6

For many participants, their own trans lived experience was intrinsically brought into focus when they were in these sporting spaces. Sport is organised along binary lines, and in such settings, the body is explicitly used, displayed, observed and talked about, with bodily presentations an important aspect of the performance of normative masculinity and femininity.

Within these spaces

> Both physical and social dominant forms of heterosexual masculinity and femininity can be established and/or challenged. In these areas, peoples' gendered bodies and behaviours are both scrutinised and disciplined by their peer group, with public and negative labelling for those unwilling or unable to conform to group norms.
>
> *(Paechter, 2003, p. 71)*

Discussions about trans people in sport feature heavily in the gender critical movement, who have strongly vocalised their belief that trans people – by which they mean trans women – should be denied access to changing rooms and toilets, and to competing with/against cis women in sport. For example, in 2019 David Lloyd sports clubs requested its trans members show a gender recognition certificate when accessing changing rooms, a request later abolished (Alibhai, 2019). The previous year, protesters from the gender critical feminist organisation Resisters UK (2021) staged a series of 'Man Friday' events at Hampstead Heath ladies' ponds in reaction to the news that trans women were welcome to swim there (Busby, 2018). At times this focus on trans women has rendered trans masculine and non-binary people's experiences invisible, which this chapter will address.

Navigating the Private and Public Nature of Changing Rooms

The changing room is a quintessentially panoptic place (Doan, 2011; Foucault, 1977). Due to the open-plan design and presence of mirrors, we can often feel like we are being watched by others, and several participants expressed feeling particularly vulnerable about their presence there. Changing rooms are spaces which have their own rules, expectations, language and etiquette, and a set of formal and informal practices which are unique depending on the gender of the person using them. In order to use this space, one must present as the gender the space is designed for and adhere to those practices expected of that gender. The changing room itself is a highly interactive and distinct social space which comes with its own social script and gender-accordant behaviour. In the context of the changing room, they are often a kind of antechamber, which one must access before entering the main sporting area.

As changing rooms were frequently mentioned by several people as causing a barrier to participation in sport, this chapter begins with discussing their significance. When talking about how it feels to use gendered changing rooms to get changed before swimming, Miles said:

> A lot of the men's changing rooms don't have any cubicles to change in, especially public pools, like the outside ones, or some of them don't even have doors on. So, when you get changed it's quite scary, you don't know who else is changing there, and you don't know what their views are. In terms of safety, I do get worried, you don't know who's changing with you. And men tend to have a more physical approach to getting angry when they feel someone is in their space who doesn't deserve it. And whereas, whenever I've been, when I was more androgynous, and I was changing in the women's spaces I would still get asked to leave sometimes.

Miles is challenging the assumption that what is considered to be a private space – a changing room – is perhaps not necessarily quite that private. Thus, even private spaces still retain a sense of ownership by those who use the space, and for those people who might not conventionally look as if they belong there, the risk of confrontation and violence was a genuine concern. A space being gender segregated does not make the occupants within it immune from the gaze of others.

Freya, whilst saying she was not personally concerned about 'negative responses' in changing rooms as she passed, was aware of how they could be 'a hindrance' for trans people. She said:

> Going to gyms and experiencing a bit of a barrier there…a lot of gyms do generally have two changing rooms and lockers outside, so it is possible for someone not to go into the changing room. Many people aren't happy with changing rooms, but most of the time in the past I've tried to go into the female changing room 'cos obviously I should be able to do that, and it can be difficult.

Unfamiliar changing rooms can feel disorientating to many people, but it can be especially so when a person moves from using one gender-segregated space to the 'opposite' one (Bladh, 2022). The layout of changing rooms and toilets are often differently configured for men and women and working out how to behave in that space might feel difficult and may perhaps have a different rules and social conventions. Many people are inhibited about others seeing their naked body, and whilst a changing room or a bathroom is designed to serve a basic (and often private) function, these spaces come with the expectation that a user will behave appropriately. Presumptions are made about the person using a particular changing room, in both explicit and implicit ways, often expressed in the kinds of behaviour and language people engage in, and how they talk to each other. For example, changing room 'banter' in men's changing rooms can often be sexually explicit and homophobic, whilst in women's changing rooms gender norms and presumptions can manifest through gender policing, addressed a little later (Spandler et al., 2020).

Concerns about violence and confrontation

The gender critical organisation Fair Play for Women state on their website that 'most sexual assault is by males, against females. For our physical and emotional safety, we need to know where men are not permitted to follow' (Fair Play for Women, 2024, n.p.). As an organisation, they have taken out full-page adverts in newspapers such as the *Metro* (Duffy, 2018, n.p.) advocating for the maintenance of single-sex spaces (for cis women only) and to oppose reforms to the UK Gender Recognition Act (2004). To be clear, this book does not deny that most sexual assault is by males against females (Women's Aid, 2021, n.p.). It also fully supports any survivor of assault to own their own story and have a right to safety. But many single-sex spaces are not off limits to men even when they claim to be, and who is guarding them from possible intrusion anyway? Many companies employ men to clean female changing rooms, and these men are not viewed with the same level of suspicion as trans women. Rather, it is the cisgender gaze, as Caudwell calls it, that is used to govern transgender bodies, and 'hostile exclusionary comments, and physical ejection all amount to "intensified policing" by cisgender people of what are viewed as "potentially contagious" transgender bodies' (Caudwell, 2020, p. 6). Perpetuating the idea that sexual assault is inflicted by strangers in public or semi-public spaces rather than by family members, friends or acquaintances in the home glosses over the reality about sexual assault and harassment in sport. Most notable is the former Olympic gymnast team doctor and American coach Larry Nassar, currently serving life imprisonment for multiple counts of sexual assualt against young athletes. Single-sex spaces are never a guarantee of safety (Freeman, 2018, n.p.).

Gender critical feminists view trans women using single-sex spaces as 'a legal and moral failure' (Fair Play for Women, 2024, n.p.), but why have such spaces, including changing rooms, become branded as 'safe spaces' anyway? After all, there has been no need to raise this concern before, and many gym and leisure centres already have open-plan changing areas with individual cubicles. Where has the need come from to frame changing rooms as 'safe spaces' which must be protected from trans women? There is also no equivalent conversation about what it means for cis men to share their spaces with trans men, undoubtedly due to the lack of moral panic associated with this. Framing trans people as deviant sexual predators who should not be allowed to use cis people's changing rooms and bathrooms bears a striking resemblance to previous moral panics, most notably the one against gay men in the 1980s, which saw them branded as paedophiles. Any mention of homosexuality was deemed to risk 'turning children gay' in the same way that there is now concern that young people will be 'turned trans' if they learn about gender diversity (Barker, 2017, n.p.). Alison Phipps (2016, p. 132) writes of how, 'this politics of fear uses the language of victimisation and emotional triggers to great effect'.

Trans people are right to feel concerned about this insinuation from the gender critical movement, impacting on it does on their own safety in sporting spaces (Barras, 2019). Participants spoke of needing to be hypervigilant in toilets and changing rooms (often due to experiences of homophobic bullying in the past), sometimes using the 'wrong' space out of desperation. Miles found having to occupy gendered changing rooms difficult because he had to say 'I'm not a boy and then I'd feel really awful. I felt like I had to pretend to be female to use it because I knew that, if I used the men's, I'd probably be in a worse situation'. For James, who often felt uncomfortable in changing rooms as a trans person, it got easier, 'because, you know, I pass…for want of a better word'. As Miles's own gender transition progressed and he grew a beard, he gradually felt more comfortable in the men's changing room, because he too passed. He said 'even when I first came out as trans, I wanted to use the men's 'cos it made me feel good. I could just be the gender I feel'.

The anxiety Miles felt about being in a 'male space', and the concern about safety and violence due to past homophobic bullying, was shared by Alix. When using the changing room at the gym, Alix always kept a towel wrapped around their lower body (Alix had undergone 'top surgery' but not had 'lower surgery'). They said:

> I've been in a situation where there were two guys having a conversation behind me, one of the men had gone out on a date with a woman and found out she was trans, and he said it was one of the most horrific things that had happened to him … I was frozen by my locker, I had a towel around me, and if I'd turned around, they would have seen that I was trans, like a really uncomfortable situation. It could get violent, so I stood there for ages in my locker, waiting for them to leave.

Such experiences inevitably have an impact on future visits. There is the very real concern about violence, due to the ways in which gender is read off the body in these spaces, and even outside of the space, the concern about violence remains. Jude confirmed this when they said, 'if you are a very visibly queer person in a straight place, you do feel uncomfortable. I would'. Whilst they passed, Alix remained on guard, because 'even if you have had top surgery, or any kind of surgery [meaning a person might pass better], you're worried that if there's a space you want to use, you worry you're going to get assaulted, or verbally assaulted. And all you want to do is get changed'.

It was not only the changing rooms which caused anxiety for participants. Craig had expressed concern when using 'macho areas, like the weights room', and completely avoided the changing rooms and toilets, where confrontation might arise. They noted: 'until something happens it doesn't feel completely real, but it's something I'm aware one needs to be mindful of'. Craig, too, had experienced homophobic and transphobic bullying.

Nonetheless, many participants were adamant that they were entitled to use that space and would continue to do so. Alix said:

> I was going to the gym for about a year before I felt comfortable to shower there … I thought, why shouldn't I be using this space the way that everyone else is? I started doing it, but you can see how uncomfortable people are, not all the time, not everyone, but there's generally at least one or two people who are staring at me in the changing room, and it's uncomfortable. And I guess they're just super gendered places.

Eric avoided transphobia by 'pre-emptively' not being in the space where it might happen, which is a difficult decision to make, as it meant Eric could no longer participate in the sport he both enjoys and finds beneficial for his mental health. If Eric wants to participate, he has to join the men's boxing team, which creates a new issue, the wearing of a binder. Eric, who is trans masculine, had to be in spaces which felt safe for him to not wear his binder, 'which realistically means women only spaces. Or women and non-binary. Which aren't working for me'.

When I asked Miles how he felt about only using the male changing rooms and toilets, and how he approached this, he explained how there was 'a point in everyone's physical, medical transition…where they don't feel like they can use either… they have to time it when no one is coming in or out. So, they run in, and find safe space, or you have friends who can go in and tell you where everything is'. In the past, Miles had experienced transphobic verbal abuse whilst using a public toilet, and these encounters subsequently altered his feelings of safety in changing rooms. Like Alix, Miles had undergone top surgery, but this was no guarantee of safety, because, as he said, 'you still know the world isn't as open as you are, or understands you, you're [always] worried [about assault]'.

Sarah, who plays tennis and darts, had a similar story. Sarah was so worried about confrontation at her tennis club that she carried around her gender recognition certificate 'just in case someone wants to see it'. When I asked Sarah if she felt safe at the club (which is an LGBT club), she said, 'of course, yes, I do, but I don't announce it, who I am, I don't even talk about it'. For Sarah, avoiding confrontation (and feeling safe) is achieved by keeping her gender identity a secret. Like Miles, who sometimes felt worried about using the men's toilets, or Craig, who did not use the changing rooms at their gym, Sarah avoided potential transphobia by not telling anyone she is trans. Sarah was also worried someone may confront her and say 'this is not fair, captain, this is not fair, that's not really a woman', and she would not be able to play tennis anymore.

Changing rooms are stressful places for many people, but especially so for trans people. Barker and Scheele (2020, p. 143) write of how trans people are 'unsafe in many public and domestic spaces, risking discrimination, ridicule and even violent attack if their transness is read. At the same time, they're often seen as a danger in places like public toilets or changing rooms'. When it comes to single-sex spaces and extending greater provision to all, this does not have to mean the reduction of provision to others. As research conducted by Spandler et al. (2020) and Erikainen et al. (2020) found, greater provision benefits not just trans people but is also likely to make sporting spaces more inclusive of other groups who face barriers to accessing sports spaces, including cis women and many cultural and religious minorities. Whilst creating fully inclusive spaces is not always possible, 'that does not mean that improvements cannot be made. The second-best solution is to re-design existing spaces to be more inclusive' (Spandler et al., 2020, p. 7).

Combining open plan with private cubicles

A common assumption is that changing rooms are gender-segregated because both men and women want and prefer this, and that many individuals simply feel more comfortable using a changing room alongside users of the (assumed) same sex (Doan, 2011, 2015). Comfort and safety play an important role in the design of changing rooms, and many of us are used to accessing gender-segregated changing rooms for much of our lives, likely starting at school, certainly at least in the United Kingdom (Berg and Kokkonen, 2022; McBride et al., 2020). The long history of sexual violence against women and/or children by men (and sometimes other women) means that changing rooms and toilets can be triggering by those who have experienced it and/or feel vulnerable in these spaces. Changing rooms, then, are designed to be gender-segregated because social and cultural norms expect men and women's bodies to be segregated when there is a possibility of nudity and vulnerability (see Mackay, 2021, pp. 101–102, for an excellent discussion about toilets).

The layout of the changing rooms also caused a dilemma for most participants. This was because open-plan areas in sporting spaces offered less privacy, and those who had surgery scars, or who were binding, felt nervous about using them. James talked about how the open-plan configuration of changing rooms put him off using them, as he did not want to reveal his surgery scars or the lower half of his body. James said a few extra cubicles would make the changing rooms more inclusive. He said:

> Just a couple of cubicles in changing rooms would be nice, 'cos I just want to change my t-shirt after the gym then I'll come home and shower. But I can't even change my t-shirt, I have to go into the loo, into the one cubicle in the whole place that's meant for men.

Whilst Alix's gym had an available cubicle for changing, this was also where the toilet for disabled people was, and they did not want to take this facility away from another person, and they 'shouldn't have to use the disabled toilet'. Craig agreed, and did not use the disabled toilets because 'it's for disabled people to use…also, it feels a bit like, hi there, why don't I just announce myself?' When I asked Craig if they felt unsafe using the changing rooms because they are trans, their response was mixed. For Craig, 'it isn't always that I'm ashamed of being trans, because I'm not, but sometimes I'm worried about safety and things like that too'.

A Trans Feminist Approach to Spaces

The retention of single-sex spaces is not the issue. For me, the issue is the gender crtical assumption that single-sex spaces are only used by cis women. Zanghellini (2020) argues that gender critical feminists therefore make a mistake on at least three points: first, in assuming or arguing only cis women are in need of the protection of women-only spaces; second, in insisting trans women's experience of socialisation mirrors that of cis males; and third, in not treating gender identity seriously as relevant to determining who counts as a woman. 'To be blunt', writes Hines (2019, p. 155), 'the abuse of trans women is not considered to be a feminist issue within some sections of feminism because trans women are not considered to be women'.

This position arguably says more about the feminist who holds such a view than the lived reality of trans people. It situates the penis as an autonomous weapon, 'an organ with a life of its own, whose threat partly resides in the fact that it is not possible to tell whether it is there or not (perchance, like the stranger rapist, it might jump out from the darkness)' (A. Phipps, 2016, p. 312). It is not enough to identify as a woman, simply trying to pass as one is viewed as deceitful, and insensitively likened to drag artists committing 'woman face' if you google this particular Mumsnet belief. For gender critical feminists, the only reason trans women want to use a single-sex space is to commit sexual violence (or win in sport). This is, according to Butler (see Ferber, 2020, n.p.), 'a rich fantasy, and one which comes from powerful fears, but it does not describe a social reality'. It also overlooks how trans women (and trans men) are frequently discriminated against in changing rooms and bathrooms. As Butler writes (2020, n.p.), 'the fact that such fantasies pass as public argument is itself cause for worry'.

What is less considered by gender-critical feminists is that changing rooms evoke unease for many people – and not just in terms of fear of male violence – but how race and culture intersect here too (Saeidzadeh, 2020; Spandler et al. 2020). After all, the ways in which bodies have been – and continue to be – kept separate in public spaces is not limited to gender, and includes race, class, disability, sexuality and age (Hines, 2019; Mansfield et al., 2017). Chapter 1. This leads us to the topic of gender normativity.

The gendered normativity of public sporting spaces

Eleven participants found language problematic. This was espeically the case during interactions with staff members, instructors and players on other teams. James talked about how gendered yoga can be, and whilst yoga, like many sports and activities, may not set out to be intentionally trans exclusive, the gendered assumptions instructors make about people's bodies may make them feel excluded. James said that he did not think yoga was 'gender neutral…some instructors talk about menstrual cycles…obviously with the assumption a person is cisgender', and he had 'definitely been to classes where if you are non-binary or trans, you are excluded from the instructions'. The language used in sports and exercise settings goes mostly unnoticed by those it does not effect. Freya reflected upon how she had experienced this during a fitness class:

> Again, there're some kinds of barriers there … there was one fitness class … one of the instructors was using [gendered] words to describe people, like, 'you can do it girl, keep going girl', and I think I got a 'keep going guy' … and I don't wear … tiny tops or tiny shorts like cis women may when they go to the gym … so it's a little less obvious for the instructor to know.

Gender identity and gender presentation do not always align harmoniously in sporting spaces, and barriers can be both overt (e.g. gender-segregated changing rooms) and covert (e.g. gendered language). Alix suggested how 'tapering' language and not making assumptions about a person's gender promoted inclusivity in sporting spaces. Alix said, 'I think sometimes it's just the way you are welcomed into these spaces, and the way you are spoken to, or how you're treated by people in the space…like what's your name, what are your pronouns? There's a lot more that could be done to make people feel welcome in those spaces'.

Whilst Herrick and Duncan (2019) argue that changing rooms are sites for queer sexuality, very often they are trans/homophobic spaces (as experienced by some participants in the past), dominated by the cisgender gaze. Many people are naked (or partially naked) in changing rooms, creating what Eng (2006, p. 58) terms 'body intimacy'. That is, 'the social relations in the locker room exist in an atmosphere of nakedness, close body contact, and focus on the body – assumptions are made about the asexual nature of them'. Changing room culture is based on the view that 'homosocial spaces are non-sexual – how changing rooms are segregated (men and women) makes heteronormative assumptions about the occupants' (Eng, 2006, p. 59). For someone who transgresses gender norms (no matter if they are trans or not), they may well experience what Doan (2011, p. 635) has termed 'the tyranny of gender', and because gendered spaces shape nearly every aspect of our lives, they can feel disorientating for some people (Warner, 2000; Yeadon-Lee, 2016).

However, whilst many cis people can experience misgendering, for trans people, this infraction has negative consequences in sport. This was the case for Katy, who plays football on a women's team. Whilst she said it was infrequent, it was, of course, highly upsetting. Katy said:

> The [other] team ... must have just gone out to get me from day one...they were quite nasty, kicking everyone, but I really got targeted. But that came from the crowd as well, so I was misgendered across the board from everybody, and the club was calling me he ... the spectators and the people to do with the club were basically just encouraging people to call me he and so on, so that was the worst experience I've had.

Although Katy said there was possibly a language barrier with the referee (who was from another country) and did not blame him for failing to notice the comments, she felt it was important to flag it for the future via training. This was because, she said, 'referees have got to be trained, and they have got to know about LGBT abuse, because they need to stamp on it, because you can't leave it to LGBT people to complain about. Because then we get targeted even more'. This is an example of emotional labour or doing the heavy lifting of activist work. Like Alix who suggested tapering language as a training exercise for all staff, Katy's suggestion of referee training in football could also be offered. This would prevent singling out any one individual and could be easily implemented to improve inclusivity. Katy had even experienced a physical assault whilst playing football, and she had been 'elbowed at a corner and I'm fairly confident that was deliberate'. For Katy, the consequences of 'the referee, he just ignored it', meant her participation in the match was over, because she 'ended up getting taken off because my manager wanted to take me off for my own safety basically, so it was that level'.

The ongoing media hostility towards trans women in elite and professional sport has been filtering down to everyday sport for some time (Barras, 2019). For instance, Charlotte said she knew there was opposition to trans women participating in sport and whilst she was able to ignore it, it undoubtedly impacted on her own participation in sport because it was 'off-putting'. She said:

> They're [gender critical feminists] putting pressure saying that it's unfair, we don't want what is classed as male bodied people in our spaces ... it's really off-putting. What do I do if I do meet one of these people at the swimming pool [or] out on a run [or] I'm told I can't participate in certain activities, and are expected to produce certificates?

Even when an individual was not confronted directly in a sporting space, there was still a residual fear that it might happen, often due to past experiences of homophobia or transphobia. For example, although Alix said, 'no one has directly said anything to me' about them being there and being trans, they still had to be on their guard. Alix said, 'sometimes I can't tell if people are amused or uncomfortable, or angry that I'm in their space, um, it's yeah, it's a difficult one'. When I asked Alix if they had experienced any direct transphobia in the gym, Alix replied that 'no one has said anything directly to me, but again, they don't always have to, sometimes it's just enough, the way someone was looking at you? It's not always about violence, really, it's just the uncomfortable situation'.

The majority of sport and physical exercise requires the negotiation of the private, gendered changing room, and the public space of, for example, the football field, and some participants keenly felt 'the fear of visual and verbal surveillance' (Caudwell, 2020, p. 6) which happens in these spaces and places. Returning to the occurrence of the word 'safety' and the term 'safe spaces', these experiences have highlighted the reality many trans people face in sport, how their participation is often fraught with both the expectation and reality of discrimination and transphobia. Within these highly gendered spaces it is evident that peoples' gendered bodies and behaviours are both 'scrutinised and disciplined by their peer group, with public and negative labelling for those unwilling or unable to conform to group norms' (Paechter, 2003, p. 71). This can make people, such as James, feel wary of using them, because '[I] felt uncomfortable in gendered spaces, like sports teams, like changing rooms ... on the surface, homophobia perhaps... but [also] there was kind of a gendered aspect to what was putting me off'. Next, we examine the frequently overlooked experiences of the trans men/trans masculine particpants (Paechter, 2003, p. 71) in relation to hegemonic masculinity.

Trans Men and Hegemonic Masculinity in Sporting Spaces

Many sporting settings, especially certain areas of the gym like the weights area, are often viewed as men-only spaces. Joe said that they 'hated the gym' because 'it's horrible...I hate the changing rooms, I hate the showers, I hate all of it. I hate that the men take up all of the free weights area. It's the masculinity, the horrible air of masculinity (*laughs*) that surrounds gyms'. Farber (2017, p. 262) discusses exactly this in and her analysis of trans men's experiences of masculinity via online fitness forums and their feeling about attending gyms. She says:

> Gyms are not neutral spaces and particular forms of self-presentation, dress, actions and vocalizations are gendered. With cisgender men often controlling the gym space (particularly the weight room), and while many people experience 'gymtimidation', transgender men faced unique challenges in accessing and using the gym.

This was the case for Craig, when they spoke about feeling confident enough to use the weights area in the gym, because they pass as male. They said how they had:

> Kind of ventured downstairs to the weights area [and] you have to be a certain kind of person to go down there, but it tends to be populated by people who appear to be cis men. Um, pretty muscular, doing their thing…I don't care anymore, and it doesn't even induce anxiety, so that's quite cool.

In Ravenhill and de Visser's (2017) study on gay men, sex and masculinity, they found that gay men, like many straight men, may utilise stereotypically masculine attributes and behaviours in an attempt to accrue 'masculine capital'. In other words, the gay men in their study shored up the social power afforded by displaying traits and behaviours associated with hegemonic masculinity. According to Ravenhill and de Visser (2017), muscularity and voice quality may contribute to gay men's masculine capital. Gender presentation matters in sporting spaces, where frequently an unspoken hierarchy exists between users of the space. Misogyny is common, and thus passing as male made acceptance easier (see Hertzog and Lev's excellent 2019 study on macho culture in Israeli gyms for more on gender power relations). Yet, interestingly, passing as male (visible facial hair, a flat chest area) was what permitted access to these men-only spaces. Proof of being in possession of the qualities valued in hegemonic masculinity (stronger, faster, more skilful) never needed verification by other users of the space. Masculine capital in this context, simply meant looking normatively male, and an assumption of male socialisation.

This (gendered) socialisation has been explored by Schilt (2010), via the experiences of trans men in the workplace. Schilt revealed the ways in which assumptions about innate differences between men and women serve as justification for discrimination, finding that some trans men gain acceptance – and even privileges – by becoming 'just one of the guys' (Schilt, 2010, n.p.). Schilt found that some trans men were coerced into working as women or marginalised for being openly trans and that other forms of appearance-based discrimination also influenced their opportunities. Schilt concluded that this research was not only valuable for the ways in which it revealed workplace inequality for both trans men and cis women, but that the trans men she spoke to in her research found their experiences and practices of masculinity more salient than other men. This was a similar experience to the trans masculine participants in this study, who found that once they passed as men in the gym they became privy to the sexist language and behaviour frequently conducted in these spaces. To be seen as a man by other men in a male space, also meant being included in displays of (unpleasant) hegenomic masculinity.

Some of the participants described their masculinity as fluid, and not fixed. That is, it was relational, often dependent on who they were with, and their environment. This is what Abelson (2019, p. 21) terms 'Goldilocks masculinity', which she explains as being 'not too masculine and not too feminine, [and] is central to the regular guy'. Trans men, argued Abelson (2014), do not become immune to the threat or reality of violence (from other men) by virtue of now being seen as men. Whilst they enjoyed increased access to public spaces or found that their body afforded them a new sense of safety, their 'geography of fear shifted' (Abelson, 2014, p. 558). That is, these trans men now experienced a new set of fears, brought on by 'the privilege of male violence' (Abelson, 2014, p. 558). This meant that for the trans men in Abelson's research, they felt that their change of position relative to women was not always a positive one, because it involved the possibility of being subjected to other men's violence in a new way. This included, for example, having to negotiate interactions with men in ways they found to be sexist or homophobic, just like Craig did and Joe did.

When Craig was in the gym using the weights area, an area in which frequently only the most experienced (cis) men worked out and was thus deemed 'notoriously masculine', they said that 'I can just laugh about it [the men showing off] … it doesn't really bother me anymore'. Here Craig derides the absurdity of hegemonic masculinity and, in doing so, adapts it to suit them, a trans masculine man in a (predominantly) cis man's space. This is an example of a way in which hegemonic masculinity can be thought of as 'incorporating or appropriating aspects of subordinate or marginalised masculinities in order to retain the gender order' (Abelson, 2019, p. 17). After all, Craig has not sought out a new space in the gym nor challenged the users in the existing space. Rather, they have established their own place in the gender hierarchy. Thus, the gym provides an opportunity to witness hegemonic masculinity in action.

Changing rooms are also sites for the production of hegemonic masculinity. One very distinct aspect of changing rooms is the reality of encountering another person's naked body and having your own observed. This could make people feel vulnerable. This vulnerability was both a bodily one, and one which required these participants having to 'newly orientate themselves to being accountable to gender expectations for those who are sex categorised as male' (Abelson, 2014, p. 558). This was in part due to safety and in response to other (cis) men's dominating practices and potential for sexist banter and even violence in these spaces. This was Craig's concern, and although they had not felt threatened inside the gym, they worried someone 'may notice something and accost me outside that space'. Similarly, Harry said he had friends on his squash team who could not use the showers, as they 'don't want anyone else seeing that they haven't got a willy, basically' and suggested more individual cubicles with doors would be welcome. The fear of the discovery of the visible signs of their trans heritage, as Craig described it, was more of concern for trans male/masculine participants. This raises questions about safety in (private) sporting spaces for many users, not just those who are cis women.

The participants in Abelson's 2014 research also identified particular bodily characteristics as important for their sense of safety. Like the participants in this research, their perceptions of safety changed based on their own body, the space they were in and the communities they engaged with. Abelson's research highlights similarities with the trans masculine participants in this research, because these perceptions of safety, such as in the changing room or the showers, become 'central to how they account for their masculine practices as they orient to their sex category and transgender status' (Abelson, 2014, p. 562).

The trans men in this book had genuine concerns about their own safety, but so long as they passed, or did not disclose what Craig called their 'trans heritage', they were able to participate in sport. Both Craig and Harry were able to use their trans masculinity as a way to find their own place at the gym and in the changing rooms, both spaces which are often considered to be subject to displays of hegemonic masculinity. For example, when Harry was asked about his surgery scars whilst changing after football, he did not pretend they were from having heart surgery, as his teammate assumed. Instead, Harry disclosed the reason, which was having had top surgery.

Joe, Alix and Craig were critical of the policing of other people's gender in these spaces and used their own passing privilege to look out for their cis friends and family. In doing this, they reconceptualised hegemonic masculinity as a tool to promote equality and make cis men feel uncomfortable. Joe talked about this when they went to the gym with their teammates from the women's rugby team:

> It was disgusting, and I'd get a lot of looks like, they'd look at me, like yeah, well done, you're doing well. And I'd be like, I just want to come to the gym. They would just stare at all my friends, especially when they were squatting, so they could stand behind and see their bums, and think they couldn't be seen, like, there are mirrors you know! Disgusting.

Alix talked about how they go swimming with their younger brother, 'but it's not generally a pleasant experience, because people will just stare at you. Which I find bizarre, and it used to bother me, but now I enjoy staring back at people, and making them as equally uncomfortable for what they're doing'. In this example, Alix is turning their gaze back on to those who are staring at them, which arguably still counts as a display of hegemonic masculinity. There is also the sense some of the trans masculine participants are in the privileged and unique position of experiencing both perspectives of how hegemonic masculinity works, offering a unique insight into the ways it is interpreted. This sheds light, for example, on the ways in which sporting spaces are gendered to permit easier entry to those who fit standard representations of what a cis man looks like. Whilst this research did not make a specific decision to ask participants whether they had better (or worse) experiences once they were re-entering sporting spaces as trans men, it could be argued that they practice masculinity more consciously than cis men due to their gender identity.

A similar perspective is found in Abelson's (2014) research on trans men, masculinity and spatial safety, and Schilt's (2010) study on trans men's experiences of gender inequality in working life, where she details the interactional process of 'achieving social maleness (2010, p. 48), that is, the work of being recognised as male by others. In this way, Schilt argues (2010, p. 48), trans men may gain acceptance and some privileges as (cis) men but may also experience 'marginalisation and discrimination if they choose to live openly as trans (men)'.

with Men

Over time, participants such as Joe and Craig found they were able to construct their own version of (trans) masculinity, establishing their own gender identity and subsequent integration into that same space. Humour was key, with three participants poking fun at the overt (hegemonic) masculinity in these spaces. However, this was only possible due to their passing, because they were reassured their gender presentation 'matched' those of the other users. Returning to Abelson's (2019) and Goldilocks masculinity, these trans men, like some cis men, 'do not want to be hypermasculine, but neither do they want to be too feminine. Instead, the ideal may be somewhere in-between' (Abelson, 2019, p. 5). The trans men here constructed themselves as manlier by criticising cis men, embodying a innovative form of trans feminist masculinity, undermining and challenging sporting spaces, whilst also feeling affirmed in their gender (Saeidzadeh, 2020).

As Connell and Messerschmidt (2005) noted in 2005 when writing about hegemonic masculinity as an embodied practice, masculinity tends to be considered as something that only cis men's bodies do, yet in these examples the participants bodies are also 'doing' masculinity (see also Nigel Jarvis, 2015). Both Edie Sedgewick (1995) and Jack Halberstam (1998) have critiqued that there is a tendency within masculinity studies 'that everything pertaining to men can be classified as masculinity, and everything that can be said about masculinity pertains in the first place to men' (Sedgewick, 1995, p. 12). Expanding on the participant's experiences, I suggest that masculinity is something that' not only some specific bodies (those assigned male at birth) have or own but is more situational and can be deployed and activated by a variety of bodies' (Gottzén and Straube, 2016, p. 221). Indeed, as Sedgewick (1995) wrote, sometimes masculinity has got nothing to do with men: rather masculinity is both situational and relational.

In Abelson's 2014 research examining how trans men construct their masculinities in public spaces such as on public transport or in the gym, she found that respondents' masculine practices changed depending on who they interacted with and the level of safety (or potential violence) they perceived. Abelson (2014, p. 549) wrote of how 'respondents' concerns for safety, and their masculine practices, changed according to variation in transition, physical location, audience and their physical stature'. this observations chimes with Joe's experience.

Whilst Joe was transitioning and still legally female, they stopped playing (women's) water polo and instead joined a women's (LGBTQ+) rugby team. They described how passing as male caused confusion for the opposite team:

> My breasts were really small to start with [before top surgery]. I'm tall, I'm 5ft 11, my voice got deep, at that point I was quite hairy, and they were like, what are you doing here (laughs)? And like I'd play at the back and yell and everyone would turn around and say there's a man on the team!

Joe's masculine appearance stood out to the other players on the field, not least as it was a women's team. This is an example of how using the lens of trans feminism can help to reorientate our cisgender epistemology towards the needs of trans people and their bodies. According to trans feminist activist and author Emi Koyamo (2001), there are two primary principles of trans feminism that each trans feminist lives by, strives to follow and wishes for all individuals. Firstly, all people should be allowed to live their own lives in whichever way they choose and define themselves. Secondly, they should also be respected by society for their individuality and uniqueness. Included is the right to individualised gender expression without the fear of retaliation. When this focus shifts in sporting spaces, a person can sometimes feel differently about their body when this fear is removed, as was the case with Joe playing on the women's rugby team whilst passing as male.

Overall, those participants who reflected on masculinity found they did not aspire to emulate the kind of (cis) masculinity they witnessed in these spaces, which they found to be sexist and misogynistic. James talked about using a gym where cis men were not allowed to join, and how different the experience was as a trans person, because of 'the way that cis men behave'. In fact, three of the trans masculine participants shared this view of spaces being felt as masculine. Alix called the weights area in their gym 'notorious ... just big men down there, lifting weights...grunting...all very uncomfortable or intimidating'. In James's experience, it was specifically cis men who were the problem in gyms. It is imperative, then to give some consideration to how we can rethink gendered public spaces.

Rethinking gendered public spaces

Sports spaces are often organised in ways which assume women and men might engage in different sporting activities (or have to depending on who dominates them). One assumption is that when women go to the gym, they will do cardio and muscle toning activities, whereas when men go, they will do weightlifting and muscle-building activities (Spandler et al., 2020). The way in which the gym floor is organised can reinforce these invisible gendered territories, and a number of masculine presenting participants reflected upon how uncomfortable they found these 'male spaces' to be when they first started using them. Much like in male changing rooms, public spaces are still subject to gender stereotypical behaviour which can manifest in overtly sexist and/or masculine behaviour and/or language from users.

This means that for many trans people who are going through transition (and even once they pass), negotiating sporting spaces is anxiety inducing, where the cisgender gaze is strongly felt, and there might be pressure to conform to a certain gender stereotype, or risk being confronted. A person's gender identity is intrinsic to their participation in sport, but this was not always easy to achieve when people were worried about how their gender identity would be read by others (Bradford and Syed. 2019).

Passing and being read as your preferred gender requires the constant repetition of behaviours considered normative by others (Carrera-Fernández and DePalma, 2020), which can not only be labour-intensive for some trans people, but not engaging in this performativity or, worse, failing at this performativity can often have consequences (Bernstein Sycamore, 2006). The ways in which spaces such as changing rooms and gyms are laid out could be reconfigured in the future to accommodate not just gender-diverse people, but those who may have cultural or religious needs. Gendered clothing and pronouns are easily adapted, and bodies of all shapes, sizes and ages might feel more welcome in these spaces (Spandler et al., 2020). Trans men can feel unsafe in cis spaces, and overall, the experiences of trans men in these discussions are frequently overlooked. Such 'valuable testimonies on embodied subjectivities' (Caudwell, 2014, p. 398) are hopefully captured in enough detail here to demonstrate that it is time to reconsider sporting spaces for everyone's comfort and safety.

A Need for Trans-Only Sporting Spaces?

The existence of spaces and sessions designed only for trans people was mentioned by Miles, Jude, Alix and Freya. Like passing privilege (and single-sex spaces), there are both benefits and limitations for these spaces and sessions. As Miles said, 'it's nice that there are trans specific places and clubs, like swimming, that's really important, 'cos it's intimidating. You feel very self-conscious'. These spaces (and the trans-inclusive organisations who run them) enabled users to feel safe, accepted and removed the need to negotiate many of the issues already mentioned in this chapter. Jude said they thought 'that's what brings it all [doing sport] together. 'Cos there's a space where you can support each other during a game'.

Alix agreed with Jude and said, 'people know they can go to those spaces [and feel ok], which gyms in general just aren't doing. I think what Trans Can Sport [a Brighton-based trans inclusive sports organisation] is doing is really important'. Miles also found public swimming 'a bit difficult', and when swimming on their own, Alix would only swim 'at a trans specific swim group'. As Persia explained, for many trans people swimming was an almost-impossible activity to access and enjoy, because:

> When they have the physical, sexual anomalies that they can't hide. Like I would never had gone swimming before I had surgery, which I've had...before then, what would I have done? You don't want to go anywhere near that.

Jude said that even though they knew there were trans swimming groups around, 'which are really great, and I know a few friends have been and have had positive experiences', they would 'not go swimming, that's a definite'. This was because, they said, 'swimming is obviously one of the things that people find difficult because you wear as little clothing as possible. There's nowhere to hide'. However, James said when he went swimming, 'I still feel self-conscious, [but] it doesn't stop me from going'. James found going to a trans-only swimming session meant he was still able to do the activity he enjoyed. However James knew that:

> Some people won't go [or] wouldn't feel comfortable going alone...they go with another, usually trans person, so they feel safe, or they'll go to a trans only space like the swimming ... people really rave about that, it's really given people an opportunity to do something they otherwise wouldn't have done.

The existence of trans-only sessions and spaces, arguably much like the spaces branded as women only/single-sex or LGBTQ+ friendly, certainly provide an important and necessary service. This is clearly of great benefit to those participants who feel self-conscious about being involved in sport, but trans-only spaces and sessions are limited and not always reliably available. This meant some participants such as Alix would still use, as they called them, 'straight' sporting spaces, which are more readily available. When trans-only spaces and sessions are not routinely available, they become hard to depend on. Another disadvantage to trans-only spaces and sessions was raised by Jude. Jude acknowledged that whilst trans-only spaces and sessions are 'a really, really important thing, it's really hard for people who want to be really competitive in sport'. That is, the trans population is small, and opportunities for competition are limited. Jenny, who competes in cycling, agreed, saying, 'very few women compete in the mountain bike orienteering...if you had a separate category, I am always going to win that...I don't always want to win it!'.

Joe felt that many of the issues in sporting spaces 'weren't even a trans thing … I think lots of people find gyms horrendously uncomfortable'. Sporting spaces, like bodies, are gendered, where intense social interactions between people often take place, becoming sites of meaning for individuals to perform and confirm their gender. In these spaces, people often draw upon dominant social and cultural understandings of gender to define themselves and others as legitimate users of that space (Abelson, 2014; Kauer and Rauscher, 2019). The body exposure these spaces require can be a significant barrier, making people unwilling or unable to use sports facilities because of that, or, if they do, using clothing or a binder to help them negotiate the space.

Trans eminism in porting paces

Many participants found themselves having to negotiate sporting spaces to some degree, whether public or private, which both function as sites 'for the gendered display of hegemonic forms of heterosexual masculinity and for the subordination of alternatives' (Paechter, 2003, p. 47). Social science in particular has mobilized queer theory to highlight the mutual interdependency of gender normativity and hegemonic masculinity (Giulianotti, 2016) within sport, but one of the most powerful challenges to these concepts in sport over the last two decades has come from trans feminism. Serano (2013, p. 5) said:

> Existing feminist and queer movements (much like their straight male-centric counterparts) always seem to create hierarchies, where certain gendered and sexual bodies, identities, and behaviours are deemed more legitimate than others.

In other words, it is through the repeated practice of hegemonic masculinity (and gender normativity), regardless of who is promoting it, 'which come to organise social life, either sustaining a patriarchal order, or challenging it in unprecedented forms' (Gottzén and Straube, 2016, p. 219). Conceptually, trans feminism is different to hegemonic masculinity in that it does not advocate for gender hierarchies. Rather, trans feminism champions bodily autonomy and living as a person's authentic gendered self, even if that means finding a place in that hierarchy. Because trans feminism places trans people at the heart of its thinking, it respects the rights of any trans individual to find happiness in that hierarchy, so long as it is affirming for them. Centring trans people epistemologically in all research concerning them encourages a looking beyond the common or popularised sporting narratives which value gender normativity and hegemonic masculinity.

Trans feminism strives to closely listen to the uncommon narratives, those of the trans participants themselves. Arguably this is no different than any perspective which privileges a particular minority group. In fact, the centring of the voices of participants in this research are a given when adopting a trans feminist perspective, and thus this research meets the first and fundamental aim of what trans feminism does. Sara Ahmed (2017, p. 227) writes:

> Trans feminist politics illuminate not only how the sex-gender system is coercive, how it restricts what and who can be, but how creativity comes from how we survive a system that we cannot dismantle by the force of our will alone.

Trans feminist theory acknowledges that a reliance on binaries in sport can create accessibility issues for those people whose gender identity might not be situated along normative binary lines. Some participants both celebrated how they were transgressing conventional or binary boundaries in sport, found a binary gender idetity affirming. binary. For them, this sporting disruption was something they acknowledged, but not something they necessarily wished to permanently change. For example, rather than directly confront the hegemonic masculinity and gender normativity prevalent in sporting spaces, the trans masculine participants at times re-essentialised it and were themselves sometimes more salient in their masculinity than the cis male users of those spaces.

The epistemological position of trans feminism, which argues a reconsideration of how sport is organised – that is, not by anatomy but by ability, in order to achieve equality for trans people, was not necessarily what every participant vocalised. Rather, some found affirmation and an end to their gender dysphoria once their own gender identity was aligned, and, for some, this meant identifying as binary trans. For trans feminists, it is 'the confines and coercive nature of the sex-gender binary structure, especially in physical activity and sport, which is problematic and in need of change' (Caudwell, 2020, p. 8). However, whilst some participants acknowledged this, not all of them found this problematic, and no one expressed a wish to radically change it. Rather, their very presence in sport and sports settings meant they were involved in redefining gender from within and counteracting this coercive nature by continuing to participate in sport. This was achieved by continuing to occupy gender-segregated spaces such as changing rooms and occasionally recognising (as trans feminism does) where cissexism and transphobia intersected.

Trans feminism brings to conversations trans people's participation in sport the opportunity to be creative when thinking about inclusion, and seeking out alliances with others who also feel excluded in sport. Trans feminism has also provided a lexicon to better understand how cis narratives dominate sport and looks to ways to examine how gender normativity and hegemonic masculinity create barriers for many people in sport. These considerations about equality were vocalised by five participants, in the ways in which they had internalised the essentialist view they would possess an innate competitive advantage over their cis teammates. For three trans masculine participants they often had the perception of being good at sport conferred upon by them by others, due to passing as cis men. In this way, all of these individuals were subverting gender performativity to their own advantage, allowing for the possibility of change. In this way, 'the very freedom of the subject who is called upon to repeat and reinforce the gender normative, can open fissures that may eventually lead to a destabilization of power' (Butler, 1990, p. 67), which is fundamentally what trans feminism strives for.

Summary

Sport is built on two millennia of heteropatriarchy and body politics (Waldron, 2019). Engaging with trans feminism helps to critically evaluate why sport continues to be based on binary competition. Modern sport has always been a crucial cultural domain for the construction and reproduction of dominant, heterosexual masculine identities, and sports institutions at professional and amateur level still harbour formal and informal hierarchies which limit participation for those who sit outside of these identities (Mumford, 2021; Patel, 2021). These hierarchies were experienced by participants as they navigated their way around sporting spaces and how they both encountered hegemonic masculinity and adapted it to their own version of (trans feminist) masculinity.

Major barriers to participation in sport still exist for trans people, yet they still found a way to participate. It is clear that these examples of hegemonic masculinity being both adopted and derided are situational and relational. These lived experiences contribute to the existing literature on hegemonic masculinities, especially where hegemonic masculinity is performed by bodies which are not cisgender. However, more research is required to fully understand the constructions, meanings and displays of the range of (masculine) gender identities reflected upon in this book.

Discussion Questions

1 Why do you think trans men and trans masculine people are so overlooked in sport?
2 Are trans-only sporting spaces and activities facilitate inclusion, or do they create more barriers to participation?
3 Imagine you can redesign a gym/exercise studio/your dream sporting space. How might you do this to promote more inclusion and accessibility for all of your users?

References

[Fair Play for Women]. (2024). https://fairplayforwomen.com
[Women's Aid]. (2021). Women's aid. https://www.womensaid.org.uk

Abelson, M. (2014). Dangerous privilege: Trans men, masculinities, and changing perceptions of safety. *Sociological Forum*, *29*(3), 549–570. https://doi.org/10.1111/socf.12103
Abelson, M. (2019). *Men in place: Trans masculinity, race, and sexuality in America*. USA: University of Minnesota Press.
Ahmed. S. (2017). *Living a feminist life*. USA: Duke University Press.
Alibhai, Z. (2019, March 9). *David Lloyd gyms insist trans members have 'have gender certificate' before they can use their preferred changing room*. i-news. https://inews.co.uk/news/uk/david-lloyd-gyms-trans-gender-certificate-267576
Barker, M.J. (2017). *A trans review of 2017: The year of transgender moral panic*. Retrieved from: https://theconversation.com/a-trans-review-of-2017-the-year-of-transgender-moral-panic-89272
Barker, M.J., & Scheele, J. (2020). *Gender: A graphic history*. London: Icon.
Barras, A. (2019). *Hostility to elite trans athletes is having a negative impact on participation in everyday sport*. Retrieved from: https://theconversation.com/hostility-to-elite-trans-athletes-is-having-a-negative-impact-on-participation-in-everyday-sport-113296
Berg, P., & Kokkonen, M. (2022). Heteronormativity meets queering in physical education: The views of PE teachers and LGBTIQ+ students. *Physical Education and Sport Pedagogy*, *27*(4), 368–381. https://doi.org/10.1080/17408989.2021.1891213
Bernstein Sycamore, M. (2006). *NOBODY PASSES: Rejecting the rules of gender and conformity*. New York: Seal Press.
Bladh, G.H. (2022). Spatial bodies: Vulnerable inclusiveness within gyms and fitness venues in Sweden. *Social Sciences*, *11*(10), 455. https://doi.org/10.3390/socsci11100455
Bradford, N.J., & Syed, M. (2019). Transnormativity and transgender identity development: a master narrative approach. *Sex Roles 81*, 306–325. https://doi.org/10.1007/s11199-018-0992-7
Busby. (2018, May 29). *Trans rights campaigners say 'Man Friday' Hampstead Heath protest was 'transphobic'*. Independent. https://www.independent.co.uk/news/uk/man-friday-hampstead-heath-protest-transphobic-lgbt-rights-a8374651.html
Butler, J. (1990). *Gender trouble*. UK: Routledge.
Carrera-Fernández, M.V., & DePalma, R. (2020). Feminism will be trans-inclusive or it will not be: Why do two cis-hetero woman educators support transfeminism? *The Sociological Review*, *68*(4). UK: SAGE. https://doi.org/10.1177/0038026120934686
Caudwell, J. (2014). [Transgender] young men: Gendered subjectivities and the physically active body. *Sport, Education and Society*, *19*(4), 398–414. https://doi.org/10.1080/13573322.2012.672320
Caudwell, J. (2020). Transgender and non-binary swimming in the UK: Indoor public pool spaces and un/safety. *Frontiers in Sociology*, *5*. https://doi.org/10.3389/fsoc.2020.00064
Connell, R.W., & Messerschmidt, J.W. (2005). Hegemonic masculinity: Rethinking the concept. *Gender and Society*, *19*(6), 829–859. https://doi.org/10.1177/0891243205278639
Doan, P.L. (Ed.). (2011). *Queerying planning: Challenging heteronormative assumptions and reframing planning practice*. Farnham: Ashgate.
Doan, P.L. (Ed.) (2015). *Planning and LGBTQ communities: The need for inclusive queer space*. London: Routledge.
Duffy, N. (2018, October 10). *Metro newspaper runs full-page ad attacking transgender rights reforms*. Pink News. https://www.pinknews.co.uk/2018/10/10/metro-newspaper-full-page-ad-attacking-transgender-reforms/

Elling-Machartzki, A. (2017). Extraordinary body-self narratives: Sport and physical activity in the lives of transgender people. *Leisure Studies*, *36*(2), 256–268. https://doi.org/10.1080/02614367.2015.1128474

Eng, H. (2006). Queer athletes and queering in sports. In: J. Caudwell (Ed.). *Sport, sexualities and queer/theory* (pp. 49–61). Abingdon: Routledge.

Erikainen, S., Vincent, B., & Hopkins, A. (2020). Specific detriment: Barriers and opportunities for non-binary inclusive sports in Scotland. *Journal of Sport and Social Issues*. https://doi.org/10.1177/0193723520962937

Farber, R. (2017). 'Transing' fitness and remapping transgender male masculinity in online message boards. *Journal of Gender Studies*, *26*(3), 254–268. https://doi.org/10.1080/09589236.2016.1250618

Ferber, A. (2020, September 22). *Judith Butler on the culture wars, J K Rowling and living in "anti-intellectual times."* New Statesman. https://www.google.com/search?client=firefox-b-dandq=the+new+stsatesman+butler

Foucault, M. (1977). *Discipline and punish: The birth of the prison* (2nd Vintage Books ed.). New York: Vintage Books.

Freeman, H. (2018, January 26). *How was Larry Nassar able to abuse so many gymnasts for so long*? The Guardian. https://www.theguardian.com/sport/2018/jan/26/larry-nassar-abuse-gymnasts-scandal-culture

Giulianotti, R. (2016). *Sport: a critical sociology* (2nd ed.). Cambridge: Polity Press.

Gottzén, L., & Straube, W. (2016). Trans masculinities. *NORMA*, *11*(4), 217–224. https://doi.org/10.1080/18902138.2016.1262056

Halberstam, J. (1998). *Female masculinity*. USA: Duke Press.

Hargie, O.D.W., Mitchell, D.H., & Somerville, I.J.A. (2015). 'People have a knack of making you feel excluded if they catch on to your difference': Transgender experiences of exclusion in sport. *International Review for the Sociology of Sport*, *52*(2), 223–239. https://doi.org/10.1177/1012690215583283

Herrick, S. & Duncan, L. (2019). *Locker-room experiences among LGBTQ+ adults*. Semantic Scholar. https://doi.org/10.1123/jsep.2019-0133

Hertzog, E., & Lev, A. (2019). Male dominance under threat: Machoism confronts female defiance in Israeli Gyms. *Journal of Contemporary Ethnography*, *48*(6), 836–866. https://doi.org/10.1177/0891241619834662

Hines, S. (2019). The feminist frontier: On trans and feminism. *Journal of Gender Studies*, *28*(2), 145–157. https://doi.org/10.1080/09589236.2017.1411791

Hook, J.N., Valentiner, D.P., & Connelly, J. (2013). Performance and interaction anxiety: Specific relationships with other- and self-evaluation concerns. *Anxiety, Stress and Coping: An International Journal*, *26*(2), 203–216. https://doi.org/10.1080/10615806.2012.654777

Jarvis, N. (2015). The inclusive masculinities of heterosexual men within UK gay sport clubs. *International Review for the Sociology of Sport*, *50*(3), 283–300. https://doi.org/10.1177/1012690213482481

Kauer, K.J., & Rauscher, L. (2019). Negotiating gender among LGBTIQ athletes: sport as a space for disruption and reproduction. In: K. Krane (Ed.). *Sex, gender, and sexuality in sport: Queer inquiries* (pp. 49–66). UK: Routledge.

Koyamo, E. (2001). *The transfeminist manifesto*. https://transreads.org/wp-content/uploads/2019/03/2019-03-16_5c8d1897c5d96_15tfmanifesto.pdf

Mackay, F. (2021). *Female masculinities and the gender wars*. London: I. B Tauris.

Mansfield, L., Caudwell, J., Wheaton, B., & Watson, B. (2017). *The Palgrave handbook of feminism and sport, leisure and physical education*. Basingstoke, Hampshire: Palgrave Macmillan.

McBride, R.-S., Neary, A., Gray, B., & Lacey, V. (2020). *The post-primary school experiences of transgender and gender diverse youth in Ireland.* Limerick: University of Limerick and the Transgender Equality Network of Ireland. https://doi.org/10.13140/RG.2.2.32011.52002

Morris, J.F., & Van Raalte, J.L. (2016). Transgender and gender non-conforming athletes: Creating safe spaces for all. *Journal of Sport Psychology in Action*, *7*(2), 121–132. https://doi.org/10.1080/21520704.2016.1184732

Mumford, S. (2021). *A philosopher looks at sport.* UK: Cambridge University Press.

Paechter, C. (2003). Masculinities and femininities as communities of practice. *Women's Studies International Forum*, *26*(1), 69–77. https://doi.org/10.1016/S0277-5395(02)00356-4

Patel, S. (2021). Gaps in the protection of athlete's gender rights in sport- a regulatory riddle. *The International Sports Law Journal*, *21*(4), 257–275. doi:10.1007/s40318-021-00182-2

Pérez-Samaniego, V., Fuentes-Miguel, J., Pereira-García, S., & Devís-Devís, J. (2016). Abjection and alterity in the imagining of transgender in physical education and sport: A pedagogical approach in higher education. *Sport, Education and Society*, *21*(7), 985–1002. https://doi.org/10.1080/13573322.2014.981253

Phipps, A. (2016). Whose personal is more political? *Feminist Theory*, *17*(3). https://doi.org/10.1177/1464700116663831

Phipps, C. (2019). Thinking beyond the binary: Barriers to trans participation in university sport. *International Review for the Sociology of Sport.* https://doi.org/10.1177/1012690219889621

Ravenhill, J.P., & de Visser, O.R. (2017). Perceptions of gay men's masculinity are associated with their sexual self-label, voice quality and physique. *Psychology & Sexuality*, *8*(3), 208–222. https://doi.org/10.1080/19419899.2017.1343746

Resisters United UK. (2021). https://resistersunited.org/

Saeidzadeh, Z. (2020). "Are trans men the manliest of men?" Gender practices, trans masculinity and mardānegī in contemporary Iran. *Journal of Gender Studies*, *29*(3), 295–309. https://doi.org/10.1080/09589236.2019.1635439

Schilt, K. (2010). *Just one of the guys?* USA: University of Chicago Press.

Sedgewick, E.K. (1995). *Gosh, Boy George, you must be awfully secure in your masculinity!* https://latinomasculinities.files.wordpress.com/2012/01/sedgwick-gosh-boy-george1.pdf

Serano, J. (2013). *Excluded.* USA: Seal.

Spandler, H., Erikainen, S., Hopkins, A., Caudwell, J., Newman, H., & Whitehouse, L. (2020). *Non-binary inclusion in sport.* Leap Sports. https://leapsports.org/files/4225-Non-Binary%20Inclusion%20in%20sport%20Booklet.pdf

Waldron, J. (2019). Four perspectives for understanding LGBTIQ people in sport. Krane, V. (Ed.) *Sex, gender, and sexuality in sport: Queer inquiries* (pp.15–32). Abingdon: Routledge.

Warner, M. (2000). *The trouble with normal: Sex, politics, and the ethics of queer life.* Cambridge, Mass: Harvard University Press.

Yeadon-Lee, T. (2016). *Trans bodies, trans selves: A resource for the transgender community.* UK: Oxford University Press. https://doi.org/10.1017/S0047279416000167

Zanghellini, A. (2020). *Philosophical problems with the gender-critical feminist argument against trans inclusion.* UK: SAGE. https://doi.org/10.1177/2158244020927029

6

SPORTING COMMUNITIES

Introduction

This chapter considers what people had to say about their sporting communities. Sporting communities are understood here as consisting of teammates, family, friends and allies, but also include those organisations responsible for deciding the criteria for inclusion for trans people. Sporting communities had a big impact on people's experiences as they were often intrinsic to their sense of belonging in sport, for instance, by feeling valued, affirmed, supported and welcome.

Barriers to inclusion for trans people in sport are not isolated to a single issue, such as transitioning, or changing rooms. Rather, they intersect with other factors, such as other people and environments, making participation more complex and unpredictable. Participants spoke about how being trans sometimes felt overwhelming and sport sometimes offered a way to forget about those feelings for a time. Often this was attributed to having a supportive sporting community around them.

The Value of Supportive Teammates

Participating in sport helps people feel connected to other people (Griffiths et al., 2017). Physical activity is known to increase both our social and emotional capital and our physical and psychological well-being (Barras et al., 2021). For trans people, whose bodies are frequently policed and politicised in sporting contexts, there can be fear and hesitation in participating in sport. Trans people have reported that sporting spaces are not always a welcoming environment (Caudwell, 2014, 2020), and the binary organisation of sport in general can cause significant barriers to participation (Afroozeh et al., 2023). This can result

DOI: 10.4324/9781003385486-7

in trans people 'choosing not to participate in these activities or choosing to participate in individual sports that avoid body exposure and are less demanding in terms of social recognition' (Piggott, 2020, p. 7).

The active support and encouragement of teammates were cited by several participants as key to their feeling included in sport. For example, Tom said they felt more comfortable about joining a water polo team when they went with a friend who is also trans. Tom said 'I wouldn't have gone alone but having another trans person with me...we decided to go along together and try it out [because] I was expecting it to not be particularly trans friendly'. Annie, who participates in motor racing, said, 'in general everyone is very, very supportive, and also, I've never had any hassle [from teammates]'. Freya, who only started playing roller derby after she had come out as trans, spoke about how both the sport and her teammates helped her feel better about herself and her gender identity. She said:

> I know how important it is for my wellbeing … the running is how I process things, and the roller derby is how I made friendships and community. If I didn't have those two things my life would be in a much, er, I want to say dark, it would be less complete in a way … sport is really important to me, and I want other people to have access too.

Being with like-minded people helped participants feel accepted as an equal member of their team. Sport can give meaning to a person's sense of identity and is often a shared experience (Bale 2003; Carter, Burdsey and Doidge, 2018). Sharing a love of sport with others helps to establish feelings of teamness, which can reinforce a sense of communality (Ehrlén and Villi, 2020). In turn this helped people strengthen social ties and create bonds within sports settings (Barras and Frith, 2023; Hinch and Kono, 2018).

For example, Joe spoke about how much they valued their teammates' support, and it was 'really nice' how their rugby teammates did so much to welcome them. When I asked Joe for some examples, they explained how it was not just one thing, but many different things, such as using inclusive language (Joe's pronouns) and welcoming Joe into the women's changing rooms whilst they were transitioning. Together these things made Joe feel supported, accepted and safe on the rugby team for who they are, making them feel equal. Joe said:

> They [Joe's teammates] all would actively not gender the team … and they would … call the coaches out and say, please don't say girls, can you try and say team … if we were changing, someone would let me know what the showers looked like. All of them without thinking were very inclusive of me … exclusively used male pronouns … without fail … that was a massive thing … they would see me get changed … that was really validating … I still looked like a stereotypical cis woman, so it was great.

As previously discussed, the transition period for some people can be difficult to navigate, as it can bring about changes to an individual's sporting habits, such as moving from a men's to a women's team. Having supportive teammates can greatly improve this process. Joe talked of how during transition it became 'quite difficult … but I carried on because I love playing, and my teammates were great, I loved my team mates, and they were like, we don't know what you're doing but it's fine, just, do what you want (laughs)'.

Jude, who plays roller derby, was also able to share the changing facilities without worrying, and said, 'after a game everyone goes and showers together and nobody like, bats an eyelid, like everyone's just like, cool, and it feels really inclusive … regardless of my body, I'm going to be accepted in this team'. In this way, teammates all have a part to play in building effective alliances. Joe, who had previously played water polo on the women's team, switched to playing rugby on an LGBTQ+ women's team once they started their transition. They talked about their reservations, and how these were alleviated by the presence of other trans players on the team. Although they had never played rugby before, Joe joined a queer team at university. Joe said that because 'there were two, three trans people who had played with them before, and there was one there that I was friends with … I knew it was safe it was just a far more relaxed environment. It wasn't we're here to win, it was we're here to have fun'. Understandably, it can be less daunting to join a new sport when others we can relate to are already visibly playing. Representation matters.

Katy talked at length about how supportive her football teammates were. Some teammates had even told Katy that it was 'really unfair that you can't play [because of the FA's rules] … they were aware of the fact that it was upsetting for me that I couldn't play and they could, so they were really good about it, the club as a whole was really good about it'. When I asked Katy how her teammates had supported her during a difficult period of hormone testing which the Football Association requested she do, she said she thought 'it captured their imagination a bit, and that brought with it that whole kind of like, this is an injustice issue'.

Sport is meaningful and creates bonds between people because they may share an identity, a passion or certain values. In their paper on boundary work and the construction of a body-positive dance community, Hill, Sandford and Enright (2016) interviewed dancers at an LGBTQ-friendly adult ballet school about what their participation meant to them. The authors found that the opportunity of taking a class which was gender inclusive, gender neutral and body positive encouraged individuals to enjoy dance as 'a space in which participants can challenge and rewrite the boundaries and meanings of their physical culture through the co-construction of shared localized values' (Hill et al., 2016, p. 673). Being alongside other like-minded people, as the participants in this research sometimes were, helped to create shared values, shared experiences and shared stories. Tom, who 'loves being part of a team, or something competitive or training,' also said:

> I just like achieving things as a group and having someone to share the achievement with … like the feeling of just scoring a goal and maybe two or three people are involved in it, and looking at each other and smiling and thinking yes, we did that together. For me that's a really fulfilling feeling, more than when I go swimming or set a better time, or maybe do a few more lengths than I've done before.

Tom's experience was improved by a shared motivation for their team's success and their part in achieving this. As Gleaves (2017, p. 29) writes, sports inherently involve the creation of 'a story we tell ourselves about ourselves' (Gleaves, 2017, p. 29). That is, taking part in sport helped the participants to create meaningful narratives about themselves which went beyond the more usual reasons for participation, such as health, well-being and socialising. This was Katy's experience at her community football club. Katy said because her teammates were openly trans inclusive, by extension the football club saw they had 'a chance for them to say they can genuinely be inclusive, because there are people who fall short of that, and they were really good about that'. Sport does promote physical health, but what makes it so 'enduringly captivating' (Gleaves, 2017, p. 30) is the way it 'carves out this space through its ability to create meaning through explanatory stories, or narratives that people have shaped sport to tell' (Gleaves, 2017, p. 30). For Katy and her teammates, her participation in football became a social justice issue, too, and one of allyship.

Gleaves (2017) goes on to argue how these meaningful sporting narratives can subsequently increase in meaning when a person's sporting identity becomes aligned with their gender identity. As demonstrated in this book, sport's meaningful narratives are not the work of individuals alone but can be boosted by a welcoming sporting community. Gleaves (2017, p. 36, drawing on Schechtman, 2011 and Nelson, p. 33) describes this as 'social scaffolding', because these narratives involve collaboration between us and our teammates. As such, narratives both emerge *from* and belong *to* the community (my emphasis).

Having supportive teammates made a significant difference to people feeling welcome. Although Sarah has family 'who are accepting, which is great', it was being able to play tennis with others at her new club which contributed to her to feeling 'stronger and more confident'. Without this trans-inclusive support from her teammates, Sarah said she would 'be in trouble with my confidence'. Miles felt the inclusive nature of circus and the other performers he worked with ('everyone is cool, I feel the most at ease') also helped him to continue participating. In contrast, Alix found being around cisgender people in sport, 'very, very taxing, most of my friends are trans, so when I listen to them, I don't hear a lot of gendered nonsense'. Experiencing non-judgemental and unconditional support from fellow teammates was also mentioned by Jude, who said, when they started playing rugby, 'I didn't have a clue what was happening, but carried on going and just met a great bunch of people'.

Supportive teammates were also essential for Joe to continue playing rugby. They said their teammates were:

> Really accepting and loving and trans people had played for them before, and there was still one there, and like it was just the most accepting bunch of people that I've come into contact with. And honestly, they did so much for me.

Like Katy, Joe had teammates who stood up for them when they were not permitted to play by their sporting organisation. When Joe faced issues from the organisation British Universities and Colleges Sport (BUCS, National Governing Body of university sport in the United Kingdom), regarding their eligibility to play whilst transitioning, it was their teammates who advocated for their inclusion. Joe described how their 'teammates [said] … we have a trans guy playing for us, and your policy is bullshit … my three teammates, they couldn't change it, they were three small people, but they were trying'. When I asked Joe why it mattered so much that their teammates were so active in their support of them when disputing the BUCS policy, they said it was because:

> I was Captain of the women's team. I care a lot about this team, I don't want them to get in trouble. 'Cos BUCS are really arsey about games, and if you like miss some … you get charged a lot of money [and] the team suffer.

The stories here all demonstrate that being with their teammates provides a sense of feeling welcomed and included and supported for participants. In some cases, cis teammates went out of their way to challenge the existing criteria for (trans) inclusion in their own club and advocate for better inclusion. This empowered participants to shape and influence their own involvement and ultimately have a meaningful experience in sport.

The Value of Supportive Sporting Organisations and Trans Role Models

Sports organisations often only accommodate those individuals who conform to the gender binary, which in turn can 'enforce social constructions of gender, effectively excluding many transgender participants from sport' (C. Phipps, 2019, p. 4). Many sporting organisations at local, national, amateur and professional levels often have different policies for inclusion for trans participants. However, as Jenny explained, 'most of them fall into line with UK Sport guidance for domestic competition, and with the IOC for international competition'.

Even those organisations which are openly LGBTQ+ inclusive still often subsume trans people's issues and experiences within a single LGBTQ+ policy (Caudwell, 2014), failing to consider specific barriers trans people may face in sport. Jenny's own experiences with British Mountain Bike Orienteering (BMBO), the national governing body for her own sport, cycling, was, she said, 'amazing, they have got a really, really positive trans policy, and actually they just let people self-declare'. However, Jenny had 'mixed feelings' about other organisations, such as the U.K.'s Sports Council Equality Group,[1] who she felt had a disproportionate focus on testosterone as a measure of criteria to determine whether a trans participant had any advantage over other participants. Jenny's experience with BMBO was 'very, very positive, my experience with them has been brilliant'. Jenny concluded, 'if everyone had policies which were much more like BMBO's ... that would be a definite step, it would cease putting people off'. When I asked Jenny what she felt the reasons might be for some organisations being less inclusive than others towards trans people, she said it was 'sad' that some organisations 'are so wrapped up in putting barriers up in place to prevent people, and you sort of wonder what their motivation is, is it institutional transphobia, or is it a few individuals in those organisations who are pulling the strings?'

Jenny raises a good point. Trans feminist academics and activists have long been thinking of ways in which alliances can be formed between different groups by instead looking towards shared inequalities, such as sexism and misogyny, and how they might collectively challenge these for a greater impact on change (Olufemi, 2020; Pearce et al., 2020). One way to build these alliances is by encouraging all sporting organisations, not just those who position themselves as being LGBTQ+ inclusive, to be visibly trans inclusive, rather than expect an individual player to request a change. For example, Tom, who plays water polo with an LGBT club, said that whilst his own LGBTQ+ club had been active in being inclusive towards trans players, there were still occasional issues. They said the water polo club had:

> Told us we can decide what our gender is for the matches ... if anyone has a problem with it, then they will take on the battle. Which is nice, but it takes confidence to play in a match, but also, it sounds like it's going to end up with a lot of pressure on us.

Tom's experience shows how it is crucial for a club to do the work of inclusion themselves, rather than expecting the excluded person to do the emotional labour of changing the culture at an organisational level. We know visibility and representation in sport have a measurable impact, for example, the *This Girl Can* (UK) campaign has shown that 'a targeted, high profile initiative can drive participation in a group that has traditionally been known for poor take up of sporting activity' (Pride Sports, 2016, p. 4). Past experiences of homo or transphobia have resulted in some participants feeling worried about being, as Jude said, 'visibly queer' in sporting spaces if cannot preempt how friendly those spaces are going to be.

In other words, being able to just turn up at a club or sports facility was not always possible for trans participants, because they worried beling, as Katy previously said, 'allowed' to play. Katy had been subjected to intensive and intrusive testing by the Football Association before she was allowed to play on her local, amateur team. She said how hard it was going to training every week where 'everyone was allowed to play, and I wasn't … it created this social barrier, that I wasn't quite one of the team because I was different'.

Although her teammates understood the reason for Katy being excluded (due to invasive hormone testing), this did not help Katy's feelings of isolation. Being part of the team both on and off the pitch was a very important part of Katy's sporting identity.

Creating Inclusive Spaces

According to research carried out by Pride Sports for Sport England (Pride Sports, 2016), 64% of LGBT people who identified as something other than male or female (e.g. genderfluid or genderqueer) were not active enough to maintain good health. As there is an established link between recreational sport participation, self-esteem and reduced levels of stress (Jewett et al., 2019), this is an important consideration for anyone whose mental health would benefit from inclusion in physical activity. The difficulty of engaging with sport for trans people menas potentially being excluded from the substantial positive change participation may bring. This not just mental and physical health, but the feeling of community belonging which participation in sport often creates. Sport is not always about the activity; it can offer a valuable and meaningful connection to a person's wider community, increasing their social capital.

This was the experience of Freya, whose experience of roller derby was welcoming, and of Miles, who found the circus community to be 'just great, they were so accepting [of me]'. When a sporting community or organisation is accepting from the very start, as Freya's and Miles's had been, the positive experience increases. The alternative, as Charlotte explained, is that:

> You have all the sporting bodies putting out policies … you need to have the right hormone levels … or surgery…you think … can I join, and then it's hang on a minute, I'll have to check,… so you don't ever turn up … you don't really know if you'll be accepted or not, unless you really, really want to play that sport, you end up just giving up.

The importance of best practice, social justice and the centring of the personal accounts and lived experiences of trans people in sport are becoming more prevalent in some areas of research, with the aim of providing practical and helpful suggestions for creating inclusive environments within sport, on and off the field (Kauer and Rauscher, 2019; Spandler et al., 2020; Lawrence, Hill and Mowatt, 2024). Whilst six participants had specific ideas about sport and sports settings being more inclusive, there was also the suggestion about mainstream sports settings becoming more inclusive generally, not just for trans people, but for all. For trans people to feel welcome, it is important to embed trans inclusion in policies and practices and actively identify ways in which this can happen. For example, Freya suggested staff could use more gender-neutral language, 'such as folks rather than guys', and Alix suggested training could be provided for gym staff about exercising in a binder. Gym membership forms can be easily adapted to include titles such as Mx or adding a text box for people to write in their gender identity.

It is not enough for an organisation to appear inclusive; it needs to be visibly so. Tom's experience of playing water polo with an LGBT-friendly club was that there was 'a real effort at including us'. Tom explained the club were making an active effort 'trying to get more trans people involved, they run free polo sessions'. Harry said changing the way in which teams are organised may encourage him and others to participate more. He said, 'if it was kind of mixed sport, or all gender sport, or something like that, I still like competition and stuff, but, if that aspect was removed, I think I'd be much more inclined to engage'. Mixed teams were also suggested by Tom, who said trans young people can be encouraged to participate by not always enforcing gender segregated teams. Tom said:

> I think the most important thing is, for team sports … is the long-term shift of having more mixed teams. Especially for younger people, so there's a tendency to split groups up from about 11 or 12, into boys and girls. I think it would be better to not do that … for young non-binary or trans people whose friends might be different genders, being able to continue playing sports with your friends without having any pressure to join different teams, or stop entirely, would make a really big difference in playing sports later on.

This means that the onus should be on the wider sporting community such as organisations and sporting bodies to 'proactively facilitate inclusion … and actively create an inclusive environment, so trans people feel welcome enough to come along in the first place' (Erikainen et al., 2020, n.p.). Sports community organisations need to be visibly supportive at all times and seek to engage with trans people and considerations about inclusion. And whilst, as Ahmed (2017) argues, considering this arrangement is still often left to trans and non-binary people to instigate, this chapter has shown that there are teammates and allies already supporting their trans friends with great success.

Visible Role Models for Everyone

Another way to improve and promote trans inclusion in sporting organisations is by encouraging visible role models, and this was mentioned by Annie, Freya and Katy. Sport is inspirational and role models are important, and the positive impact of initiatives like *This Girl Can* (2015), *Kick It Out* (2024) and *Title IX* (2024) are well known for encouraging underserved communities to take up sport. Such recognition of the power of these initiatives makes a difference when promoting inclusivity and encouraging participation, and this was reflected in the narratives of some of the participants. The benefits that friendships and social interactions can foster are well documented (Knoppers and McDonald, 2010)., Sport can help to reduce social isolation, and sports organisations have a duty to change this and encourage more trans role models and visible representation.

Spandler et al., 2020 Types of role models can include a family member, peer or celebrity sports person (Gilani et al., 2021; Young et al., 2015), and can be defined as an individual who inspires others through personal contact and relationship (Ingall, 1997; Yancey, 1998). Annie's own commitment to being visible in her sport, motor racing, for example, was because 'lots of trans people do not want to engage with sports, they are worried about other people'. For Annie, who considered herself a role model to other racers, she liked to be able to say to others, 'it's alright, go ahead, there're always nice people even when you least expect them'. Alice talked about how seeing a trans woman and former pro-cyclist commentating on a mainstream, popular television programme made her feel more confident about being visible herself at sporting events. As such she understood the significance of being a role model for younger gender non-conforming cyclists. Alice said she can 'understand how people can feel different and separated from other people … how do we make these people feel included … how do we make it a good day for them?' Katy found that her identity as a trans woman footballer opened up new ways to connect with sport and she 'had something to fight for'. Katy said:

> It's got me involved in LGBT sports activism ever since, because I met a lot of people through it, people who were advocating for me, and got some help. So that was actually a positive, but of course you shouldn't have to need to have these hardships to get that, but I guess that's normally how that happens.

When I asked Katy how barriers might be reduced to participation, the importance of role models was her first answer. She said:

> There are obvious ones, visible role models. I hear this a lot from trans people who want to get involved in sport, and don't feel they can, is that first interaction … some things we might need to check, but please come on down.

When Jude first watched roller derby, they said it made them feel like they 'wanted to be part of that. I wanna do that too', and that they were also inspired to take up rugby after watching women's rugby on television. Jude said they wanted to do the same, because they 'just love running around outside, you know, being free'. Jude's health and well-being were greatly improved not just by playing rugby and roller derby, but by being with others who also enjoyed it and accepted them as a fellow player. Jude had been inspired to try rugby and roller derby because they had watched others and felt a connection.

Realistic role models are not only important for trans people. Cis women and, to a lesser degree, cis men also endure discrimination and bodily objectification in sport, and this book has drawn attention to the ways in which sport continues to use gender normativity and hegemonic masculinity to maintain and sustain this. Vescio et al.'s (2005) evaluation of 25 Australian good practice case studies identified that a lack of positive role models for adolescent girls can impede their participation in sport (Young et al., 2015), and this finding has been replicated across a number of countries including the United States (Women's Sports Foundation, 2024), Canada (Canadian Association for the Advancement of Women and Sport and Physical Activity, 2012) and Britain (Tibballs, 2013). There are similar findings within LGBTQ+ studies on the importance of visible role models for trans young people. A report by Mermaids (Barras, 2023), a UK charity which supports trans, non-binary and gender diverse young people, gathered data from 180 participants aged between 11 and 16 about their experiences in sport. The report found that positive, visible role models across all media helped encourage participation and continuation in sport for young people.

Similarly, Katy explained, in her experience, inclusion in sport for LGBT+ people is generally not always well attended to, because 'often, sports is so bad at LGB+ plus stuff quite frankly, and we're [trans people] just tacked on the end of that, and sports is one of the areas where the key to inclusion works quite differently to LGB inclusion'. When I asked Katy what could be done to improve inclusivity for trans people in sporting organisations, she said, 'trans stuff really needs to be about including us in mainstream clubs'. This could extend to those involved in sport in other ways, Katy said, 'it doesn't always have to be playing, it can be administration or officiating as well'. When I posed the same question to Alice, she replied that 'openness … in clubs, in governing bodies, and national federations … if it was made more visible [like] … we don't care what your gender is … if you want to come and cycle, swim, you are more than welcome … that we are for everybody, really'.

Sport Is Meaningful, Pleasurable and Can Create Alliances

What the lived experiences of all the participants revealed was, no matter what barriers they might have encountered in relation to their sporting body, sporting spaces or sporting community, they still found a way to be involved in sport. Whilst in part this was for their own physical, mental and physiological health and well-being, it was also because sport was meaningful to them. That is, participants found something which fundamentally transcended the more commonly noted health benefits of sport.

According to Chen (1998), meaningfulness in sport and physical exercise involves consideration of the purpose and goals of movement, judgements related to the emotional value of the experience, and a sense of coherence that provides a 'big picture' comprehension and connection between these and other life experiences. Chen (1998) sees personal meaning interpretations as being constructed in relation to the world, where individuals make connections to 'something that reaches beyond the actual experience, linking it to something else' (Chen, 1998, p. 286). Persia spoke of how swimming and yoga had 'made my body strong and lithe, they made my body basically'. Miles, who enjoys swimming, said it was 'so good for you, you just get in the water and ahhhhh'. For Alice, whose gender dysphoria dates back to her early teens, taking part in open water swimming meant she could 'put on a wetsuit with electric blue toenails and no one will give a damn, because I'm just there for a swim'. Sarah felt tennis had 'saved me, basically, it saved me', and without it in her life she would 'not be very confident'. Evident inall these recollections are moments of joy, where pleasurable connections between the body and sport helped people to establish and affirm their own athletic performance, gender identity and sporting ability. This is discussed by Caudwell, who calls it 'collective pleasure' (Caudwell, 2020, p. 7), and was something she observed in her research with adults at a local trans swimming group. Caudwell (2020, p. 7) writes of how after being in the pool, participants reported feeling 'happy, content, calm, relaxed, confident, healthy, body confident, relieved, refreshed, peaceful, natural, energized, and motivated to do more exercise. In addition to these feelings, there is evidence of a collective pleasure'.

In her study, Caudwell (2020) linked this pleasure to the opportunity swimming provided for positive displays of the body, and this physical joy was shared by some participants in this book. In the context of recreational sport, face-to-face contact and shared physical experiences are also important for establishing emotionally meaningful social relationships (Ehrlén and Villi, 2020). This interaction not only is a facilitator of social relationships but can also be perceived as a meaningful social practice which is integral to feeling good (Serafinelli, 2017). Katy said:

> Team sports [helped] me get out of social isolation … it did help me to get out and see people and socialise more … even when I couldn't competitively play, or be involved at all, that would help me to get out and meet people a little bit more, which is a thing we see in LGBT communities, especially trans communities.

Like Katy, Joe was well supported by their manager and teammates, but felt the wider issue of transphobia and positive representation for trans players is still not fully addressed in the sporting community. For Katy, there was the wider issue, that 'you can't leave it to LGBT people to complain. Because then we get targeted even more'. The necessity of allies and strong support from teammates are essential for fostering shared attitudes, common interests or goals for many participants. Whilst sport can be empowering and inclusive, it can also be intimidating and stressful, especially when reflecting upon all the intersecting barriers at play between sporting bodies, sporting spaces and sporting communities. It is also unfair to expect the trans community to do all of the heavy lifting in challenging transphobia.

Rather than divide women and erase their achievements in sport, the lived experiences of participants demonstrate that there is an opportunity for shared meaning and relevance with those they play sport with. By experiencing these moments of meaningfulness, participants were able to engage deeply with their sporting community and connect with others in an enjoyable environment (Hill et al., 2016).

Summary

Sporting communities are made up of teammates, organisations and role models, all of whom can have an impact on a person's sporting experience. One way in which alliances can be formed in sport is by working together to challenge and change the structural inequalities in sport and create new approaches. Instead of an over-reliance on inconclusive science, the common-sense position and biological essentialism, feminist alliances can work together in addressing the continuing marginalisation of (cis) women's sport, organising for solutions to end discrimination in sport. New feminist alliances could be formed, to 'better collectively speak back and organise against oppressive structures like sexism on a local and global scale, by unsettling the idea that binaries divide us' (Olufemi, 2020, p. 158.). Trans-exclusionary voices within feminist circles only serve to divide feminists and support a cis normative and oppressive status quo. Trans feminist theory operationalises a deconstruction of the sporting heteropatriarchy, 'debunking the assumed naturalness or normalness of the sex, gender, and sexuality binaries that the institution of sport works so hard to enforce' (Kauer and Rauscher, 2019, p. 55).

Trans feminism and queer politics and perspectives have been fundamental in their contribution to challenging discrimination in sport, and as Heyes (2003, p. 1094) wrote, 'feminists of all stripes share the political goal of weakening the grip of oppressive sex and gender dimorphisms in Western cultures'. If one of the primary goals of feminism is to challenge biology as destiny, then examining the enforced binaries within the nexus of sex, gender and sexuality (Heyes, 2003) can offer up new ways of thinking about how alliances might be forged. According to de Vries (2015), the lives of women and trans people are considered less valuable in a patriarchal society, a shared suffering resulting in a shared claim to feminism. In the face of this shared oppression, taking a trans feminist perspective, the lived experiences of the participants supports the view that forming alliances is 'a far more effective political strategy than fomenting divisions and creating false debates about who 'really' gets to be considered a woman, and therefore share in feminist movements' (Carrera-Fernández and DePalma, 2020, p. 757).

Trans feminism asks that the similarities between the oppressions faced by cis and trans women (and others who are positioned on the margins in sport, including intersex athletes) need to be recognised. There is more potential for collaboration between communities than division. This collaboration might include cis women who choose not to (or do not want to) conform to unrealistic beauty standards and gender normative stereotypes, wear revealing sports clothing or be subjected to other patriarchal expectations demanded of them in sports environments.

The alliances which could be formed here in sport could be focused on what Butler called in *The New Statesman* 'gender freedom ... the political claim to live freely and without fear of discrimination and violence against the genders that we are' (Ferber, 2020, n.p.). That is, the idea that all people get to make a political claim about their gender, and to be open about the ways in which traditional gender presentations might be constraining for some people. The lived experiences of participants in sport has helped to challenge the gender binary: even when people are comfortably situated at one end of it, their very presence in sport leads to a better understanding of the value of supportive sporting communities, and a greater appreciations of what it means to be a trans person in sport. The fight for equality and the connection made with trans feminism in sport starts with questioning who is included/excluded, and why. As Humphrey (2020, n.p.) reflected in *The Guardian*, 'a trans and feminist dialogue can only work through respectful alliance, not divisiveness. It can only be effective through abandoning the dead-end of territory-claiming wars over biology and rights'. Rather than focusing on what might be lost for cis women in sport when trans women are welcomed, the focus needs to be on what could be gained from rethinking conventions of sex and gender and to deal 'generously, not defensively, with change' (Humphrey, 2020, n.p.).

These lived experiences, which carry the same importance as feminist and cis people's experiences, allow what Rofes (2005, p. 87) called a drawing upon of 'status queer' to 'rethink our efforts and our role in either maintaining or radically transforming the status quo'. They are also fundamentally, as Krane

(2019) argues, about treating trans athletes with dignity and respect. The socially constructed gender binary, and, with it, a gender normative and essentialist expectation serve to exclude those who transgress this normativity, and sporting communities have a role to play in acknowledging and being sympathetic to those who feel excluded. As Butler concluded in their interview in *The New Statesman* (Ferber, 2020, n.p.):

> We fight those misrepresentations because they are false and because they reflect more about the misogyny of those who make demeaning caricatures than they do about the complex social diversity of women. Women should not engage in the forms of phobic caricature by which they have been traditionally demeaned. And by 'women' I mean all those who identify in that way.

Participants talked both about the value of visible role models for themselves and of being role models to others in the wider LGBTQ+ community. Adopting a trans feminist approach has a focus on community building, including representatives of diverse groups in organisational roles, better support for non-binary and other gender-diverse people and working towards facilitating access to sport. Feminism has long acknowledged that different experiences and identities open up shared goals, and solidarity remains at the heart of most feminist thinking. Trans feminism welcomes alliances and dignity and questions notions of authenticity – of who is, or can be, considered to be a 'woman'. By ecluding trans people from sport, this authenticity 'breaches the goals of equality and dignity [and] runs counter to the ability to fulfil a liveable life or, often, a life at all' (Hines, 2019, p. 155).

There is a clear opportunity for us all to reconsider ways in which alliances can perhaps be formed with others and look towards ways to reduce hostility in practical ways in sport, an idea shared by participants. After all, 'one of the most distressing aspects of the hostile narrative', writes Kim Humphrey in *The Guardian* (Humphrey, 2020, n.p.), 'is that it side-lines a reality of alliance'. Gender critical feminists are unnecessarily set in opposition within public discourses against trans people 'on a seemingly unrelenting path of mutual antagonism … trans rights have been pitted against sex-based rights for "real" women, with conflict forever spiralling into charge and counter charge of hate speech and silencing, and into bitter social media wars' (Hines, 2019, p. 155). Some people in this book had a long history of participating in sport, whilst others had found a new connection with sport, one which helped them to both establish and affirm their gender identity. The importance of participating in sport for physical, mental and psychological health and well-being and social change are woven together with the benefits friendships and interactions bring (Hill et al., 2016).

Before turning to the next chapter to read how to put this book into practice, spend ten minutes reflecting on your own thoughts on this book. What actions might you instigate to make your workplace or classroom more inclusive, not just for trans people, but for everyone?

Putting Theory into Practice: Top Ten Recommendations

This book has shown the importance of visibility of trans people in sports spaces, and the part role models, coaches and teammates all have to play in promoting inclusion in sport. Because the book is grounded in the voices of the participants, practical suggestions have been identified to facilitate inclusion and reduce barriers in sport for trans people. One of the most effective ways to do this is to encourage more trans people to participate, by making the sporting environment inclusive and friendly. Here are some suggestions:

1 Use signage and other symbolic objects (such as posters, social media, websites and other public-facing communications) to convey that a space is trans inclusive and friendly. Changes to membership forms, for example by adding 'Mx' to the list of titles, are a simple way to achieve this when a person joins.
2 Offer gender-neutral changing facilities, which have single cubicles with doors, so privacy is assured. This is often seen in swimming pools, where cubicles are poolside and anyone can use them. Sanitary bins and products should be placed in all changing rooms, baby changing facilities, and toilets.
3 Give sensitive and relevant training to all staff as standard on gender-inclusive practices. LGBTQ+ organisations such as Pride Sports UK and Trans Can Sport should be used. Using more gender-neutral language (such as 'folks' rather than 'guys') should be introduced where possible, whilst recognising that such changes can take time, and mistakes are part of the learning process.
4 Include cis staff in all discussions to promote allyship and work through any concerns as a whole. This can help to alleviate reservations they may have about trans people being included and help with challenging the misconceptions some cis people have about trans people in sport; this was an idea many participants raised. This will help form stronger alliances between users of sporting spaces and amongst the sporting community.
5 Having an organisational-wide policy which makes it clear that LGBT+ abuse will not be tolerated and do not hesitate to enforce this policy when it happens.
6 Academic research about practical ways to improve inclusion for trans people in sport should be freely shared with universities and sports colleges, organisations such as British Universities and Colleges Sport (BUCS) and places teaching sports studies.

7 Information should also be provided for local authority run leisure facilities which have dedicated diversity and inclusion officers. Many private businesses who provide gym and fitness facilities for their staff may also benefit from information about improving inclusion for trans people in sport.
8 Organising spaces such as gyms to reflect they are used by a mix of people. Where possible, adjusting the layout of these spaces would help to accommodate not just gender-diverse people, but those who may have cultural or religious needs. For example, exercise equipment stereotyped as 'feminine', such as resistance bands or balance balls, could be placed in the 'masculine' weights area.
9 Clothing policies could be relaxed (when safe to do so) to allow people to wear what they feel comfortable in. This would promote inclusion for bodies of all shapes, sizes and ages.
10 Offering trans-only sessions which are regular, not at inconvenient times, or cancelled at short notice.

This book acknowledges that some changes – such as reconfiguring outdoor spaces – may be harder to instigate, but this does not mean small changes such as those listed above could not be made.

Note

1 Jenny was right to feel concerned: in 2021 the Sports Council Equality Group published their new guidance for transgender inclusion in Domestic Sport (SCEG, 2020). You can read a critique of this report at https://sportsmedialgbt.com/new-trans-guidance-is-backwards-step-say-uks-leading-lgbtiq-sports-organisations, which I co-authored.

References

[This Girl Can]. (2015). https://www.thisgirlcan.co.uk/

[Title IX]. (2024). https://titleix.harvard.edu/what-title-ix

[Women's Sports Foundation]. (2024). https://www.womenssportsfoundation.org/

Afroozeh, M.S., Phipps, C., Afrouzeh, A., Mehri, A., & Alipour Asiri, Z. (2023). "The spectators ask, is it a boy or a girl? What is it?": Cultural cisgenderism and trans men's sporting experiences in Iran. *International Review for the Sociology of Sport*. https://doi.org/10.1177/10126902231162270

Ahmed. S. (2017). *Living a feminist life*. USA: Duke University Press.

Bale, J. (2003). *Sports geography*. London: Routledge.

Barras, A. (2023). *Young People and Sport: understanding the experiences of young transgender, non-binary and gender diverse people in sport and physical exercise the UK*. Mermaids. https://mermaidsuk.org.uk/research/

Barras, A., & Frith, H. (2023). 'Cos not everyone wants to talk, they prefer to do, to move': circuits of trans embodied pleasure and inclusion in sport and physical exercise. *Sport, Education and Society*. https://doi.org/10.1080/13573322.2023.2266755

Barras, A., Frith, H., Jarvis, N., & Lucena, R. (2021). Timelines and transitions: Understanding transgender and non-binary people's participation in everyday sport and physical exercise through a temporal lens. In: S. Bekker, I. Costas Batlle, B.C. Clift, J. Gore, S. Gustafsson, & J. Hatchard (Eds.). *Temporality in qualitative inquiry: Theories, methods and practices* (pp. 57–71). London: Routledge.

Canadian Association for the Advancement of Women and Sport and Physical Activity. (2012). Available at: https://cwhn.ca/en/node/14578

Carrera-Fernández, M.V., & DePalma, R. (2020). Feminism will be trans-inclusive or it will not be: Why do two cis-hetero woman educators support transfeminism? *The Sociological Review*, *68*(4). UK: SAGE. https://doi.org/10.1177/0038026120934686

Carter, T.F., Burdsey, D., & Doidge, M. (2018). *Transforming sport: Knowledges, practices, structures*. London: Routledge.

Caudwell, J. (2014). [Transgender] young men: Gendered subjectivities and the physically active body. *Sport, Education and Society*, *19*(4), 398–414. https://doi.org/10.1080/13573322.2012.672320

Caudwell, J. (2020). Transgender and non-binary swimming in the UK: Indoor public pool spaces and un/safety. *Frontiers in Sociology*, *5*. https://doi.org/10.3389/fsoc.2020.00064

Chen, A. (1998). Meaningfulness in physical education: A description of high school students' conceptions. *Journal of Teaching in Physical Education*, *17*, 285–306. https://doi.org/10.1123/jtpe.17.3.285

de Vries, Kylan Mattias (2015). Transgender people of color at the center: Conceptualizing a new intersectional model. *Ethnicities*, *15*(1), 3–27. https://doi.org/10.1177/1468796814547058

Ehrlén, V., & Villi, M. (2020). "I shared the joy": Sport-related social support and communality on Instagram. *Visual Studies*, *35*(2–3), 260–272. https://doi.org/10.1080/1472586X.2020.179030

Erikainen, S., Vincent, B., & Hopkins, A. (2020). Specific detriment: Barriers and opportunities for non-binary inclusive sports in Scotland. *Journal of Sport and Social Issues*. https://doi.org/10.1177/0193723520962937

Ferber, A. (2020, September 22). *Judith Butler on the culture wars, J K Rowling and living in "anti-intellectual times"*. New Statesman. https://www.google.com/search?client=firefox-b-dandq=the+new+stsatesman+butler

Gilani, M., Wallach, P., & Andreas, K. (2021). Levels of physical activity and barriers to sport participation in young people with gender dysphoria. *Journal of Pediatric Endocrinology and Metabolism*, *34*(6), 747–753. https://doi.org/10.1515/jpem-2021-0007

Gleaves, J. (2017). Sport as meaningful narratives. *Journal of the Philosophy of Sport*, *44*(1), 29–43. https://doi.org/10.1080/00948705.2017.1280407

Griffiths, K., Bullough, S., Shibli, S., & Wilson, J. (2017). The impact of engagement in sport on graduate employability: Implications for higher education policy and practice. *International Journal of Sport Policy and Politics*, *9*(3), 431–451. https://doi.org/10.1080/19406940.2017.1359648

Heyes, C.J. (2003). Feminist solidarity after queer theory: The case of transgender. *Signs*, *28*(4), 1093–1120. https://doi.org/10.1086/343132

Hill, J., Sandford, R., & Enright, E. (2016). 'It has really amazed me what my body can now do': Boundary work and the construction of a body-positive dance community. *Sport in Society*, *19*(5), 667–679. https://doi.org/10.1080/17430437.2015.1073946

Hinch, T., & Kono, S. (2018). "Ultramarathon runners' attachment to place: An interpretation of runner generated images during on-site training camps." *Journal of Sport and Tourism 22*(2), 109–130. https://doi.org/10.1080/14775085.2017.1371065

Hines, S. (2019). The feminist frontier: On trans and feminism. *Journal of Gender Studies*, *28*(2), 145–157. https://doi.org/10.1080/09589236.2017.1411791

Humphrey, K. (2020, July 7). *Trans rights have been pitted against feminism but we're not enemies*. The Guardian. https://www.theguardian.com/commentisfree/2020/jul/07/trans-rights-have-been-pitted-against-feminism-but-were-not-enemies

Ingall, C.K. (1997). *Metaphors, maps and mirrors: Moral education in middle schools*. Frenwich: C.T. Ablex Publishing Company.

Jewett, R., Kerr, G. & Tamminen, K. (2019). University sport retirement and athlete mental health: A narrative analysis. *Qualitative Research in Sport, Exercise and Health*, *11*(3), 416–433. https://doi.org/10.1080/2159676X.2018.1506497

Kauer, K.J., & Rauscher, L. (2019). Negotiating gender among LGBTIQ athletes: Sport as a space for disruption and reproduction. In: K. Krane (Ed.). *Sex, gender, and sexuality in sport: Queer inquiries* (pp. 49–66). UK: Routledge.

Kick it Out. (2024). Available at: https://www.kickitout.org/

Knoppers, A.E., & McDonald, M.P. (2010). Scholarship on gender and sport in Sex Roles and beyond. *Sex Roles*, *63*(5), 311–323. https://doi.org/10.1007/s11199-010-9841-z

Krane, V. (2019). *Sex, gender, and sexuality in sport: Queer inquiries*. Abingdon: Routledge.

Lawrence, S., Hill, J., & Mowatt, R. A. (Eds.). (2024). Routledge Handbook of Sport, Leisure, and Social Justice. Routledge. SBN 9781032485607 (hardback) | ISBN 9781032485645 (paperback) | ISBN 9781003389682 (e-book). https://www.routledge.com/Routledge-Handbook-of-Sport-Leisure-and-Social-Justice/Lawrence-Hill-Mowatt/p/book/9781032485607

Olufemi, L. (2020). *Feminism interrupted*. UK: Pluto Press.

Pearce, R., Erikainen, S., & Vincent, B. (2020). TERF wars: An introduction. *The Sociological Review (Keele)*, *68*(4), 677–698. https://doi.org/10.1177/0038026120934713

Phipps, C. (2019). Thinking beyond the binary: Barriers to trans participation in university sport. *International Review for the Sociology of Sport*. https://doi.org/10.1177/1012690219889621

Piggott, L. (2020). Transgender, intersex and non-binary people in sport and physical activity: A review of research and policy. https://doi.org/10.13140/RG.2.2.20795.64805

Pride Sports for Sport England. (2016). *Sport, Physical Activity and LGBT*. https://www.sportengland.org/media/11116/pride-sport-sport-physical-activity-and-lgbt-report-2016.pdf

Rofes, E.E. (2005). *A radical rethinking of sexuality and schooling: Status quo or status queer?* United States: Rowman & Littlefield Publishers.

Serafinelli, E. (2017). Analysis of photo sharing and visual social relationships: Instagram as a case study. *Photographies*, *10*(1), 91–111. https://doi.org/10.1080/17540763.2016.1258657

Spandler, H., Erikainen, S., Hopkins, A., Caudwell, J., Newman, H., & Whitehouse, L. (2020). *Non-binary inclusion in sport*. Leap Sports. https://leapsports.org/files/4225-Non-Binary%20Inclusion%20in%20sport%20Booklet.pdf

Tibballs, S. (2013). Female sport in schools: The future of school and community sport. The Smith Institute, 44–51. Available from: https://www.womeninsport.org/wp-content/uploads/2015/04/Changing-the-Game-for-Girls-Policy-Report.pdf

Vescio, J., Wilde, K., & Crosswhite, J.J. (2005). Profiling sport role models to enhance initiatives for adolescent girls in physical education and sport. *European Physical Education Review*, *11*(2), 153–170. https://doi.org/10.1177/1356336X05052894

Yancey, A.K. (1998). Building positive self-image in adolescents in foster care: The use of role models in interactive group approach. *Adolescence*, *33*(130), 253–268. PMID: 9706313.

Young, J.A., Symons, C.M., Pain, M.D., Harvey, J.T., Eime, R.M., Craike, M.J., & Payne, W. R. (2015). Role models of Australian female adolescents: A longitudinal study to inform programmes designed to increase physical activity and sport participation. *European Physical Education Review*, *21*(4), 451–466. https://doi.org/10.1177/1356336X15579574

7

CONCLUSION

I hope you have enjoyed reading this book and found it both interesting and useful. Its purpose was to examine the lived experiences of trans people in everyday sport in the United Kingdom, in order to identify any potential barriers to their participation. It has done this in order to find ways to improve inclusion and offer recommendations for practitioners, as well as helping to break down some of the common discourses around fairness and safety. At the heart of this book are the stories of the 18 people who were kind enough to share these with me. In doing so, this book has placed trans people's narratives at the centre of LGBTQ+ scholarship which can often render trans people invisible. As Elling-Machartzki (2017, p. 256) notes:

> Physical activity and sports can be regarded as particularly challenging social practices for trans people, regarding the centrality of the body, gendered structures like changing rooms and competitions, and normative gender ideologies. In the emerging body of literature on trans people and sport, the main focus has been on mainstream, competitive sports as non-inclusive.

It was clear that, for the majority of participants, their lived experiences, individual actions and responses to their sporting environments were 'part of a wider social order that permits some actions and disallows others' (Lawler, 2008, p. 104). Here are the key points from the book.

DOI: 10.4324/9781003385486-8

Key Points

People's experiences are complex and heterogeneous

The intersections between people's sporting bodies, the sporting spaces they exercise in and the sporting communities they exercise alongside can be difficult to navigate when gender is viewed as non-conforming by others. Sometimes a person's sporting experience was a journey of both disruption and resolution, due to taking time out to transition, or when negotiating their own feelings about using changing rooms. Other times it was uninterrupted. Either way, participants needed to (re)learn gendered norms and behaviour in sporting contexts. Frequently, these experiences were emotional, with stories of joy, meaning, success, pleasure, fear and even sadness being shared.

People find a way to participate

Because trans people's bodies are frequently policed and politicised in sporting contexts, participants often felt anxious when involved in sport. Nonetheless, participants found a way to be involved in sport, and vocalised their involvement as a vital and valued aspect of their lives, giving them considerable joy. In some cases, sport was an opportunity for someone to (re)confirm and affirm their gender identity. Participation in sport was meaningful.

People had negative experiences...

All participants had both negative and positive experiences. Negative experiences included feeling anxious about being welcomed and accepted in gender-segregated spaces such as changing rooms, and concerns about being confronted in them and asked to leave. Often these concerns were based on past experiences of trans/homophobia, such as at school. Negative experiences also included being misgendered or incorrect pronouns being used during sport, or feeling uncomfortable wearing gendered clothing, such as a swimming costume. Sometimes these negative experiences could be mitigated by going to an activity with a friend or by attending trans-only sessions.

...and positive ones

Positive experiences included the support and allyship of teammates and friends in sport, such as the advocation for a person's inclusion on a team they had formally belonged to or on a new team. The experience of being welcomed in sport whilst transitioning was felt to be especially meaningful, because it allowed a person to maintain a relationship with their sporting identity, stay connected to friends and not feel socially isolated. In addition, many participants enjoyed the opportunity to become visible role models in their communities and to seek out ways to further include sport in their lives and careers. Participants also enjoyed engaging in everyday sport for the physical health and fitness benefits it brought. People took pride in being good at their sport and celebrated their accomplishments. Other positive experiences included the chance for someone to forget about the worries they might be dealing with in their everyday life, such as gender dysphoria. Sport was intrinsic to their overall identity, and a positive influence.

People were political with a small p

Many participants worried about using gendered spaces such as changing rooms and the ways in which gender-segregated teams caused a barrier. These spaces were often difficult for trans people to navigate and they sometimes felt unsafe. Discussions about passing revealed that some participants did not want to disrupt or challenge the gender binary in sports settings, and felt euphoria when their gender identity was affirmed by others and they were addressed correctly.

Participants were mostly discrete about the ways in which they were challenging gender normativity and hegemonic masculinity in sport: some individuals embraced binary models of sport, and did not want to break down gendered structures, though passing was sometimes necessary for safety in sporting settings. This did not mean that participants did not notice or care about the presence of gendered structures such as changing rooms in sport. In some cases, they identified examples of where cissexism, misogyny and transphobia intersected, and challenged it.

Trans men/trans masculine experiences are often overlooked

I spoke to more trans men/trans masculine people than trans women in this research. Their stories are frequently overlooked, and their experiences of (hegemonic) masculinity and passing are crucial in our understanding of how the social construction of sport continues to privilege the male body. Trans masculine participants were able to challenge sexism and misogyny and defended their cis teammates and friends when they experienced it in a way cis men often do not. Their experiences of being challenged in sex segregated spaces such as changing rooms also revealed the ways in which it is not just cis women who feel vulnerable in these environments. It was clear that passing as male conferred an assumption of competitive advantage, even if it did not exist.

Improving inclusion for everyone takes time and effort

The lived experiences of participants provide us with recommendations for reducing barriers in sport in a number of ways, and some of these are listed earlier on page. Although some participants had specific ideas about making sport and sports settings more inclusive, there was also the notion that mainstream sports would benefit from improved inclusion overall, not just for trans people, but for everyone. Participants noted certain spaces, even when labelled as LGBTQ+ friendly, were often still sites for the marginalisation for trans individuals in sporting contexts, creating barriers. As this book has consistently shown, gender identity matters, and gender identity and are always open to individual interpretation. Change also takes time and effort.

Understanding gender critical feminism

The lived experiences of the participants have revealed that trans people are frequently the victims of hostility in sport, with much of this abuse focused on the body. Yet the presence of competitive advantage being an innate quality all trans women possess never materialised. Rather, it was a person's skills (or not) in a particular sport which provided them with an advantage, or the appearance of a beard which provided the illusion of being better at sport. As this book has identified, participants were aware that the unwanted attention they sometimes faced was not dissimilar to the sexism and gender discrimination their cis friends and teammates also experienced in sport, such as in the gym. I think that gender critical feminists are frequently set in a manufactured opposition against trans communities in the UK media, and as such possible alliances are overlooked. By looking towards shared oppressions, such as discrimination in sport, we can collectively mobilise towards challenging these things whilst acknowledging our different needs.

Cis people can endure discrimination and bodily objectification in sport, and this book has highlighted how sport continues to use body politics to maintain and sustain this. Challenging the sporting heteropatriarchy means offering solidarity to those who are closest to the material impact these oppressions have on their bodies, and this means all genders, cis and trans included.

The contribution of trans feminist theory

Using trans feminist theory to examine the lived experiences of the participants offers two original contributions to the research field. Firstly, some participants in this book said they did not always wish to challenge the way sport is organised along binary lines. Trans feminist theory regards the reliance on gender binaries in sport as problematic for trans people. It calls for, if not a complete dismantling of gender binaries in sport (and more widely in society generally), then at least a calling into question the ways in which sport uses anatomy as a criteria for organisation, as well as the ways in which sport normalises binary gender structures, such as sex-segregated teams and changing rooms. Supporters of trans feminism celebrate gender fluidity, self-identification for gender and a blurring of the socially constructed reliance on gender essentialism in wider society, not only in sport. In addition, trans feminism recognises that such binary gender structures can cause barriers to participation for trans people, resulting in lower participation rates in sport than the cis population.

However, this was not always reflected in the data. Rather, a number of participants did not want to dismantle or challenge the ways in which they engaged with sport. Instead, once they established their own gender identity in relation to sport, they celebrated this, and found affirmation in being able to participate, for example, on a women's football team, or using a gendered changing room. This does not mean that such examples of gender binaries were not at times oppressive and difficult to negotiate; they were nonetheless a positive experience for many, particularly for those individuals who passed. Arguably, this could be interpreted as a matter of some participants wishing to feel safe and to conform to societal norms, but people revealed that this was only one aspect of their participation in sport. What was fundamental was the embracing and celebrating of their gender identity being situated as binary (male or female), and to not be challenged in sport or within their day-to-day lives. In this way, gender identity mattered because it felt affirming for a person to be able to participate in sport as their authentic gendered self.

Trans feminism recognises that some people are not immutably tethered to an innate experience of womanhood or manhood simply by being designated male or female at birth. Many participants found the ways in which sport is organised along gendered binary lines difficult to navigate and would agree that such an emphasis on anatomy is reductive. What trans feminist theory argues for in sport is not the complete doing away of gender binaries or some kind of categorisation for participation, but the opening up of the ways in which trans people can be included. Trans feminism places the lives of trans people at the centre of its discussions and, within sport, advocates for trans athletes to compete and participate as themselves. This includes those athletes, like some of the participants, who wished to compete and participate on a gender-segregated team. Trans feminism recognises not only the discrimination and barriers trans people face in sport but also the complexity of these barriers and works towards an ethics of inclusion. Trans feminist theory brings to the forefront trans people's experiences and makes room for what has been diminished and marginalised and asks for lived experiences and narratives to be considered with dignity and respect. In this way, trans feminism can help work towards change through alliances.

Gender segregation in sport

Participants had different thoughts about gender segregation in sport. For example, whilst some recognised the importance of trans-only sporting spaces and sessions to enable people to exercise safely and confidently, others enjoyed the gender-segregated organisation of sport and the increased opportunities for competition this brought. Trans people in the United Kingdom make up less than 1% of the population (Olufemi, 2020)., Those participating in this book talked about how they wanted to continue participating in sport alongside their cis teammates and friends, or else there would be no competition. Whilst trans feminist theory advocates for making space for trans people in sport, perhaps with more mixed teams or thinking of different ways to organise sport other than using non-binary models, some participants rejected this. For these people, reducing the opportunity to compete alongside other athletes took away what they enjoyed about sport – the chance to win or to benchmark their performance. Not being able to be involved in sport with their peers might lead to their leaving sport, because there was no opportunity to measure their ability against others. What is assumed about trans people's lived experiences in sport do not reflect the reality of their lived experiences or their opinions.

Recommendations for Future Research

This book makes three suggestions for future research, with the aim of improving inclusion for trans people in everyday sport. Firstly, greater awareness of the issues and barriers facing trans young people under the age of 18 would greatly help to mitigate the issues they may face in the future. This will also help to build awareness amongst friends and peer groups and will help those young people who want to stay in sport, to continue doing so. Concering physical education (PE) and school sports, there is little theoretical and empirical knowledge about trans youth, though the field is rapidly growing (see Barras and Frith, 2023, for some examples of these). Community work with schools and on the PE curriculum could help to prevent dropouts at certain key points (like puberty) and encourage mental health and well-being generally, which is frequently cited as a concern for gender-diverse young people and adolescents.

Secondly, research which looks over the whole life course would be beneficial for trans people, and not just children and young adults. As this study has revealed, sport and exercise are a valued part of participants' lives, and, even when it was sometimes difficult to access, people still found a way to be involved. Finding ways to engage older trans people at any stage of their lives, for example during transition, could offer new and inclusive ways to encourage people to get involved in everyday sport and physical exercise. This is especially significant since the impact of COVID-19 has highlighted the importance of daily exercise and access to green spaces and concerns about isolation amongst older populations. In addition, high-quality data are required to monitor health trends, assess health needs and evaluate the effects of policies and other interventions. However,

> valid sources of quantitative data for trans people can be difficult to find, and population-based surveys are limited by the lack of standardised survey items used to identify trans respondents, and are often too small to provide meaningful samples of trans people.
>
> *(Thomson and Katikireddi, 2019, p. 369)*

There is an opportunity, then, to encourage more quantitative research which could sit alongside qualitative findings in this area.

Thirdly, future research with cisgender teammates could help to develop wider understandings not just of trans people's sporting experiences but also of those who form part of their sporting communities. This could help to foster suggestions about how to improve inclusion for people in sport generally, which will lead to stronger alliances between different groups. It is also important to listen to cis voices and experiences if this is to be achieved. Whilst the qualitative nature of this book has been fruitful in producing a rich understanding of trans people's lived experiences in everyday sport and physical exercise in the United Kingdom, other study designs could produce equally rich contributions in this area. Quantitative research could yield important insights regarding sporting participation rates in the trans population. Ethnographic research which examines how cis and trans athletes exercise and interact alongside each other could also be useful.

As gender identity exists and influences all our lives, understanding how it also intersects with participation in sport specifically for trans people should not be hard to accommodate. This book contributes to widening discourses on how barriers can be reduced in sports settings, emphasising the importance of foregrounding trans people's voices to achieve this. I strongly believe that foregrounding these experiences also has the added potential to make sport more inclusive for others. Thinking about barriers for trans people helps to move the focus away from measuring eligibility and instead focus on the importance of participation for people, the enjoyment and pleasure doing sport brings. The rich and varied experiences shared by participants demonstrated this study has contributed a different perspective.

It is important to reiterate sporting practices are historically produced, socially constructed and culturally defined to serve the interests and needs of powerful groups of society. The prevalence of gender normativity and hegemonic masculinity in sport shows that whilst much of the literature is supportive in its advocating for trans people's inclusion in sport, sport remains difficult to access, and those who experience gender incongruity will often face significant barriers when attempting to participate in sport and physical activity. However, as this book has shown, the literature in this field is growing and there is more visibility and representation of trans people in media, popular culture, politics and sport.

We all benefit from taking part in everyday sport and physical exercise. At the time of writing circumstances have been very challenging for many people in the United Kingdom due to lockdowns and the closure of playgrounds, gyms and leisure centres, and the importance of daily exercise and its connection to mental health and well-being have become a priority for many people. There is now an even greater recognition of not just the physical health benefits sport brings, but the additional benefits such as socialising, having fun and belonging to a community. To deny any group of individuals these benefits, whether they be trans people or those who cannot access a green space, sends the message that access to sport and exercise and by extension access to health and well-being are the preserve of the privileged.

Trans people's inclusion in sport has been under constant attack around the world, and a 2021 statement from the North American Society for the Sociology of Sport (NASSS), challenged what they called anti-trans laws and bills in sport, saying, 'in the USA and beyond, there have been spikes in attacks legally, physically, culturally, and politically against gender and sexual minorities, both in and out of sporting institutions' (NASSS, 2021, pp. 1–2). The common goal should always be to raise awareness, understanding and compassion for a group of people in sport facing more unnecessary barriers than others. It is also unfair to expect the trans community to carry the burden of challenging transphobia, and this was a concern of several participants. Martinez-San Miguel and Tobias (2016, p. 5)' In keeping with a trans feminist perspective, this book reflects on the words of Alice, who had this to say about their experiences of cycling and being trans:

> Sport gave me an identity that wasn't around being trans, and as you know, I'm proud of being trans, it's been really good for my mental health, and for my happiness as well, to have that. And I've made a lot of friends through it, yeah, it's been a really big part of the last few years, a big part of my life.

Above everything, for me, sport is a human right, something which should always start from a place of inclusion. As someone who swims often to both unwind and to sooth my aching joints, to not have this in my life would be unimaginableMoving my body brings me great joy, relief and pleasure, and to deny that right to another goes against everything I believe sport should encompass: kinship, community and well-being. These sentiments align with my trans feminist position, whose point 'is to challenge societal sexisms and other forms of marginalisation' (Serano, 2013, p. 47). When applied to trans people's inclusion in sport, we can open up, not shut out, a chance to celebrate diversity, where sport becomes a place where we can all thrive. Fundamentally, the misuse of girls and women's sports to promote discrimination against transgender individuals needs to stop, and we can only do this through collaboration and dismantling those systems which oppress us all.

References

Barras, A., & Frith, H. (2023). 'Cos not everyone wants to talk, they prefer to do, to move': circuits of trans embodied pleasure and inclusion in sport and physical exercise. *Sport, Education and Society*, 1–15. https://doi.org/10.1080/13573322.2023.2266755

Elling-Machartzki, A. (2017). Extraordinary body-self narratives: Sport and physical activity in the lives of transgender people. *Leisure Studies*, *36*(2), 256–268. https://doi.org/10.1080/02614367.2015.1128474

Lawler, S. (2008). *Identity: Sociological perspectives*. UK: Polity Press.

Martinez-San Miguel, Y., & Tobias, S. (2016). *Trans studies: The challenge to hetero/homo normativities*. US: Rutgers.

North American Society for the Sociology of Sport. (2021). https://nasss.org/wp-content/uploads/2021/04/NASSS-statement-TransAthlete-Ban.pdf

Olufemi, L. (2020). *Feminism interrupted*. UK: Pluto Press.

Serano, J. (2013). *Excluded*. USA: Seal.

Thomson, R.M., & Katikireddi, S.V. (2019). Improving the life of transgender people: The need for good data. *The Lancet*. https://www.thelancet.com/action/showPdf?pii=S2468-2667%2819%2930129-X

GLOSSARY

Although some of the key terms listed are discussed in greater detail within this book, this glossary appears here to provide a quick explanation of what they are. Wherever possible all terms in the glossary originate from sources written by trans and non-binary authors, artists and activists.

Binder A binder is a compression undergarment that looks like a vest and is usually made of durable nylon and spandex. Wearing a binder ('binding') flattens the breasts to the body, creating a flatter/more masculine silhouette, helping to curb gender dysphoria. It can help with 'passing' since the appearance of breasts often increases the chance of strangers using female pronouns.

Bottom or Lower Surgery The common term for genital affirming surgery. This can be vaginoplasty, where a vagina is surgically created; metoidioplasty where clitoral growth from hormone therapy is used to shape a penis; or phalloplasty, the type of surgery where a penis is surgically constructed from another part of the person's body.

Cis(gender) People who are not transgender, whose gender identity aligns with their assigned sex at birth. Often shortened to 'cis'.

Cisnormative/cisnormativity The assumption that all or almost all individuals are cisgender.

Cissexism Prejudice or discrimination against trans people.

Gender Dysphoria A medical term for the experience of discomfort or distress in a person's body, due to having a gender identity that does not align with their gender assigned at birth. Not to be confused with body dysmorphia, a mental health condition where people perceive flaws in their appearance.

Genderqueer An older version of non-binary.

Heteropatriarchy A feminist term to describe a hierarchical society or culture dominated by heterosexual males whose characteristic bias is unfavourable to gay people and women in general.

Intersex People who are born with a reproductive or sexual anatomy that does not fit the 'standard' definitions for female or male. Intersex people are sometimes included under the trans umbrella, though some argue they differ with regard to their physical sex, not their gender.

LGBTQ+ This book uses the abbreviation LGBTQ+ to encompass lesbian, gay, bisexual, transgender, questioning (or queer) and intersex identities.

Non-binary People who do not identify within the male/female binary, and instead may identify as being neither woman or man, a little of both, or as being gender-fluid (i.e. moving between different genders over the course of their lives).

Packer A packer is the term for any object used to create a bulge in a person's underwear or trousers, to create the illusion of a penis. Accordingly, 'to pack' is the act of using a packer.

Passing A person being read by strangers as their preferred gender.

Testosterone or 'T' Testosterone, or 'T' as it is often called, is a hormone usually prescribed either as a gel or an injection. Testosterone can bring about dramatic changes to a person's body, including increased hair growth, deepening of the voice, easier muscle building and changes in fat distribution.

Top or Chest Surgery The common term used to describe the removal of breasts and/or fatty tissue to create a more masculine physique.

Trans feminine The term used to describe someone whose gender presentation is feminine looking.

Trans(gender) People whose gender identity does not align with their assigned sex at birth. The term 'transgender' is typically used as an umbrella term to describe all people who defy 'straight' mainstream notions regarding gender. The trans umbrella may include (but is not necessarily limited to) people who are transsexual, crossdressers, drag artists, androgynous, two-spirit, genderqueer, agender, feminine men and/or masculine women. Often shortened to 'trans'.

Transition The steps a person may take to align their gender identity with their gender presentation. Transition can be social (such as using a new name), medical (such as taking gender-affirming hormones) or surgical (such as having gender-affirming surgery). There is no 'right' way or time to transition, and everyone is different.

Transsexual An older version of transgender. Many trans people find this definition objectifying as it places undue focus on body parts rather than the whole person but is still respected as a term of self-identification.

Trans man A person who has transitioned/is transitioning from female to male (socially, medically, legally or all three).

Trans masculine The term used to describe someone whose gender presentation is masculine looking.

Transmisogyny The way in which cissexism and misogyny intersect in the lives of trans women and others on the trans/feminine spectrum.

Trans woman A person who has transitioned/is transitioning from male female (socially, medically, legally or all three).

INDEX

Pages followed by "n" refer to notes